The Land of No
Horizon

Kevin and Matthew Taylor

**The inner Earth holds the secret to
the origins of humanity.**

First published in 2001 by:
tlonh.com
PO Box 1175
Runaway Bay Qld 4216 Australia

Web: www.tlonh.com

Produced by:
Kevin J. Taylor and Matthew J. Taylor

National Library of Australia Catalogue-in-Publication entry:

> Taylor, Kevin, 1949- .
> The land of no horizon : the inner Earth holds the secret to the origins of humanity.

> Bibliography.
> Includes index.
> ISBN 0 646 41057 1.

> 1. Curiosities and wonders. 2. Parapsychology. 3. Human beings - Origin. I. Taylor, Matthew, 1975- . II. Title.

001.94

Printed and bound in Australia by:
Southwood Press Pty Limited
76-82 Chapel Street
Marrickville NSW Australia 2204

The Land of No
Horizon

Introduction

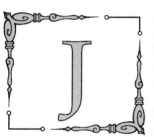

ust how much does each of us really understand about the complexity of the world around us? Are we sure what we believe is right? Is what we currently accept as fact drawn from our own conclusions? Or are they drawn from the conclusions and beliefs of others?

Today we are faced with so many mysteries. Amongst countless numbers of unknowns, we hear of past ice ages, continents that drift across the globe, UFOs from outer space and humanity's missing evolutionary link. The existence of so many mysteries presents a problem. They reflect serious flaws in our basic understanding of things around us.

How much do each of us really know about these things? Do we truly understand the reasoning behind scientific theories proposed to solve such issues? Are the claims made by theorists right? How many of us have seriously considered the need to examine the evidence for ourselves?

These are vital questions for each of humanity to contemplate.

Unfortunately, few in the community are scientifically versed. Most encounter problems with the complexity of explanations given. The maze of mathematical formulae and scientific terminology creates an impenetrable barrier to our understanding. Invariably, hypothesis supporting answers are just too complicated for us to even begin to question. For most, it is easier to simply agree with the "experts" and accept what they say must be right.

Yet, how can we be sure established beliefs and concepts are correct? How carefully have the workings behind them been assessed? Have all elements been equally considered?

Complacency over important issues such as this, has allowed others to make up our minds for us. Instead of thinking for ourselves, we have permitted those in authority to lead us

Introduction

as they see fit. Unfortunately, once a belief is established and supported throughout the community, it is difficult to change. Even when new contradictory evidence is found, such beliefs invariably remain firmly intact.

This presents us with a dilemma.

Whether scientific or otherwise, close scrutiny of many of our beliefs reveal beginnings built on questionable evidence. Some dubious ideas have been treated as fact for generations. These in turn have become the springboard for new understandings which themselves rely heavily on the authenticity of those conclusions made before. Because of initial error, a serious inherited problem has been accumulating for generations. A significant portion of our accepted understanding rests upon shaky foundations laid down in the past. It is this flawed concept of things around us that justifiably gives rise to the growing list of mysteries confronting humanity today.

If we are to overcome our unfortunate predicament, it is first necessary to rectify those errors made in the past. But this task will not be easy. With minds already made up, change to established beliefs is extremely difficult.

How is it that such a situation like this has been allowed to occur?

Relying on blind faith has been our downfall. Unconditional acceptance of answers without proper knowledge of the workings behind them is the reason. It has made us vulnerable to errors made by others. Being able to evaluate the evidence is as important as the answer itself. This way, conclusions can be assessed to our own satisfaction before accepting them as correct.

"The Land of No Horizon" is a book that digresses from convention. It examines the unexplained from a different perspective. It emphasises equal evaluation of all material involved in our mysteries. This includes every aspect from individual elements right up to and including the overall larger picture. This method of investigation promptly exposes those simple errors from the past.

Awareness of the fact that most are not entirely acquainted with science has created the need for language that is not only commonsense, but also easy to comprehend. This has been used throughout the book to provide both answers and crucial reasoning behind them. Without both parts, "The Land of No Horizon" would have been less than complete. Scientific methods of achieving solutions, the complexity of human nature, as well as the possibility of cover-ups, have all been taken into consideration in providing the final outcome.

The truth has consequences much greater than we think. It will move us all.

Part I

The Barrier of Mysteries

One simple misunderstanding from our past
is responsible for the countless unknowns of today.

Chapter 1

The Missing Link

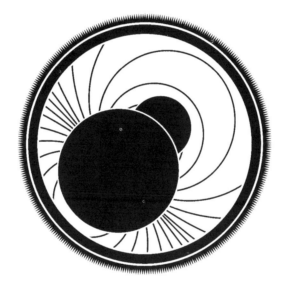

Science cannot find the missing link...
because they are looking in the wrong place.

The Missing Link

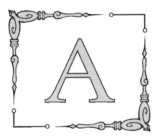nd suddenly we are standing there...

We feel the ease of lightweight freedom in this beautiful imaginary land. Visions of tranquillity pass before our eyes. With heads raised, we now watch as the entire world covers us, a world that is wonderfully distorted.

The sun is dim. Its flare consumes the land above. The whole world is bathed in soft filtered light. In the haze of humidity, the outlines of grand forests stand. But their shapes somehow do not conform. Life is everywhere. Eerie calls echo from the shadows, but they are sounds we do not recognise. The scene around us is one of allure and mystique. Senses seeking things familiar, become strained in a place where normality does not apply.

We stand in awe, captive and lost in a world unknown. Questioning eyes have found no answers. With growing apprehension consuming our thoughts, the wonders around us are quickly forgotten. Where are we? What is this strange place? Nothing looks as it should. As minds begin to focus, anxiety closes in. What are we doing here? And, who are these strange people with us? We try desperately to understand. Then all of a sudden a fearful grip takes hold as we realise...

...this is not a dream.

Evolution of life on Earth

Planet Earth is a lonely island, a speck of minuscule proportions in the vast emptiness of space. Silently orbiting its star 150 million kilometres distant, it is our unique world, a sanctuary containing every life form known to humanity, a refuge isolated by the endless vacuum of space.

Incredibly, life is found teeming over the four corners of this tiny solitary globe. Nature's optimum designs inhabit every land mass and every ocean, from the poles to the Equator. Species in their millions exist right here, on the surface of the place we accept as home.

For generations, the source of so many different species has raised questions and intense debate. However, with time and ongoing scientific investigation, vital evidence has provided us with the currently accepted theory known as "evolution".

"Evolution" is the theory of survival based on what is known as "natural selection". The concept operates through reproduction where slight changes in successive generations can be beneficial, thus improving the species. Stimulated by a need to compete and adapt to ever-changing conditions, offspring that are better suited to the surrounding environment are inclined to reproduce and survive in greater numbers replacing those existing before. This allows each species to evolve and adapt to remain in line with the changing environment. Over time this process has allowed life to adapt and branch out, into increasing numbers of new varieties.

The theory of evolution was initially published in 1859 when A. R. Wallace and Charles R. Darwin compiled the necessary scientific evidence to produce the first edition of Darwin's "Origin of Species". This new understanding became known as "Darwinism".

Unfortunately, Darwin's theory fell short of satisfactorily explaining how an organism passed on its new characteristics and therefore how new species evolved. This became an apparent difficulty with the concept. A solution arrived however at the beginning of the 20th century, when the science of genetics provided an important development. In 1901, De Vries presented the theory of evolution aided through "mutation". Mutation allowed a well defined sudden random development of a new species. This provided a credible solution to bridge some of the gaps in Darwinism. The gene being the carrier of genetic make-up determines the characteristics of a life form. Because genes are passed on, any changes in them can likewise be passed on to an offspring. Mutations beneficial to the species as a whole improved the survival rate of the life form.

Today, evolution is generally accepted as the reason for the diverse existence of life on Earth. It now embodies the view that all of life is in fact related and interconnected in the form of a huge family tree. The first simple organisms are represented as the roots. The most advanced represented as the upper canopy. Each species forms an integral part of the tree and can be traced back through the connecting branches to its origins and all other life.

Fossils likewise support this view.

Like all planets, Earth suffered a violent past. Today, extensive sedimentary layers conceal the remains of many. By piecing together remnant fossils, we see the story of evolving life mirrored in stone. This is a story that confirms the interconnected tree of evolution. It is a map showing how each species adapted and developed to meet the reshaping course of Earth's evolution.

To the uninitiated, it would seem at first, all plants and all animals fit perfectly, forming

The Missing Link

their own exclusive niche in the evolutionary tree. But this is not the case. There is an exception. One species is unique. It is one that has not followed the same lines of evolution as other life has.

That species is humankind.

Evolution and the human species

As each species adjusts and adapts to meet changing conditions, new varieties evolve. Over evolutionary time, these new varieties branch out over and over again creating ever more new species. The end result is multiples of similar species closely linked in common groups or families. These multiples of related species form the backbone of the evolutionary tree connecting all variations of plant and animal life on the planet.

Accordingly, If theories are correct and mankind evolved naturally from other existing life, then we too should be closely related and similar to multiples of other species. However, this is not particularly true. The human species provides an exception to the rule. Paleontologists searching to establish the origins of humanity, are continually confronted by an intriguing enigma within the structure of the evolutionary tree. Anticipated connecting branches, vital for linking Homo sapiens with other life, don't appear to be there. There are several gaps. This is confirmed by examination of fossil remains. Despite years of intensive searching, evidence supporting the assumed story of humans evolving from primates remains sketchy and inconclusive.

It is true Homo sapiens share a clear anatomical and genetic relationship with other primates. But the problem lies in the fact that the evolutionary gap between the two is vast. It is a void too great to have been spanned in a single progression of evolutionary development. Paleontologists realise the need to find tangible evidence of smaller progressive stages linking our development from primates. However, such evidence continues to elude them. Without it, the true origins of the human species remains speculation.

It is this yet to be discovered, assumed connection between ourselves and the rest of the animal kingdom that sets us apart. It has become known as "the missing link".

Today, "the missing link" is an evolutionary gap fully recognised by science. It is a persistent issue that needs be unraveled if we are ever to decipher the mystery surrounding the origins of humanity.

This is where "The Land of No Horizon" comes in. The following chapters will bring forward new material not properly considered in the past. Science discovering the missing link is not an accident. It genuinely exists. Presented evidence logically points to where the missing clues can be found. They in turn expose the reason for the gap in the evolution theory. This is the purpose of the book. It provides answers to the source of the origins of humanity, explaining why we are different to other life on the planet.

However, before any solution can be reached, it is firstly necessary to understand the extent of the problem. The missing link is a complex issue, one that isn't solely about a lack of fossil evidence or other similar species. There are several other factors equally as important that need to be considered.

The Missing Link

The environment and mankind

The surface of the Earth is a domain of diverse environments. It is a place of land and sea where alternating conditions rule all life. Temperature extremes fluctuate enormously across the planet. Climates vary from frigid regions near the poles through to oppressive heat at the equator. As the Earth orbits its Sun on a tilted axis, seasons follow in sequence. Environmental temperatures vary dramatically as winter replaces summer on an endless cycle through time.

As the Earth rotates, night follows day. Without the warmth of the Sun, nighttime temperatures plummet, often below freezing. This adds to the extremes and frequency in temperature changes experienced across the surface of the planet.

All environments open to natural sunlight are exposed to varying degrees of ultraviolet light (UV light). Radiated from the Sun, ground level UV light can be damaging to unprotected life. Whilst levels are low in polar regions, UV intensity increases significantly towards the Equator.

Other factors governing conditions within the environment include aspects such as variations in rainfall, atmospheric and oceanic currents, elevation of the land or sea floor and active forces within the planet.

Most importantly is gravity. It is the power source that unites the mass of the planet as one. The weight of matter reflects its strength. All variations in all environments are sourced and controlled by this single common force. It governs all.

To survive the multiple environments and climatic regions of the Earth, each species has evolved in its own specialised way. Some animals have developed thick coats of fur and fat layers suitable for life in colder parts. Others have adjusted for subsistence in dry deserts. Nocturnal animals are adapted for the night. Aquatic life inhabits the rivers, lakes and oceans. Many have mastered the art of flight. Insects thrive and multiply in micro environments. Plants and forests exist. They clothe the land and provide food and shelter for others. All life is protected from the damaging potential produced by ultraviolet light radiation and ideally structured to cope with the level of gravity present in every habitat.

From the smallest microbes to ocean going whales and giant Redwood forests, life fills the environments of the Earth. This is the miracle of our small blue planet, a unique place where all species live, reproduce and survive. Fine tuning through evolution is mirrored in the structure of the evolutionary tree as each species fills its own particular niche in the many varied climates and living conditions across the face of the Earth.

If mankind is a product of the same evolutionary process, then we too should be adapted to fill our own particular niche within the environment. But are we? Further analysis provides another intriguing anomaly, one found in a biological comparison between Homo sapiens and other existing life.

Human skin

At the beginning of each day everyone performs an essential ritual. We establish an artificial environment for our bodies to live in. This undertaking is necessary no matter

The Missing Link

where we live. The man-made environment is achieved by wrapping protective layers around ourselves thus insulating us from the outside world, a world so harsh that we would not survive without clothes.

Perhaps we have become so complacent with this, our daily ritual, that we rarely stop to consider why. The act of adding protective layers is a necessity totally unique to mankind. It is an act performed by intelligence.

When studying the harsh world around us, it is not surprising to find animals cloaked with coats of hair or fur. Others have heavy layers of fat concealed beneath. For them protection from the extremes of heat and cold is assured. Some species have heavily pigmented skin. This naturally protects from the burning action of ultraviolet radiation. For all, skin has evolved with thickness and strength, to alleviate damaging effects from the pull of gravity. Clothed in skins that insulate and protect, life has evolved with a natural ability to cope.

But the human species is an exception. Our skin is unique. Its biological structure is different.

We possess one of the thinnest and most delicate skins of all species of comparable size sharing the same environment. It offers little in the way of protection. We have minimal hair and insufficient fat for the required insulation. The majority of our bodies are naturally exposed with virtually no hair at all. Despite the development of adequate skin pigmentation in many native races, for others it is lacking. Sunburn and skin breakdown result from over exposure to ultraviolet light. This leads to problems such as premature ageing and varying degrees of skin cancer.

The inadequacy of our skin creates difficulties when searching for a suitable environment for the origins of humanity. In our unprotected naked state, places warm enough to survive winter become hazardous in summer. Unable to avoid strong ultraviolet light, those with low pigmented light skin encounter the ominous consequences of sunburn damage. Because ultraviolet light is a natural product of our Sun, we would normally assume the Earth's surface has been exposed to it for millions of years. And accordingly, if life has evolved with protection to cope, then why hasn't mankind?

Our fragile skin is also effected by gravity. Delicate and poorly structured, it fails to meet the forces ever-present in the environment. Over time it distorts, stretches and wrinkles as it is pulled down. This is another factor instrumental in prematurely ageing each and everyone of the human race.

Our skin is out of tune with other life and the environment in so many ways. The pertinent question here is, if we evolved as other life has, then why does such a situation exist at all? Fortunately for us, there was a solution. We have been able to cope, not through evolution, but by developing an artificial environment around us. We use intelligence to protect ourselves against the drastic extremes of the world's environment. Our acquired ability to think, reason and understand has so far secured our continued existence. Without it we would not have survived.

Human eyes

Second only to intelligence, human eyes are our most advanced development. Yet again they too are not fully in tune with the environment around us.

A great many species have eyes developed to see and survive in the low light of the nighttime period. But for humanity, our night vision is very poor. Supposed millions of years of evolution has not adapted our eyes to cope in the dark at all. The predicament is, prior to reaching intelligence, the primitive human species would have encountered considerable difficulty defending themselves, hunting or even performing the most basic of tasks during the dark hours of night. How did they survive through evolutionary time against other competitive life around them? Today, only for our intelligence, we would spend half of our lives virtually blind and non-functional.

If our eyes are not adapted to see during the night, how well are they suited during the day?

Not surprisingly, in these health conscious times, we are rigorously warned to protect ourselves from the harmful effects of the Sun. This is emphasised particularly in warmer climates. In the brightness of day we artificially dim our world. This is done by positioning protective glass over the eyes to reduce sunlight. Sunglasses shield our eyes from the harmful rays of naturally occurring ultraviolet light. This, the same light that damages our skin, has been present in the environment, ever since life first emerged on the Earth.

We look with eyes not equipped to cope. The same eyes that fail us at night, fail us in the brightness of day. Our most developed sense is out of tune in a world from which we supposedly evolved.

Again we overcome this hardship using technology developed from intelligence.

The human skeleton

Homo sapiens as a species is upright in stature. Because of this, our skeleton is subjected to stresses over and above that of other animals supported on four legs. Accordingly, it would be normal to expect evolution would have supplied us with bone structure that is stronger to compensate. But when we investigate, we find this is not the case. Rather than stronger, our skeletal structure is actually finer than that of other animals of a comparable size. Again, the question is why? If our bodies evolved in the same environment, why are we different?

Because of our structural weakness, we encounter certain hardships. Gravity acting on our bodies contributes to many common medical complaints. Problems in the spine, hips, knees and other joints afflict many as bones wear down under the weight of the harsh environment.

The same gravity that destroys our skin also damages our bones.

Once again, technological advances derived from intelligence are used to minimise this problem.

Allergies

Why are common allergies such as asthma, hay fever and skin irritations invariably caused by natural products, pollens, grasses and animal fur? We show a negative reaction to

The Missing Link

simple life forms that supposedly evolved along with us.

Medications developed through intelligence, are used to help.

Competition within the environment

Evolved species are readily equipped to be competitive within the environment. Many have acquired long claws, horns and teeth designed to attack and defend. Others possess powerful limbs, developed for speed to capture victims or escape predators. Birds exist in endless varieties having mastered the art of flight. In the world today, we are witness to multiples of species. Each is the product of natural selection, highly developed and biologically designed to compete with others to achieve food, water, shelter and so, survive.

But what about humans? How naturally competitive are we?

In comparison, Human beings are not physically powerful at all. Such qualities are altogether lacking in the species. Humans do not possess claws or long teeth. Our running speed is slow and unsustainable. We are not equipped to attack or escape as other life is. We survive solely because of our intelligence. Without it, the human species falls a long way behind other competitive life.

Acquired reasoning has enabled us to compete by developing fire, weapons, and protection with clothing and providing food and shelter.

Reproduction and mankind

The world around us is ruled by changing seasons and weather conditions. Depending on our location, environmental circumstances regularly improve at certain times of the year. Life has adapted to take advantage of this ensuring preservation of future generations. Adaptation has been achieved by each species aligning its reproduction cycle with those seasons or circumstances more favourable for the protection of new life. Such well organised cycles are the consequence of life's slow development over millions of years.

But what about the human reproduction cycle? How does it fit in?

Our reproduction cycle is surprisingly different. It is not one that follows normal seasonal changes. Instead it repeats every 28 days, and despite adversities, continues throughout the whole year. Why is this so? If we all developed in the same environment, why does our cycle deviate from other life around us?

Is the human reproduction cycle an oddity or is it aligned with something else? If so, what could it be?

There is however, one cyclic phenomenon equivalent to our reproduction phase. It is the orbit of the Moon. It likewise completes one cycle every 28 days. Is this peculiarity a part of the key or just pure coincidence? Is it possible the Moon had a bearing on the development and reproduction of the Human species? If so, how and why?

We overcome this reproduction dilemma using intellect to create artificial environments, environments necessary to shield offspring from adverse seasons outside.

The Missing Link

Human intelligence

With our intelligence we are alone on the face of the Earth. No other species shares our capacity to think, reason and understand. Surely all would agree, acquired intellect represents the pinnacle of achievement in evolution.

This however leads to another appropriate question. If we currently survive in our natural habitat, then why has evolution on the one hand given us advanced intelligence but at the same time biologically equipped us so poorly we cannot meet the basic requirements of the environment around us? To this, no satisfactory answer has been proposed.

Remarkably, the span between human intelligence and other life presents evolution's widest and most dubious gap.

Fortunately for us, acquired intelligence has been our greatest saviour. It is used to bridge the evolutionary rift. It has allowed us to adjust and live throughout the globe. We have used aptitude and knowledge to artificially change the environment to suit our needs. But sadly, modern times see humankind taking eagerly and returning little. It seems our very survival depends on continued exploitation at the expense and depletion of the environment around us. This is something no other species has to do. Many now consider, the arrival of the human species has had disastrous consequences for the rest of life on Earth.

But this is not where the enigma ends. Our unique intelligence leads to one final question for those who support natural evolution of the human species.

If we look at our assumed development as one of natural evolution, there would have been a primitive period prior to acquiring intelligence. This would have been a time without the ability to create such things as fire, weapons and clothes. These did not exist for mankind. Instead, it would have been necessary for the evolving human race to rely on natural protection to cope and compete for survival, as does all other life throughout the world today.

This presents a definite problem for believers of the evolution theory. When considering the extent of how mankinds's current biological makeup is poorly suited to the environment, how could the human species have possibly survived the important pre-intelligent period of evolution? Totally outclassed, early Homo sapiens surely would have succumbed to the stronger and more competitive species and died out.

Some evolutionists have a different proposal. It has been suggested mankind lost his compatibility with the environment after reaching intelligence. The reasoning behind this is, once acquiring such an intellectual state, environmental protection was no longer necessary.

Unfortunately, there is a fundamental flaw with this concept. Evolutionary adaptation occurs when it is beneficial to a species as a whole. Such adaptation is essential as it allows life to align and cope to meet changing situations. But what force would influence an already adapted species to develop away from existing conditions that are ideal to it within its environment? Evolutionists are yet to come up with an appropriate reply. The suggested deviation in the human species is unique. It is one that regresses away from the most basic of daily needs, needs that help us to cope in the fluctuating climate and

The Missing Link

daylight, exposure to ultraviolet light, competition with other life and even the inescapable effects of gravity. Such changes seemingly oppose all laws of natural evolution. Is this what really happened?

In addition, as already discussed, where are the branching subspecies that would have evolved alongside human beings connecting us to all other life? They simply do not exist. And why has not a single species on the planet followed in this path?

We are unique and alone on the face of the Earth.

Humankind, the misfit species

The origins of humanity is a baffling mystery. There is an obvious imbalance. Fossil evidence is sketchy and incomplete. There is a lack of similar species. Our bodies are biologically out of tune and not physically structured to be competitive with other existing life. Our reproduction cycle is different. And, we are alone with our intelligence.

Homo sapiens appear virtually as an orphaned species on the Earth.

So, what is our story? Do we really fit in with the environment at all?

Evidence suggests, to a degree we do. Fossils exhibit a partial connection. There is an indisputable genetic relationship with other primates. Our internal structure mimics that of many other species. We share remnants of common features visible to all such as hair and skin pigmentation. Humans gain continued nourishment and sustenance from the produce of the environment. We are able to consume its food, water and atmosphere.

Conflicting factors leave us with two intriguing considerations. On the one hand, we must assume, a part of our genetic makeup did evolve here, alongside other life sharing the same environment. But then secondly, where did our other unique characteristics come from, characteristics of intelligence and those that put us out of tune with the environment? Is it possible they came from somewhere else?

The very existence of an abnormal rift in our evolution raises obvious questions. It is as if humans appeared suddenly on the Earth already equipped with intelligence. Because of this, new concepts lean towards the possibility of an interruption to the natural evolutionary process having taken place. Many perceive interruptions were instigated by others of higher intelligence.

Examination of historical writings tend to support the same point of view. Ancient texts narrate the actual creation of a man and a woman and their introduction into the new world. This is the story of "Adam and Eve". Unfortunately, authenticity in biblical history has remained unresolved for centuries. So, what significance do these historical pages really hold? If we are to achieve any sort of satisfactory answer, all available material must be investigated thoroughly. No portion of evidence or information should be knowingly omitted from scrutiny. Is it just possible, such writings describing the creation of mankind conceal a critical part of the key?

So, what is the truth concerning the origins of humanity?

Three theories have been proposed in an attempt to explain the origins of the human

The Missing Link

species.

1. Natural evolution
2. Creationism
3. An interruption took place to the natural evolutionary process, instigated by intelligences unknown.

Firstly is "natural evolution".

This is the most widely accepted theory in scientific circles today. But one should ask, why? As already discussed, there are serious inherent problems in this concept. What initially may have seemed feasible, encounters multiple complications hidden beneath. Natural evolution on its own is incomplete. It does not provide necessary answers to unravel this intriguing mystery concerning humanity. Other factors have to be involved.

Second is "creationism"

Some seek religion as the answer. They believe their biblical records teach them we were created by an all loving, perfect, and all powerful God, the creator of the world, its environments and all its creatures.

But once again, we encounter certain difficulties with this concept.

If we were created by God, why didn't this perfect God create us biologically in tune with his perfectly created environment as other life is? What would be the logical reason for not doing this? One is left to wonder. Unfortunately for believers of creationism, it would appear this single question has not been properly addressed.

Those not satisfied with such ideology, seek more feasible alternatives. Many look outward from the Earth to the realms of space in search of an answer.

This leads to the third concept. An interruption to the natural evolutionary process took place, instigated by intelligences unknown.

It is easy to be consumed by the awesome size of the universe. None of us are able to comprehend the infinite dimensions around us. The combinations allowing life to exist on Earth must reoccur over and over again throughout the endless reaches of space. And so, the thought of other intelligent life has become a definite probability in our minds. Many direct telescopes, looking and listening for the slightest sign. But although we are searching, our deserving questions are yet to be answered.

Is it possible a part of the seed of humanity originated not from the Earth, but from worlds far away? Could this offer the single solution to both the "Missing Link" and why we are biologically out of tune with the environment?

Recordings of unidentified flying objects, abductions and unusual encounters with "gods" and other "strange beings" have been documented throughout history.

Many who support the UFO phenomenon, subscribe to the belief that from ancient times, we have been periodically visited by beings from civilizations more advanced than our own. This concept together with the prospect of one day meeting other intelligent life,

The Missing Link

has excited many. Some dream of higher worlds and how their technology will help us. They look to the future with optimism, hoping for vital answers.

These thoughts foster a complete set of new possibilities. Is another intelligence someway responsible for the arrival of humankind? If so, do we still posses a part of their genetic pool? Is that why we are different from all other life on Earth? Will this prove to be the ultimate solution to the enigma confronting the human species?

As a consequence, pondering the origins of humanity now sends new images through our minds. Thoughts no longer revolve around evolution, as opposed to God. They now include sources from other worlds deep in space. Questions being asked include: Was the creation of humankind orchestrated by extra terrestrial life? If so, why? What was their purpose? Were they the authors of the ancient biblical texts? And are we to believe the reported encounters occurring today are simply ongoing guidance and observation of the progressing Human race?

For many, this offers the only logical reasoning behind the origins of humanity and our place here on the Earth.

But, are they correct? Many think not.

In our delusion, we tend to grasp at any information available, because we need to believe in something. But with so much still to be explained in the world today, it is difficult deciphering the genuine from the ridiculous. Unfortunately, we have often been a little too quick to form judgment in the past. As a result, today it is generally accepted as fact that UFOs are spacecraft manned by extra terrestrials traveling across space.

But can we be sure?

Whilst there is little point in denying the existence of the UFO Phenomenon, the concept of extra terrestrials traveling from other planets in distant space is nothing more than pure speculation. There is no evidence whatsoever to support this line of thought. This basis of thinking relies heavily on firstly, a long chain of unproven assumptions and secondly, our desire for it to be so.

So what is the truth? Are UFOs traveling to Earth from deep space or not? Is it possible they originate from a world not too distant from our own? If so, where could it be? And, how would their environment differ from that experienced on the surface of the Earth? Are they somehow responsible for the origins of humanity? Could this provide the reason for the disparity in our biological makeup? And, does this offer a possible solution as to why we are unique on the face of the Earth?

The biological characteristics of each species reflect the type of environment in which it evolved. Millions of years of natural selection has adjusted life by providing specific features to enable it to cope with conditions present in any of the Earth's habitable environments. In other words, an animal's individual characteristics communicate a great deal about the type of environment it is from.

For example, a polar bear's heavy insulation tells of a species evolved in an environment of intense cold. Even the colour of its coat has the purpose of acting as camouflage in a world of snow. Similarly, if we look at a camel, we see an animal able to survive for long periods without water. It has splayed hooves and specialized nostrils enabling it to contend with shifting sand. These along with its other characteristics tell of a species evolved in arid lands and desert regions of the Earth.

Such biological features do not evolve unless there is a definite need. Life's physical requirements are dictated by conditions encountered in each individual environment. Variations in physical characteristics between species are simply the result of adaptation to differing conditions. Such variations are naturally beneficial to each species' ongoing survival. This is how the evolutionary process works. Adjustments improve the strain allowing life to meet changes as they occur in the environment.

So what does this tell us about the human species?

Keeping in mind, characteristics evolve only because they are dictated by conditions within an environment and in turn advantageous to the survival of the species, what do our characteristics tell us about the type of environment we are from?

If we accept a part of our biological makeup is out of tune because we evolved to some degree in an environment elsewhere, then examination of those physical characteristics unique to us will shed some light on this most amazing mystery. It will give, not only an incite into existing conditions in mankind's evolutionary environment, but also provide the first clue as to its actual location.

An environment responsible for the evolution of humankind

Because our biological makeup is poorly adapted to cope with fluctuations in temperature and seasonal changes, we can safely assume the environment responsible for our evolution would have been a place relatively free of such extremes. In other words, in order to explain our unique biology, we must have partly evolved in a world where temperature changes were minimal, a place supporting ongoing stable warmth.

Because both our skin and eyes have developed with insufficient protection to avoid the burning action of ultra violet light, we must also assume the environment responsible for the evolution of these characteristics would have been a place where this type of radiation was low. The human species developing to some degree in an environment exposed to low levels of ultra violet light provides the only reason why we have little protection from it.

Human eyes are poorly equipped to see in the darkness of night. As discussed, this feature is unlike most other life around us. However, like all other biological characteristics, human eyes evolved according to the particular needs of an environment. If we lack the ability to see adequately in the dark, then it must be assumed there was no need for such a development in our evolutionary world. This raises an obvious question. Would the source of light have been different in the environment responsible for the evolution of humankind? Are we to assume this was a place without familiar night periods as experienced on the surface of the planet? If such a place were to exist, does an environment free of nighttime chill further legitimize our lack of protection from the cold?

Homo sapiens is a species upright in stature. As discussed, this unusual posture imposes additional stresses on bones and joints in the human skeleton. Despite this we evolved

The Missing Link

with a skeletal structure much finer than other comparable life sharing the environment with us. Realization that our bones would not have developed as fine as they have unless it was advantageous to us, tells us something about the environment responsible for our evolution. It must have been a place where the skeletal requirements for bulk and strength were less.

The question here is why?

The level of gravity experienced in any environment determines the required strength of bones in a skeleton. The stronger the force, the stronger bones need to be. As human bones have evolved finer, we should consider the probability of the environment responsible for the evolution of humankind being a place where the force of gravity was less.

Human skin, reflects the same environment. It is adequately designed for conditions of both low gravity and even warmth. It is finely structured, without the added burden of heat trapping fat layers or surface insulation such as fur or hair.

Evolution has equipped life with reproduction cycles precisely designed to ensure the survival of each species. Because the Earth has a rotating seasonal pattern, reproduction cycles align annually with those seasons where conditions are more favorable. This has obvious benefits for the preservation of new life. However as already stated, human reproduction is different. Instead of following the Earth's normal annual pattern, our cycle repeats monthly and continues throughout the year.

Why is the timing of our cycle different?

The very fact that all the human race share the same reproduction cycle implies its significance as a part of our evolution. It tells us more about the environment responsible for the evolution of humanity. The fact that Homo sapiens are endowed with a 28 day cycle suggests the environment where we evolved must have also cycled every 28 days.

Our unique biological characteristics indicate we partly evolved from an environment with significant differences to the surface of Earth. Evidence suggests, the place responsible for the evolution of humanity is a world of constant light and warmth. It is a world where ultra violet radiation is low. It is a place where gravity was less. And one with a time frame that cycles monthly.

As unusual as it may seem, such an environment offers a logical explanation for the existence of the exotic characteristics of mankind.

Is it possible such a place exists?

Scientific views would like us to think otherwise. But unfortunately for science, this viewpoint is wrong. The purpose of "The Land of No Horizon" is to show how and why such a world does exist. It is a place responsible for the origins of mankind, an environment from which we partly evolved, a world where we are not alone.

Other life has evolved here as well. Forged from the same ingredients that produced us, multiples of other species have acquired similar biological characteristics. Just as families of similar species evolved on the surface of Earth, the same has occurred here. Now the

The Missing Link

genus of humankind includes numerous other group types, those who developed alongside us. All are genetically related and close in appearance to humanity.

In this world we evolved to be naturally competitive with other life around us. Having our beginnings here means allergic reactions to natural life products are less of a problem.

But there is an issue remaining. If we are partly from this different world, then how did we end up on the surface of the Earth?

The answer lies in the fact that the environment responsible for the evolution of humanity is also responsible for our evolved intelligence. Other life, having shared the same evolutionary time period, has likewise acquired varying degrees of intellect. However, as exists in all environments, not all species have developed to the same extent. Whilst some life forms have remained rudimentary, others have progressed forward attaining higher levels of advanced intelligence.

It is the existence of those of higher intelligence that provides the reason for the existence of humans on the Earth.

In mankind's evolutionary world our roots are found firmly embedded in the evolutionary tree. Its branches connect us to all other life. All the vital answers are hidden here.

This is why science has not found the missing link. They have been searching in the wrong place.

So, where should they be looking?

The repeating cycle of our reproduction phase conceals a clue.

Our 28 day cycle mirrors the time clock governing mankind's evolutionary world. But, what is the source of a force capable of aligning a world to a 28 day repeating phase? Such repetition would not occur without a logical reason.

As stated, this cycle is not unique. Is it just a coincidence our Moon orbits the Earth in the same 28 day phase?

What bearing does this have?

If our evolutionary environment is also aligned with the phases of the Moon, then the environment responsible for the origins of humanity may not be distances away in space. It may be closer than we think.

And suddenly we were standing there...

We looked up at the stars and the moon, our faces reflecting insecurity and fear of this strange place. But with generations of work now complete, the moment was finally here. By the time the sunset dimmed and faded away, those who brought us had long since disappeared beyond the horizon. But even though we were now alone, our creators would never be forgotten. Wondrous memories had been left behind, miracles and writings serving as a reminder. A bond with their world

The Missing Link

and ours. A bond with themselves and us.

They left us mysteries, mysteries which our future would unlock.

They gave us life, something we must cherish forever.

They gave us their world, a place we must protect and care for.

And they gave us intelligence, intelligence which would enable us to survive in this different world, a world of day and night, where somehow we don't belong. We fought back the tears and pain and learned to live alone. We would adapt. But, through all our hardships our eyes would never leave the horizon, for it was during that final sunset they had promised...

"One day we will return"...

The Missing Link

Chapter 2

Earth's Mysteries

There are those who believe, some things are not meant to be understood...
They live in fear of what the truth may hold.

And there are those who say, there are things we will never know...
They see no purpose in pursuing an answer.

But there are others who share the understanding, all mysteries have a solution...
They will find the truth, and see its value to humanity.

Earth's Mysteries

 he origins of human kind could arguably be the paramount question throughout history. Yet, this compelling mystery is certainly not alone. Countless other unanswered enigmas span all areas of science today. As incredible as it may seem, virtually everything around us is involved to some degree. It is now apparent, precious little escapes the long list of unknowns before humanity.

Mysteries do not result from accurate understanding. They are a sign of something wrong in our perception of things around us.

Whilst most may be aware of those mysteries more familiar, there are others not so frequently discussed. Despite this, all are important. None can be dismissed. The unknowns before humanity are in fact interconnected. All are related because each stems from a common problem in our understanding. For this very reason, the missing link cannot be treated as an issue on its own. It is a part of everything else.

This is the key.

To identify this common problem in our understanding is the first step towards finding the common solution.

A clue as to its source is revealed by taking a brief look into some of the mysteries before us.

Extinction of the dinosaurs

It is known great dinosaurs once roamed the Earth. They survived for an incredible 160 million years before disappearing into extinction. The reasons for the loss of such massive life forms provides our first mystery.

Earth's Mysteries

Why would a species developed naturally through evolution just die out? It would be normal to expect they would have been perfectly adapted to the Earth's environment at the time. So, what happened to them?

Today, the most widely accepted theory surmises their loss resulted from the adverse effects of an enormous celestial impact. It is believed cataclysmic circumstances that followed destroyed most of life on Earth including the dinosaurs.

With little else in the way of other proposals, this theory has been generally accepted as being correct and is now treated as virtual fact throughout the world today.

But is this what really happened? Unfortunately, evidence to support the theory is limited and inconclusive.

The relevant factor is; extinction brought on by a celestial impact is speculation only and accordingly, should never be treated as absolute fact. Exactly what earthly changes were responsible for the end of the dinosaur age? This is still to be authenticated. If the celestial impact theory were correct and other life survived, why not the dinosaurs? And, why have none of those who survived developed to fill the niche left by their extinction? No land animal exists on Earth to match the size and bulk of these incredible creatures from the prehistoric past.

The loss of the dinosaurs has mystified humanity ever since the discovery of their amazing fossilized remains. However, as with all mysteries, this too has an answer.

Re-examination of the evidence sheds new light on why this great age came to an inevitable end. It is part of the key.

So, how does the disappearance of these magnificent beasts fit into the confusing puzzle of evolving life? And, what clues does this give as to changes that took place during the evolution of the Earth itself?

Drifting continents

Due to overwhelming evidence, It is now considered fact, that all the continents of the world were originally joined as one giant supercontinent. Science has named this super landmass "Pangaea".

It is speculated, at the time of the supercontinent, the Earth's surface was divided into two distinct areas, one being the supercontinent itself, and the other, a huge 200 million square kilometre oceanic expanse that encompassed the rest of the world.

It is theorised everything changed when an estimated 200 million years ago a major event took place. Unknown forces, assumed sourced from within the planet, fractured the supercontinent breaking it into a multiple of smaller pieces. Thought to be motivated by the same unknown force, we are informed the fragmented supercontinent pieces began to mysteriously drift away from each other across the surface of the globe.

Continental drift is perceived to have continued for the duration of the past 200 million years and as observed, still continues today. This ongoing action has relocated all the supercontinent fragments into the world map we now recognise.

Earth's Mysteries

Scientific study of continental movement and forces responsible for it, is currently known as "Plate Tectonics". However, to this point, all proposals of how the process of continental geology works are known to be flawed None escape obvious inherent problems. This has been the source of much debate within plate tectonics research ever since the discovery was made.

As a result, today many important issues remain unexplained.

Why would the Earth have evolved with all its dry land in the one place?

What are the forces responsible for breaking the supercontinent apart and continental drift?

Whilst the evidence supporting continental drift is overwhelming, the physics involved in providing a force sufficient to relocate whole continents thousands of kilometres from their origins seem totally implausible.

So, what is the real story behind this mystery?

How significant is this part of the key? And, what effect will it have on our understanding of the evolution and structure of the Earth?

Continental shelves

Every continental land mass on the Earth has a common undersea geological feature. All are completely surrounded by a sharp edge known as the "Continental Shelf". Not visible from the land, these cliff structures mark the place where present day continents broke away from the original mass of the assumed supercontinent Pangaea.

By joining continents back together at these edges, we see Pangaea reformed. But then, just as the task nears completion, an obvious problem begins to emerge. The supercontinent has a continental shelf of its own. Like all others, it continues fully around its perimeter.

Adding to the confusion, geological examination of the surrounding shelves reveal them to be of a similar structure and age as all other shelf breaks. They too occurred at the time of the fragmentation of the supercontinent.

This presents a dilemma. If the supercontinent was complete in itself and so had nothing to break away from, why do these shelves exist around its exterior?

Are theories supporting the idea of a supercontinent correct?

Was the Earth's surface divided into the two distinct areas of a supercontinent and a superocean as claimed? Or, as the evidence indicates, did the geological mass assumed as Pangaea break away from something else?

Is it possible it broke away from itself? What effect does this have on our understanding of the evolution and structure of the planet?

Earth's Mysteries

The age of Earth's surface geology

The very latest in technology is used to explore the hidden world beneath the sea. But once again, each new discovery uncovers more mysteries. Tests confirm, all the ocean basins of the world today have been formed in recent geological times.

Whilst continental land masses are estimated to be as much as 4,000 million years old, the oldest sea floor has only been in existence for a mere estimated 200 million years. In other words, oceanic crusts formed up to 3,800 million years after continental land masses. This means, all 200 million square kilometres of the Earth's present oceanic basins did not exist at the time of the supercontinent, Pangaea. What's more, there is nothing at all in the way of evidence, such as geological remains, to suggest the existence of the ancient superocean floor that supposedly surrounded the original supercontinent. Nothing of it has ever been found. All the sea floors that exist in the world today are recent developments, formed since the breakup of Pangaea. None of them existed before that time.

What does this mean?

If an ancient super sized ocean did exist, what happened to it? How could 200 million square kilometres of ancient ocean floor just disappear? Surely some remnants of it would exist. If, as evidence suggests, this assumed ocean surrounding Pangaea is in fact an incorrect presumption, what would the Earth have been like before the present ocean basins formed?

Is it possible the Earth was smaller?

Mountains

Mountain ranges dominate over the land all around the globe. Scientists know mountains are the result of compression forces acting horizontally within the Earth's surface crust. But, what generates the force is not completely understood. Put quite simply, no-one has been able to adequately explained why mountains even exist. Despite our modern technology, we are still to find the source of the energy that creates these countless geological wonders across the Earth.

Why?

If we don't understand forces clearly in operation on the surface, how can we claim to understand the processes of geology working within?

Earthquakes

Another enigma concerns earthquake activity. Today, most regard earthquakes as natural happenings that reoccur in faulted regions throughout the world.

But, what is the true cause of this type of movement within the Earth's crust? Do we really understand the geological workings behind them, or even why they occur at all?

Are scientific theories concerning earthquakes correct?

Earth's Mysteries

What sort of answers will a better understanding of the geological structure of the Earth provide?

The great flood

We are told of Noah, his ark and many animals saved from an historical flood, a flood that swept the Earth for a whole year. This famous event is clearly recalled in biblical history, and numerous other ancient texts and cultures right throughout the world. Most reports are strikingly similar. They tell of a catastrophe that inundated the land and brought an end to the evil of mankind. It was a deluge supposedly brought about by divine intervention.

Today, many express doubt as to the authenticity of the story of the great flood. Was this man Noah really saved from an event that ravaged the Earth? Or, is it just another nonsensical myth handed down from generation to generation? What about geological evidence? Is any present to support such an event? If in fact the flood did occur, what caused it? Where would enough water have come from to inundate the entire world? And more importantly, where would it have all gone in order for the flood to subside?

If the flood did occur, what part does it play in the evolution of the Earth?

And what clues does it give as to its inner geological structure?

Changes in sea level

Throughout the world there is considerable evidence to suggest that sea level has changed in the recent past. Undersea exploration has discovered old riverbeds, remnants of forests and even ancient ruins on many of the world's continental shelves. These are remains from a different age, now lying submerged, beneath the waters of the sea.

What could cause the ocean to rise on a global scale?

Is it really the result of a melting ice age as proposed by theorists, or were coastal lands inundated by the sea for other reasons?

Was the rise in sea level a result of the great flood?

Ice ages

Scientists tell of great ice ages in the past. These were times when the Earth supposedly turned cold. Huge sheets of glacial ice are perceived to have advanced from the poles as the climate changed. But, what would be the cause of such an astronomical event? On what evidence is the ice age theory based?

With current confusion concerning the geological processes involved in continental drift, ocean floor construction, mountain building, and the cause of earthquakes together with the occurrence of numerous global floods following past celestial impacts, should we not be a little more cautious as to deciding just what the evidence means?

Have decisions been made prematurely?

Earth's Mysteries

Can we afford to judge "ice ages" as fact, if our basic understanding of so many things before us is still under considerable shadow of doubt?

Is it not possible the evidence represents something else, like a combination of other factors such as continental drift and the remnants of a great flood?

The surface of the sea

Most of us perceive the sea surface as being level. However, with the aid of modern satellite technology, this has been found to be not the case. Certain anomalies exist. Instead of being flat, the sea's surface contains permanent undulations. Variations in elevation, create a surface format of hills and valleys across the oceanic expanses of the world. Because changes are gradual, they are not visible to the naked eye.

Oceanic surface contours remain fixed in position and bear no resemblance to surrounding features or the spinning action of the Earth. Ongoing investigations revealed surprising differences between hill tops and valley floors. Amazingly, they vary as much as 200 metres (650ft.) over the oceans of the Earth.

What could be the cause of such deviations in sea level?

It is now theorised the variations result from irregularities in the strength of surface gravity. This is thought to be brought about by differences in mass concentration within the matter of the planet.

Unfortunately, in order to satisfactorily explain the amount of variation experienced, mass deviations need to be greater than that normally expected.

What does this tell us about the inner structure of the planet?

Other gravity anomalies

Gravity anomalies have also been discovered elsewhere across the Earth. Deep sea trenches traverse the geology of the oceanic abyssal plain. The bottoms of some trenches are in excess of 11 kilometres beneath the sea surface. It is here gravity anomalies occur.

It is known, as one descends beneath the surface of the planet, the strength of gravity naturally decreases. The rate of reduction has been scientifically calculated on a scale measured with depth. However, for reasons unknown, problems persistently arise with the mathematics supporting it. It has been found, the strength of gravity in the floors of deep sea trenches is less than that calculated. Other experiments carried out deep beneath the ice in Greenland and in various bore holes in mines around the world also prove scientific estimates are wrong. They confirm gravity reduces much quicker with depth than thought.

Why? What is the cause of this? And again, what effect does this have on mankind's upheld theories regarding the inner structure and mass density of the planet?

Mysteries at sea

Humans enter a foreign world every time we cross the domain of the sea. This is a place

Earth's Mysteries

of mystery, a lonely world of unexplained events. Unsolved incidents record tales involving hundreds of ships and planes that disappeared without trace. Observations have shown that large numbers of disasters have been confined within the boundaries of specific oceanic areas. Witnesses and survivors often recall similar but strange events. Fear of the unknown has given rise to varying extravagant thoughts. There are suggestions of super powers from the deep, UFOs and even other dimensions. As a result, questionable oceanic areas have now been given infamous names such as, "The Bermuda Triangle" and "The Devil's Sea".

On the other hand, some respectable authorities claim there is nothing unusual at all. They believe the losses are the result of normal everyday circumstances. Disasters occur more frequently because the regions in question are notorious for sudden weather changes, strong currents and freak wave conditions.

So, what is the truth? Are the losses just normal happenings? Or, is there some other unseen force, mysteriously at work, responsible for the phenomenon?

Does the unseen inner structure of the Earth hold a vital clue?

The Earth's magnetic field

The Earth, like many other celestial bodies, is surrounded by a huge magnetic field. Everyday, compasses are used to follow its lines of magnetism for navigation. As happens with the Sun and other planets, Earth's magnetic field originates from the very centre of the planet. But just how and why it is generated remains a total mystery.

The most accepted explanation for the magnetic field is it is generated somewhat like a dynamo. It is suggested a combination of the spinning Earth with its theorised iron core generates a field like a huge magnet. Unfortunately, there are persistent difficulties with this theory. The required alignment between the magnetic field and the poles is not correctly orientated for the theory to work. Observation of magnetic fields originating from other planets in the Solar System show similar situations.

So what is the truth?

What generates this naturally occurring phenomenon discharging from the centre of our planet? Will a better understanding of the magnetic field reveal more about the true inner structure of the Earth? And, how will knowledge of the Earth's inner structure help in our understanding of other planets and celestial bodies.

The red spot on Jupiter

Even as mankind ventures out to explore the realms of space, information transmitted back shows just how little we truly know. Solutions are few and far between. Every new discovery simply adds more questions to the long list of confusion.

The red spot on Jupiter has been viewed from Earth since its discovery some 300 years ago. Of the many theories proposed, the most accepted suggests it is a giant storm in the planet's atmosphere. But is that correct?

If it is a storm, Where is the central eye as normally found within large storm systems.

Earth's Mysteries

Why would a storm endure for more than 300 years? And, why have no others of a similar size formed?

It was hoped the passing Voyager space craft would provide sufficient data to finally solve this unusual blemish in the planet's atmosphere. Unfortunately, the information received only served to deepen the mystery.

So, what is Jupiter's red spot? Are theories proposed by science correct? Or is something different true?

A better understanding of inner planetary structure will help solve this amazing 300 year old mystery.

Floods on Mars

Similarly, passing space probes have revealed startling information on other planets in the Solar System. Transmitted images reveal extensive flooding once took place on Mars. Photos show water erosion, drainage patterns and channel type river beds crossing the Martian surface.

The bewildering point here is, water cannot exist in its liquid state unless atmospheric pressure is sufficient, as is the case on Earth. Unfortunately the Martian atmosphere is only one hundredth of that of the Earth. And so accordingly, pressure is too low for water to exist and flow in its liquid form on the surface of the planet.

This presents an unexplainable problem for science. How could a major flood happen in the environment on Mars? What forces allowed flowing water to exist? And from where did it originate?

Is there a hidden link between this occurrence on Mars and the assumed great flood on the Earth? If so, what would it be?

Again, a better understanding of how planets are structured is vital in unravelling the facts behind these two notable inundation mysteries.

These and other unknowns confront us whichever way we turn. From the origins of humanity to the shifting geology of the Earth, few things escape the plague of unanswered questions confronting the human race today. All are part of an astonishing yet incomplete picture that identifies not only the planet we accept as home, but other worlds extending ever outward through and beyond the Solar System. Each new discovery reveals more pieces of a puzzle that for some reason don't seem to fit our view of the grand picture.

Whilst there are those who are striving for the ultimate answer, many choose to accept we will never know. However, when faced with such a situation, we need to be committed in our mission towards a solution. After all, there is a logical reason for all things.

Significantly, just as with any understanding, to attain an objective, structures must be built on sound foundations. Blind faith is not enough. Answers must be supported by

Earth's Mysteries

appropriate evidence. A convincing judgment needs as many pieces of the puzzle as possible. All of them must be considered. You cannot leave out any piece that doesn't appear to fit. A wrongly constructed concept results in an incorrect answer. And so it is with the origins of humanity. Our piece forms a vital part. It must be placed correctly. Only then will we realise the truth about our existence here on Earth.

The very fact that we are surrounded with so many mysteries covering so many areas of science, simply shows the size and significance of our error. It is obvious we have something fundamentally wrong in our understanding of basic things around us.

Because of this, we must be prepared to go back and rethink past judgements. Unconditional acceptance of conclusions made by others has led to our present situation and in turn, ignorance. Those investigating will need both an open mind and a broad overview of the facts. This way, all information will receive equal consideration ensuring a non bias conclusion.

So where does one begin?

Where is the common problem in our understanding to be found?

The fact that all these mysteries are related in varying degrees to planetary structure and gravity is not a coincidence. This is where the underlying misapprehension lies.

It concerns gravity.

Today, accepted theories on how gravity has formed the Earth and other planets lag behind modern discoveries being made. As a result, our current understanding is clearly not complete. We are missing vital points. Certain factors were not considered or even known to exist in the original decision making process. Age old concepts of planetary structure may remain to this day, but they are significantly flawed. This is a vital issue which in itself has far reaching consequences for all of humanity. It will ultimately change the way we perceive the evolution of our Earth. The planet is not structured the way we believe.

The correct understanding of how gravity operates is the clue needed to solve the origins of humanity and in turn all of these mysteries.

Chapter 3

The Great Flood

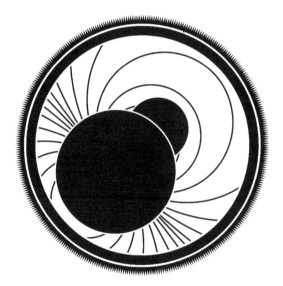

Perhaps the most intriguing question of all is not if the flood occurred...
but who warned Noah?

The Great Flood

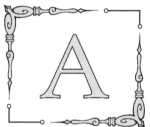nd the Earth shook. The air was still. An unsuspecting world returned to silence. But soon distant rumblings could be heard. Vibrations sent ripples across the water. Suddenly a swelling brown ulcer awoke the sea. Like a beast from the deep, it burst through the ocean surface, a liquid mountain alive with noise. The land and all its inhabitants were doomed.

The titanic force of nature had been released and no power on Earth could stop it.

Fuelled from vaults below, the great oceans grew. Moisture saturated clouds rained upon the Earth. The sea flooded the land as if the very ground itself was sinking. For the animals there was no escape. They feared instinctively, but found nowhere to run. Huge waves thick with sediment and marine life crossed the continents. Forests were bulldozed and valleys were carved. The prevailing water swept everything in its path on a destructive journey into the continents. Mountains of trees and animals were piled high and layers of sediments buried all. Huge boulders were washed great distances from their place of origin.

Growing black clouds swirled together blotting out the sun. As the flood encroached on the poles, frozen white sheets were lifted. Enormous icebergs joined the mixture and travelled with the tide. The Earth was drowning. Our once blue planet was turning brown as the thin veneer of life was wiped clean.

The water continued to rise, suffocating the world and causing massive pressure on the submerged land. The layers of debris were compressed

The Great Flood

and flattened under the tremendous weight, preserving the remains of life trapped within. Tall mountains were covered and still the water rose.

The almighty power of nature was catastrophic.

A wind filled the air and the waters came to a crest. The vaults from the deep had been exhausted. But this was just the eye of the storm. The tide had turned and the ocean brew embarked on its return journey. As the waters flowed within, the mountain peaks once again touched the sky. The Earth began to emerge. As the sea fell, the swirling tide crossed the continents, tattooing their entire length. Deep water flowing off the land carved grand canyons and giant river beds. Eventually the ocean surface receded to a final level. A new coastline formed. But the brown foamy sea was almost indistinguishable from the land. The Earth had been poisoned.

The sun shone through and warmed the world. A rainbow filled half the sky, its kaleidoscope of colours contrasting against the black atmosphere and the turbid earth below.

Nature was ready to begin again...

The great story

We have all been exposed to the legend of Noah and his Ark. This is the fabled story of how a man with his family and two of each animal were saved from a great flood. It takes us back to our childhood when we heard how a displeased God instructed Noah, "Build me an ark, for I will send rain to flood the world". In our minds we could see Noah standing beside his huge wooden boat with all the animals making their way "two by two" up the gangplank. We were told of tall giraffes, lofty elephants and wild lions and tigers. Yes, they were all there, even monkeys. The rain began just as the last of the animals entered the safety of the Ark. Then Noah closed the door behind them.

We were told of how it rained for forty days and forty nights. The water rose higher and higher. The Ark floated away on the waves with everyone safe and dry inside. We heard how the waters drowned all the animals and the evil people on Earth as the land disappeared beneath the flood.

But, eventually the rain stopped and the waters began to retreat. The Ark, with the protected ones inside, came to rest on a high mountain. God sent a rainbow as a promise never to flood the world again. Noah, his family and all the animals then left the Ark and over time repopulated the world.

What a wonderful story it was. We all remember it well. But as we matured, doubts grew with us. Questioning the events, we found some things were just a bit too fantastic to believe.

How could Noah fit so many animals into his Ark?

There are millions of different species throughout the world. It would have been a physical impossibility for one man to achieve such a task. Each animal needed enough food and water to survive the entire duration of the flood. How did Noah supply the quantities of meat needed to feed the carnivorous animals? Even if not all species were saved, the task would still have been enormous. How did Noah get all the animals to the Ark?

But, this is not the only serious difficulty encountered with the story.

The flood itself presents its own set of problems. Where did enough water come from to flood the entire world? And after the flood, where did all the water go? Even if all the moisture in the atmosphere and the polar ice caps were to join the ocean, there would be totally insufficient water for this reported event. So how could a flood of this magnitude be possible? There is simply not enough water on the surface of the planet to allow this.

Today, with so many unanswered questions, the story of Noah appears to have lost its credibility. It seems most consider it more of a fable than an historical event. It is as if Noah has been placed up on the shelf next to Santa Claus and The Easter Bunny. As with these characters, when we mature, impossibilities in their stories become apparent. Perhaps the story may have been fun as a child. But now, it is wrong for us to believe in something without supporting facts.

If on the other hand evidence is present, to ignore it would also be wrong. In pursuit of the truth, it is necessary to examine the facts for ourselves. With minds open, we can then assess the authenticity of this Great Flood.

Did the impossible happen?

Our biblical records are not the only account of this cataclysmic event. It is in fact well documented throughout non-Christian traditions too. Wherever we travel on Earth, we find records of this great inundation. It is a global event recalled in ancient history. More than 250 tribes and civilisations worldwide, speak of it in their legends. They tell of times long ago, when their angry gods destroyed mankind by sending a flood over the Earth.

Ancient people, like the Sumerians of Mesopotamia, left their account on clay tablets. Their story tells of gods who chose a family and instructed them to build a huge boat to survive a great flood, a flood sent to destroy all of mankind.

Utnapishtim, of Babylon, records, through Gligamesh, building a cubic ship with six stories. He took his family, animals and wild beasts aboard to be protected from a flood and hurricane which reduced mankind to clay.

Other legends from Peru, tell of a flood that destroyed all humanity except those who were led to safety, high in the mountains. Still more recall the ocean swelling and overflowing the coasts inundating the land.

Even 300 million Chinese have a traditional story of a great flood that covered the whole Earth.

Tribes worldwide from such places as Russia, India, North and South America as well as China/Asia, the South Pacific, Middle East and Europe all have a similar story to tell. From inscriptions, documented in the past, accounts tell of angry gods who chose a few and destroyed the rest. Those to be saved built boats or rafts or fled to safety high in

The Great Flood

mountains and caves, taking with them life to repopulate the Earth.

These are just some of the countless stories passed down from generation to generation. Even if over time, recounted memories have been somewhat exaggerated, an amazing similarity between them still remains today.

This story has stood the test of time. It has survived countless civilisations for more than 40 centuries. Incredible as this may be, are the legends enough? Is this sufficient for us to believe in this famous event? Did it actually take place? Perhaps we need something more concrete, some other evidence to offer us tangible testimony to the great flood. After all, a cataclysm of this magnitude must have left its mark. Somewhere on the Earth's surface, huge deposits would have been left behind, extensive areas would have been scoured and eroded and interruptions to the ice caps, glaciers and river sediments would have occurred.

But does any such evidence exist?

Animal remains

The early explorers of Northern Alaska and Siberia were amazed when they discovered extensive sediment areas full of animal remains. They found masses of frozen bones and trees buried together in this frigid landscape, a place devoid of any natural living trees. The harsh environment was unable to support the animals whose remains lay there. So where did they originate from? What brought them here?

Amongst the bones were those belonging to extinct species such as the mammoth, mastodon, super bison and a particular specimen belonging to the horse family. Smashed and splintered bones covered huge areas of Siberia, Alaska and islands to the north. Bones of other species still surviving today were also present in the mixture.

The explorers reported hills of crushed and splintered driftwood 75 to 100 metres in height. They could not have known the significance of their find. What caused millions upon millions of animals to be mutilated, torn limb from limb, intermingled with trees ripped from the ground roots and all, and dumped in vast sediments over these inhospitable lands?

One find, equally baffling to science, concerned the frozen carcass of a mammoth. Its stomach contained grasses and plants not indigenous to the region. The different plant species concerned, only grew in warmer climates further south. Microscopic inspection of the mammoth's skin indicated sudden death by suffocation, thought to be drowning. What force brought this and other animals like it here? Even today mammoth tusks are dredged up from the bottom of the Arctic Ocean or washed ashore after storms.

But this evidential destruction is not confined to northern Alaska and Siberia. The story is the same the world over. Right through the British Isles, Western Europe and the Mediterranean, fragmented bones belonging to tropical climate species are found buried together with those of cold climates. Remains of animals from environments thousands of kilometres apart are present in the same soils, fissures and caves. Limestone gaps, in Plymouth England, are filled with remains. Not a single complete skeleton is left, just shattered fragments. It is the same in Devonshire and Pembrokeshire. Near Paris the tops of hills are covered with deposits containing bones. Mount Genay, 440 metres above

The Great Flood

sea level, is such a place. It is capped with sediments that contain mammoth, reindeer, horse and others.

The fresh condition of the bones indicates sudden extinction in recent geological times. Animals are of all levels of maturity from foetuses to fully grown. All perished simultaneously in one single event. The absence of hardened faeces or gnawed bones indicates the animals came from somewhere else.

The same deposits reoccur, along the French coast, Corsica, Sardinia, Sicily and Spain. The cave "San Ciro" near Palermo, Sicily, contained so many bones that 20 tonnes were removed for the production of animal charcoal in the first six months of its exploitation.

One such English cave is the "Victorian" in Yorkshire, 440 metres above sea level. In Wales and France alike mutilated bones of hippopotamus, rhinoceroses, elephant, horse, cave lion, tiger, bear, wolf, deer, fox, hyena, hare, rabbit, birds and others, lie buried in marine clays, mud and sand mixed with foreign pebbles in caves. Again they are not gnawed by predators, dispelling previous assumptions of the animals having been dragged into the caves for consumption by carnivores.

There is no possible way all these animals could have lived together where their remains lie. In fact in many cases the entrances of the caves are too small for the species found inside. Bodies were obviously smashed and fragmented into pieces prior to being swept into the caves. The decayed condition of the bones and cave formation covering them suggests this is the result of a recent event estimated to having taken place within the last 5,000 years.

Even in Northern China, near Peking, caverns and fissures contain the same conglomeration of animal bones. The Siwalik hills north of Delhi, India, are situated at the foot of the Himalayas. Here lie the remains of many more species than anywhere else. Of nearly 30 species of elephant found, only one survives in India today. From Kashmir to Indochina, nature's mass destructive action wiped out huge areas of forest with all inhabitants, burying them in sand. Sediments, that now stretch up hundreds of metres above sea level, remain as testimony to the incredible powers of nature.

To add to the confusion scientists have never satisfactorily explained why large quantities of whale bones are found across Canada and the United States. What force swept large sea creatures to elevations of up to 180 metres as found in Montreal in Quebec, Canada. Bones of whale, walrus and seal are also found in marine sediments north of Lake Ontario in Canada and Michigan, Vermont, Alabama, Georgea and Florida in the United States. The deposits in Michigan reach an elevation of 135 metres and Vermont 150 metres. Astonishingly in parts of Alabama whale bones were so numerous that farmers piled them into fences to rid their fields of them. In Texas, land animals are found buried together in marine deposits.

Two other sites on the east coast of Florida are Vero Beach and Melbourne. Here in separate locations nearly 50 kilometres apart, geologists found deposits containing human bones intermixed in the same stratum with bones of now extinct animal species such as sabre-toothed tiger. Man made artefacts of pottery, arrowheads and stone tools were unearthed at the find. Geologists and anthropologists examining the find agree, the progressive mineralised state of the remains indicates all are of the same age, not much more than roughly 4000 years old, destroyed by one single event. This the same event that spelled

The Great Flood

the end forever for so many species the world over.

Scientists studying the state of these deposits agree that the worldwide conglomeration of bones in sediment indicates some sort of recent global inundation. But, the origins of such a catastrophe remains a mystery.

Those studying gypsum formations in France and elsewhere in Europe were confronted by a common problem. In many cases they found multiple layers of strata abounding with remains from fresh water and dry land plants and animals intermixed in large oceanic deposits. What event caused layers of sea sediment to alternate with land sediment in formations throughout Europe?

To reach a solution scientists came up with a theory. It was concluded that during a past catastrophic event the land in question sank below sea level. In time marine sediments built up over the submerged land. Then it necessitated another catastrophic event to lift the land back up again. Now dry sediments containing plant and animal remains formed over the marine sediments. Subsequently another event caused the land to sink below sea level again. The cycle repeating itself over and over again, resulting in the multi-layered sedimentation seen today. This offered their only solution.

Quite apart from the story being a little unusual, no-one has ever been able to offer any satisfactory explanation as to what caused this recurring incident and why. Some may be satisfied with dropping and rising lands but, even with today's technology and latest scientific discoveries, no evidence to support this belief has been found. Undersea exploration of continental shelves shows no signs of the lifting and dropping sections required to satisfy this theory.

This is because the multi-layered strata was not formed as theorised.

In recent geological times a great flood crossed the land. In one action it swept away and buried most of life on Earth, marine, freshwater and dry land species, all consumed and laid down in tidal bands of sediment as the sea washed over the Earth, such as occurs when different grades of sands, minerals, shells and corals are washed in layers on a beach during a single storm.

Fossils

Fossilised plants and animals exist all over the world. However, such remains are not the result of normal day to day events as many believe. Ordinarily, as a plant or animal dies, it is exposed to the decaying elements of its environment. Under these conditions it naturally breaks down into dust leaving little to record its existence.

When a fossil is found, a very different process has taken place. The plant or animal contained therein has been isolated in a situation where decay was impossible. The most likely cause of this is sudden burial, such as happens in a catastrophic event. Removed from the decaying environment outside, the life-form becomes partially preserved thus retaining recognisable features.

Succumbing to pressure from material above, the trapped plant or animal matter is compressed. Where large deposits exist, multiple bands may form deep below the surface. Over time surrounding minerals slowly penetrate the remains and a fossil is produced.

The Great Flood

When a fossil is found, it not only tells us about the life-form it contains but also the story of how it came to be there. The burying of an animal, tree or even a dinosaur is not a normal occurrence. A fossil is the result of a major event.

The Earth's past was filled with cataclysmic violence. Impacting asteroids and meteorites have reshaped the planet's surface many times over. Over millions of years, displaced oceans and mountains of debris have periodically buried all. Volcanic action randomly smothered forests beneath blankets of ash and stone. All these events have been recorded by life being preserved in sediments.

But there was another event, a cataclysm of recent times. This too has left its signature. Fossil beds were created on a massive scale. This time they did not result from a celestial impact but instead from the devastation of a huge flood, one of global proportions. It tore life apart and buried all in deep bands of silt across the face of the planet.

Such is the case with coal.

What exactly is coal?

Coal is a carbonaceous rock consisting of layers of compacted vegetable debris. It is categorised into different grades: brown, black and anthracite. Brown coal or lignite, as it is known, consists of vegetation partially decomposed and not completely transformed into black coal. Black coal, a later stage, is bituminous, brittle and contains sulphur. Anthracite, the final stage, is a metamorphous rock which is hard and burns slowly.

The content of coal

Coal, when analysed, can be a puzzling mixture. Its composition of vegetable matter invariably encompasses not only a wide ranges of species of both plants and trees but varieties that originate from all parts of the globe. Preserved remains from different climates and various habitats within these climates are all thrown together in turmoil. Fragments from tropical palms are mixed with cold region conifers, swamp species with dry land plants all amassed together in the one deposit. All could not have survived in the one place, in one single environment.

Many seams have upturned fossilised tree trunks encased within them. Still more contain fossilised insects and animals. Others contain pieces of rock known as "erratic boulders". They originate from mountain ranges great distances away.

In Germany, brown coal deposits (lignite) of Geiseital confirm this. The lignite is composed of tropical plant species, living today in Brazil and Java, together with other species from all other climatic regions. Insect fauna preserved in the coal is currently found in America, Africa and Asia. They have been preserved with reptiles, birds and mammals, species belonging to the ape, crocodile and marsupial families. Animals from grassy plains to swamps, birds, insects and plants from all different habitats and climates are buried together in single deposits. Leaf remains are merely torn fragments, yet chlorophyll is still present and preserved. Likewise, parts of preserved insects have retained their original colour and splendour. Animal remains found in the same deposit retain fine muscle and skin texture intact. In the normal environment, such remains would simply decay away on exposure to the elements.

The Great Flood

Where is coal found?

Coal is found at various sites all over the world. Areas range from above the Arctic Circle in the north right through to Antarctica in the south. Deposits are not related to particular climatic regions or continents. The distribution of this strange substance is random right throughout the globe.

Coal's relation to other geology

Coal's configuration with other formations is an equally puzzling factor confronting those who investigate this unusual substance. Most coal deposits are formed in layers or seams. Immediately above and in between each seam are successive sedimentary layers. These sediments are mainly of marine origin containing oceanic remains. These include abundant sea shells with weed, coral and sometimes fossilised fish. Varieties from all parts of the ocean, deep sea species to surface corals can exist in a single sediment layer. In places there are 60 to 80 or even 100 successive coal beds with marine sediment between. In many locations single seams split into numerous other seams over a short distance.

The cause of these alternating seams has mystified science ever since their discovery. Many theories have been proposed as possible explanations but none so far are really considered as convincing solutions.

Because in normal situations dead vegetation exposed to air decays away and cannot produce coal, one theory proposes coal may have been formed in peat bogs over 100's of 1000's of years. Plants and trees growing in these swamps drop their leaves or fall into the water. The matter isolated from the air is then protected from decomposition.

Suddenly a catastrophic event causes the land to sink below sea level taking with it the build up of preserved fallen matter. Silts invade and cover the vegetable remains further, preserving them underneath. Then unexplained tectonic forces cause the land to rise above sea level again, returning the area to swampland. New trees grow in the silt covering the old forest. Vegetation from the new forest falls into the swamp producing a second layer of preserved remains. The land sinks once more, the process repeating itself over and over. Sometimes as much as one hundred repetitions would have been necessary to produce the multi-layered deposits existing today.

Unfortunately, for the creators of this theory and others like it, all observations indicate a different story. No force has ever been found, capable of pulsating the land up and down to satisfy this idea. When considering the sheer number of coal deposits distributed over the Earth it becomes obvious this concept is flawed, particularly when remembering species in one coal seam are not all swamp varieties and have originated from many parts of the world.

Coal did not form this way.

Coal's formation

The volume of vegetable matter required for the production of coal is astonishing. It is estimated it takes 12 metres of plant remains to produce one metre of peat, and in turn, 12 metres of peat to produce one metre of coal. Keeping this in mind and considering some seams exceed 15 metres in thickness, this calculates to a required amount of plant remains in excess of 2000 metres deep to produce them. The question here is; how could so much material be preserved from the natural decaying process in any normal forest generating process?

Coal deposits in polar regions

When studying coal it is currently assumed the vegetation species making up the deposit originally lived and survived in that region. But, what about coal deposits in polar regions?

Antarctica is a frozen wasteland where not a single tree, bush or even grass grows. This is a place where darkness falls for six months of the year. But for scientists the discovery of large coal deposits surely indicates Antarctica once supported great forests.

Like Antarctica, Spitsbergen is a place where nothing much grows. Located 1,600 kilometres inside the Arctic Circle, this frozen wasteland experiences continuous darkness for six months of the year. Yet here, coal exists in deposits up to 9 metres thick. The species making up the coal range from tropical right through to cool climate varieties. Plants from many different regions are once again in the one location.

But how could forests have grown in such frigid regions of the world?

For those investigating, the solution was simple. The presence of coal surely indicated the climate in these regions was once much warmer. The Earth obviously went through dramatic changes sometime in its past. It was concluded, Antarctica, previously subtropical, supported widespread forests. It was these forests that produced the coal deposits of today.

However, just how or why this happened has never been properly explained.

One theory has now been generally accepted as a definite possibility. It proposes a colossal cosmic event. A large comet or asteroid from outer space almost collided with our planet. The Earth's rotation and axis was interrupted by the gravitational field of the terrestrial body. This resulted in the Earth rolling over in space. After the event, all the continents assumed different latitudes as the Earth realigned to the Sun. Tropical lands turned cold and cold lands turned warm. This is considered to be how subtropical Antarctica became the South Pole. Perhaps it should be noted, all of this is just to explain why coal is present in polar regions of the world.

Unfortunately and not surprisingly, no other evidence of such an incredible event has ever been found. This is because the evidence has been misread. The proposed climatic changes never happened as proposed.

So, if the forests didn't grow where they are found, how did the deposits come to be there?

The truth about coal

By analysing the facts concerning coal, an insight into its production becomes clear. Huge amounts of vegetable matter are required to produce a single seam of coal. The conglomeration of this matter usually originates from areas far and wide, covering tropics to cool climates. All the plant species could not have lived together at the site of the

The Great Flood

deposit. Each requires its own special climate to survive.

If catastrophic events swept bone fragments all over the world why not the plants found in coal?

Only a major event could bring all these species into the one place, an event that tore all remains into fragments, and heaped forests into piles 1000's of metres deep, an event that buried and preserved all in silts of oceanic origin. The sheer distances covered by the remains indicates the dimensions of the catastrophe. The state of preservation indicates a sudden event. Bands of marine sediment intermixed with coal deposits, indicates an inundation of oceanic origin. The range of species involved is symptomatic of an event of global proportions. The vegetable and animal matter contained in the coal did not die of natural causes. A cataclysmic flood destroyed them all.

Oceans thick with sediments and marine life flowed over the land sweeping everything in its path. Mountains of trees and animals were piled high in layers of sediment that entombed all. Bone fragments were washed into caves, fissures and cracks all over the world. Animal remains were swept to the poles.

Erosion

The landscape was scoured and changed forever by this historical event.

One such canyon in Arizona was cut for a distance of 350 kilometres. It is up to one and a half kilometres deep and to 13 kilometres wide. Today it is known as "The Grand Canyon". Multitudes look in awe and wonder at the power that created it. This canyon was sculptured, not over millions of years of slow erosion, but by a single event.

Erratic boulders

Massive volumes of debris was swept great distances. The flood broke down mountains and scattered blocks of stone across the landscape. Today, such boulders remain in foreign lands, miles from their mountain origins. Known as "Erratic Boulders", they are recognisable as being different in composition to other geological land forms around them. Erratic boulders are common the world over.

The Jura Mountains divide France and Switzerland. Here lie blocks of stone foreign to the surrounding formations. Their composition indicates they were originally part of the Alps to the west, 50 to 100 kilometres distant. Sand, gravels and clays fill the valleys in between. These erratic boulders are located up to 600 metres above Lake Geneva. Some are up to 250 cubic metres in size, all transported by a past event.

Erratic boulders in great quantities have been carried from the mountains in Norway and dumped on the shores and highlands of the British Isles, transported across the expanse of the Atlantic ocean that stretches between Scandinavia and the British Isles. Other erratic boulders from Scandinavia are massed in Germany. Stone was swept in wide arcs from Finland. Some travelled to Moscow and beyond, others over Poland and up into the Carpathian Mountains. The further from Finland the smaller the fragments, indicating transportation by a medium such as water.

Geological debris found in Russia and nearby countries has been evidently washed there

The Great Flood

by the sea. Clay, sand and gravel is spread in huge volumes over low lying areas of Russia Poland and Germany, sediments transported by the ocean. Southern Sweden, Finland and north-eastern Russia have no mountains, yet are abraded, scored and polished by erratic boulders and silts from this aqueous event.

Erratic boulders originally from Canada and Labrador are found in the north and north-eastern states of America from Main to New York to Wisconsin. They are found in valleys, coastal flats or balanced high on ridges in mountains. One such block in New Hampshire is 27 metres by 12 metres by 11 metres with an estimated weight of 10,000 tonnes. "Mohegan Rock" in Connecticut is estimated at more than 13,000 tonnes.

Erratic boulders are found on isolated islands and littering the floor of all our oceans. Pieces of stone on the bottom of the Atlantic ocean, 1100 metres below the surface, bear the scars of the flood. Originally from continental masses 1600 kilometres away, they are worn, rounded, scratched and grooved. Whilst some are of granite structure others are of sedimentary formation. On discovery scientists ascribed these to glacial action. Their theory required icebergs drifting across the sea dropping boulders torn and scraped off distant mountains. But many of the boulders are loosely consolidated mudstone, all too soft to have survived abrasive glacial action.

Sand

Sand is produced by the eroding action of waves on coastal rocks and normal weathering as occurs inland. Sand is not generated on the bottom of the ocean. There are insufficient currents for erosion to take place. This is a dark and silent world. Yet, massive deposits of eroded sand exist on the abyssal ocean floor. They are found as much as 1900 kilometres from land, five and a half kilometres below the surface. Echo soundings indicate the sand is over a thousand metres deep either side of the Mid-Atlantic Ridge.

Scientists were puzzled by its existence. When first discovered it was considered this area may have been dry land at one time. Then sank five and a half kilometres below sea level. But, any evidence to support this or how this could happen is completely unknown.

Cave paintings, ruins and the remains of ancient tools tell of once good pastures and an abundance of animal life in the Sahara and other deserts. These were places with trees, grasslands, rivers and lakes. Places where now nothing exists except thousands of square kilometres of sand. None of the animals depicted in the cave paintings could survive today in these waterless lands. Some drawings portray extinct species that lived prior to the great flood.

Fraser island, almost totally made up of sand, is the largest single sand island in the world. Located off the east coast of Australia it has an area of nearly half a million acres, is 120 kilometres long, an average of 14 kilometres wide, with dunes that reach up to a height of nearly 250 metres. Its sands have been identified as originating from The Great Dividing Range, west of Sydney over 900 kilometres away.

Loose sand is an unstable substance. It migrates in the wind and is easily eroded by the sea. It is believed the slow process of building Fraser island grain by grain started 400,000 years ago as sand travelled north on ocean currents. However, like The Grand Canyon, Fraser island was formed by a single inundation, just as a sand bank is formed by currents within a tide on a beach.

The Great Flood

The same oceanic event left sediments and erratic boulders across the landscape, washed sands thousands of kilometres out into the ocean, filled lakes and stripped the Sahara and other deserts of their fertile soils. Today, large land areas that once supported a considerable diversity of life, have been left barren.

The timing of the flood

The timing of the flood is recorded in biblical history. Its texts tell of the great inundation event commencing in the year 2,370 B.C. (4,370 years ago) and continued for more than 300 days. Whilst there are those who will always question the timing and duration of the flood, similar periods and dates are in fact recorded in many other non-Christian legends through the world as well. In addition, geological evidence also supports the Earth having experienced a major change around 4400 years ago.

Niagara Falls

The age of the Niagara Falls is calculated by its rate of erosion. Recorded observations indicate the Horseshoe Falls are cutting back into the Upper Great Gorge at a rate of more than a metre per year. The distance carved from Lake Ontario towards Lake Erie gives an idea of how long these falls have been in existence. Estimates based on a constant rate of erosion give an age of a little more than 4000 years. It seems that prior to this date these magnificent falls didn't exist. Why?

River Deltas

Each year, as the Mississippi River empties its waters into the sea, billions of tonnes of sediment are carried with it. A large part of this is deposited at the river mouth creating the famous Mississippi Delta. Studies and measurements have been conducted here for the purpose of establishing the river's past evolution. Scientific and mathematical calculations arrive at the conclusion that the volume of sedimentation comprising the delta amounts to less than 5000 years erosion.

What happened to the tens of thousands of years of sediment anticipated to be there? Surely the Mississippi is more than 5000 years old.

The Bear River Delta, on the Alaskan, British Columbian boarder, revealed a similar history. The age of its delta is estimated at 3600 years. It is thought the glacier that feeds it began to melt at this time. But here again, where are its ancient sediments?

Did the Bear River exist before this time?

Glacial ice

Snow covers many of the world's mountain ranges. When sufficient snow has fallen, it turns to ice and works its way downhill under gravity. In certain circumstances, this downward drift forms large ice sheets on lower slopes. Glaciers are formed as ice builds up on the lower contours of the mountain. The sheer weight of the ice within the glacier causes melting underneath. This melt water acts as a lubricant on which the glacier moves downhill. Resulting friction between the ice and rock below carves into and erodes the mountain.

The Great Flood

By comparing the rate of erosion with the amount of sedimentation left behind, it is possible to calculate how long the process has been taking place. Studies conducted in the Alps has uncovered unexpected results. The amount of sediment in many of these great glaciers proved them to be no more than roughly 4000 years old. What happened prior to this date? Did some Earthly event remove the glacier and its previously existing sediment? If so, does this mean the glaciation process restarted anew just 4000 years ago?

Evidence supporting a major inundation event is overwhelming.

Earth's ancient past has been shaped by a multitude of catastrophic events. Throughout its evolution, asteroids and meteorites impacted upon the surface. As a result displaced oceans spilt over the land. Volcanism blotted out life. Multitudes of life forms were periodically buried under mountains of cataclysmic sediment, trapped and preserved for all time. Ancient fossil beds bear tribute to incredible interruptions to life on Earth. Celestial impacts were a natural occurrence, not only during the early formation of the Solar System, but in recent times as well. Craters, visible on the Moon and other planets are a record of the violent nature and sheer numbers of collisions that occurred in the past.

The Great Flood was a recent event. Just four and a half thousand years ago, the face of Earth changed forever. Whole glaciers, complete with ancient sediments, were stripped clean. Deltas disappeared. Carved canyons gave birth to new and magnificent waterfalls. Sands were dispersed. Broken mountain blocks dotted the landscape. Stripped vegetation was piled high to later transform into deposits of coal, and the bones of victims were left scattered throughout the lands. The flood's signature is everywhere across the face of the Earth. It has been left for us to wonder at the power and magnitude of this famous event.

Was the flood caused by a recent celestial event?

It is hard to deny all the evidence before us. As a consequence many avenues of science agree that sometime in the recent past an inundation of immense proportions took place. Some have put forward theories in an attempt to solve this mystery.

One theory suggests the flood, as with previous catastrophes, was the consequence of a recent impact from outer space. Resulting shock waves swept the oceans across the Earth to the Poles and back again. Others suggest a passing celestial body, on a near collision with Earth, interrupted the world's gravitational field, rolling it over in space. The Poles were reversed. This change in motion caused the oceans to spill out over the face of the planet.

The problem with these ideas and others like them is, this is not how the Great flood was reported. One can only imagine the worldwide destruction taking place during a celestial interaction or collision. Unbelievable forces would have been required to empty the world's entire oceans out of their basins onto the land. How could humanity and beast alike survive such a catastrophic event. An ark or ship of any kind would offer little protection from resulting tidal waves kilometres high ravaging the Earth's surface. With life extinguished, Mother Nature would have to start over again from original primitive beginnings. With displaced oceans flowing back the entire event would have been over in a few days or weeks.

The Great Flood

The biblical portrayal

Biblical texts recall a recent cataclysm of a completely different nature. It tells of one named "Noah" who was warned. There was time to prepare. He built a boat to save himself, his family, animals and goods. It rained for forty days and forty nights. The rising waters swallowed the land. The Ark floated up on the tide, carried on relatively calm waters. Only after reaching a definite peak did the floodwaters begin to subside. The biblical flood lasted an entire year.

Evidence of the deluge is found high in mountainous areas throughout the Earth. These recorded heights are difficult to explain in the terms of a celestial impact. Firstly, a collision of the magnitude required would leave obvious crater damage on the Earth's surface. But when searching the land and sea, no suitable impact site can be found. Secondly, an impact with the power to create tidal waves to such a height would have the potential to not only destroy all of life, but also change the structure of our planet for millions of years. Subsequently, life as we know it today wouldn't exist.

A celestial interaction with Earth does not resolve the mystery of the Great Flood.

So, what was the true cause of the great flood?

Where did enough water come from to cover the Earth? And more importantly where did all the water go? A flood of these proportions defies all reasoning. No satisfactory explanation has come forward. Consequently, doubts have set in and now, for most of us, the Great Flood has faded to nothing more than an ancient mythical tale. But, to find the truth we must face the evidence. We should be asking; if the Great Flood did happen why can't we explain it?

This mystery has remained unsolved for too long. But there is a reason. It stems from a misinterpretation originating from beliefs built generations ago. We have an incorrect understanding of how gravity structures the Earth. Because of this, our geological understanding of Earth is likewise wrong. This is why we can't solve the mystery of the flood. Earth is a world shaped very different to the way we believe.

The Great Flood did occur. It was a direct result of the Earth's natural evolutionary process.

So how do we begin to understand? How and why is the Earth structured differently? What caused the flood?

Clues from biblical texts

Our interpretation of the Bible is the source of all Christianity. However the information contained therein is not so easily deciphered. This is reflected by the sheer number of religions and beliefs evolved from this singular book. But the Bible is more than just a religious book. It is a vital history book as well. Relevant information has been concealed in its ancient texts, cleverly disguised for us to unlock in the future. Mankind will find answers to mysteries obscured thousands of years ago, writings passed on by those before us. Such is the book of Genesis. Here we are told of Earth's creation and a great flood. If we examine the original words used, an amazing picture starts to build before us.

Genesis 1:6 and 7 *"And God said, Let an expanse be in the midst of the waters, and let it divide*

The Great Flood

between the waters and the waters. And God made the expanse, and he separated between the waters which were under the expanse and the waters that were above the expanse. And it was so. And God called the expanse Heavens."

Here is the first clue. In this text we are told of the world created with two separate oceanic bodies, not one. The waters were separated by an expanse. The study of Earth structure in following chapters will show how the coming together of the two bodies of water caused the Great Flood.

Genesis 7:11 *"In the 600th. year of Noah's life in the 17th. day of the month, in this day all the fountains of the great deep were risen and the windows of the heavens were opened up."*

When Genesis narrates the words "the fountains of the great deep were risen" he is telling of waters originating and rising from deep below the surface. This second body of water was the source of the Great Flood. Released as "the windows of the heavens were opened up", the waters rose under pressure as does a fountain. Rapid out-flowing water joined the oceans on the surface. This increased their volume. The seas overflowed and the dry land was inundated.

Thoughts of the flood originating solely from the rains falling upon the earth are not correct. Genesis narrates it differently.

Genesis continues.

Genesis 8:1, 2 and 3 *"And God made a wind to pass over the Earth, and the waters subsided. And the fountains of the deep and windows of the heavens were stopped, and the rain from the heavens was restrained. And the waters retreated from the Earth, going and retreating. And the waters diminished at the end of 150 days."*

This passage has great significance. It sheds more light on the source and cause of the Great Flood. "A wind to pass over the Earth" was escaping pressurised atmosphere from within the planet. It had built up over millions of years of Earth's evolution. The act of opening up the windows of the heavens had released this pressurised atmosphere. Its power forced concealed oceans of water up to the outer surface. Once the vaults of the inner oceans had been exhausted, the excess atmosphere was able to escape. Only then, after 150 days, could the floodwaters flow back into the Earth and the flood begin to subside.

This is where all the water went after the flood. With a new equilibrium reached the volume of atmosphere and sea had changed. They were now both deeper. Many previous low lying dry land areas, today lie permanently submerged beneath the new sea level, a sea level that changed less than 5000 years ago. Evidence of this is present all over the world.

Evidence of a recent change in sea level

Many major river beds and carved valleys do not end at the shore as expected. They continue across continental shelves under the sea. These drowned geological formations could only be born from erosion on land above sea level. An example is found outside New York Harbour where the Hudson River meets the ocean. Here the river bed formation continues right across the full width of the continental shelf. Another example is the

The Great Flood

River Thames. Flowing through London to the sea, the river's original route continues to be traced across the bottom of the North Sea. Surprisingly it meets up with the Rhine's ancient path near Aberdeen off Scotland. These two now famous rivers, then jointly flowed into the Northern Atlantic Ocean. Today both end their journey at the North Sea over 250 kilometres distant from each other.

Submerged continental shelves the world over, bear the markings of rivers, valleys and a previous coastline. But this is not the only evidence indicating a recent rise in sea level. Ancient forests stand in silent aquatic graveyards under the North Sea. Once splendid trees that grew on dry land, are now located 36 metres below the surface 72 kilometres from shore. The trees, mostly Oak, all fell to the north west, their roots still entwined and embedded in the ground. A calculated age coincides with the time of the flood. Other forests too have been found submerged. They exist today in numerous places such as off the east coast of America.

In other areas, the Bahamas being one example, caves are found beneath the sea. Submerged caverns and grottoes exhibit a range of formations such as stalactites and stalagmites. These have been created over long periods of time by the slow action of dripping water and evaporation, something not possible underwater.

Other caves, with entrances now concealed beneath the sea, contain prehistory humans recorded in art. One such place is Morgiou Inlet in the south east of France. Here, 36 metres below the surface of the Mediterranean, a one metre wide passage leads to the recently discovered Grotto Cosquer. Walls are decorated with prehistory art. Horses, bighorn goat, stag, bison and stencilled hands are all hidden in the total darkness. Some are partially obscured behind a thin veneer of cave formation. Experts authenticating the find estimate their age at approximately 20,000 years. The singular tunnel entrance, now submerged by the invading sea, is the only access to this amazing cave.

In the pre-flood era, much as today, the oceans were used as major trading routes. Accordingly, many cities and ports were built on the foreshore. Today their structures stand in ruin just a few fathoms beneath the new sea surface. Reminders of forgotten peoples who, with intricate construction skills, became victim to the Great Flood.

Ruins are found in locations such as; beneath the Mediterranean, Aegean and Caribbean Seas. Structures like the Bimini Wall stand a few hundred metres from the shore of Bimini, off the east coast of Florida. Its architectural design is similar to that of other ruins found elsewhere above sea level. Other remnants are reported off Andros Island. Pottery fragments brought to the surface from these sites has been dated pre-flood at around 3,000 to 5,000 B.C.

But the rise in sea level is not the result of the melting of an ice age as is generally accepted. It is part of the aftermath of a great flood that ravaged the Earth less than 4,500 years ago. The ancient world changed forever when one of Earth's evolutionary eras ended and another began. It is written in age-old texts, reported by those who knew the true structure of Earth.

And finally, the Great Flood, originally thought to be a unique event, was considered unparalleled anywhere else. But this is not so. Another similar flood has been discovered on a close celestial neighbour, the planet Mars.

The Great Flood

Scientists were astonished when their space probes sent back pictures of massive flood erosion on this dry planet. With an atmospheric pressure too low to support water in a natural liquid state, scientists remain confused by what they found. Outflow channels and chaotic terrain show where subterranean water broke through the surface crust of the planet. From here, river channels, drainage networks, and flow patterns stretch for hundreds of kilometres across the Martian landscape. Today the only water visible is the layer of ice at the Martian poles.

So what does this mean? Is there a connection between the Great Flood on Earth and this recent discovery on Mars?

As we examine the evidence for ourselves, it will be shown how the same evolutionary processes that created the Great Flood on Earth produced a similar flood on Mars.

The Great Flood was a direct result of gravitational processes at work shaping the inner Earth. It is the same inner Earth that holds the secret to the origins of humanity. To understand why this is true and how the inner Earth is structured, it is firstly necessary to investigate what is taking place on the outer surface. Here, the link between geology and seismic activity offers a crucial clue.

Chapter 4

Our Expanding Earth

What if we are not missing any pieces at all...
Perhaps the puzzle is smaller than we believe.

Our Expanding Earth

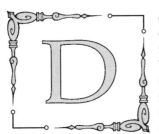eep in the past, a questioning thought entered our minds for the first time. Those from early times looked to the horizon with curiosity. Their innocent eyes pondered the surrounding environment. They observed the encompassing land, the sky and stars above and saw the world was flat. Everyone could see, and a common belief grew amongst the people. Following generations saw the same, and thus it became so. All views were alike, ruling without opposition.

As investigation of the surrounding land and sea began, a realisation arose. The explorers found something wasn't quite right. Measurements on their maps wouldn't fit. They were trying to put a round Earth onto a flat surface. Unfortunately the eventual discovery of this presented them with a serious problem. Upheld beliefs cannot be questioned. The Earth was flat and had been for generations. This was an unchangeable fact. However, whilst there were those who feared the consequences of any opposing viewpoints, there were others who were determined to tell of their find.

But the people of the day, feeling threatened, could not accept this new idea and thus ridiculed them. Naive minds argued; wouldn't those on the other side fall off? Surely the oceans would run away and besides what would a round Earth sit on? With these simplistic points of view, it was easy to show just how foolish the "round" Earth was. All were confident they were right. Everyone agreed with each other and there was no chance that the whole world was wrong. Happy again, they returned to their preconceived ideas, comfortable that the new concept hadn't changed their world. The explorers found themselves alone.

Eventually it was realised the round Earth was an undoubtable fact. But although the truth was finally known, people could not accept the reality. Mankind was not equipped with an ability to change. Stubbornness had built a wall around old ideas. Humanity

Our Expanding Earth

was unable to escape. The truth was only taken in as new generations replaced the old. Their fresh minds could examine the evidence without restriction, formulating the correct opinion. But along with these new people, an understanding was built, a knowledge of a force they called gravity.

With the discovery of gravity, an advanced understanding had arisen and fresh avenues of study were opened. With this opportunity now available, scientists eagerly calculated the internal structure of the spherical world. With their new perception of this force, they concluded all matter was attracted down towards the Earth's centre. This concept helped build the first structural models of the planet.

Heavy metallic masses within the Earth had sunk forming a central core. Then in turn, less dense material surrounded the core, creating the region known as the Mantle. It was believed pressures created within the Earth caused solidification of the lower Mantle despite the upper reaches remaining molten. This molten region is where the Mantle meets the outer crust, the solidified skin with its continents and ocean basins completing the picture. (Fig. 4.1)

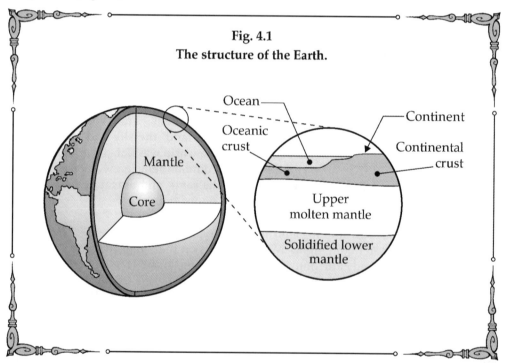

Fig. 4.1
The structure of the Earth.

Gravity was the answer to all their problems. It was responsible for the Earth being solid, compressed and round. It kept all the planets in their orbits and held us, the oceans and everything on the Earth. Mankind was once again happy. We had created a brand new comfort zone, a realisation which was so much better than the last. It was right, because everyone believed without question, and the whole world could not be wrong.

Many generations passed and the explorers mapped the coastlines. Gradually the round Earth was unveiled. But as the continental shapes came into view something very unusual was noticed. The shapes of continental edges either side of the Atlantic mimicked each other. For the first time, it was proposed that these continents were once joined and had somehow broken and moved apart leaving the Atlantic ocean in between. (Fig. 4.2)

Our Expanding Earth

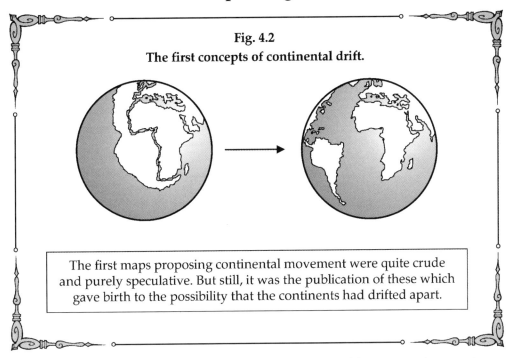

Fig. 4.2
The first concepts of continental drift.

The first maps proposing continental movement were quite crude and purely speculative. But still, it was the publication of these which gave birth to the possibility that the continents had drifted apart.

This new idea upset the beliefs of the human race. How could entire continents migrate across the globe? No such force existed on their solid stable Earth. Everyone knew the land was stationary, so the idea of continental drift was immediately discounted. It was considered nothing more than a preposterous theory which lacked substance and reality.

The continental puzzle

Exploration continued, but eventually it was discovered that the continental shapes were not the only parts which appeared to fit together. Mountain ranges on both sides of the Atlantic could also be reunited. This evidence injected new life into the continental drift theory. It was decided a closer examination was necessary. Geological studies in both South America and Africa revealed not only mountain ranges, but soil types, rock strata and even glacial remnants matched as well. The overwhelming evidence was conclusive. Science likened it to a huge jig-saw puzzle where not only did the shapes fit but the picture matched also.

Ongoing investigations revealed more. It was found, not only the continents either side of the Atlantic were once joined, but in fact all the continents of the world were involved. Scientists were astonished to discover each and every continent was just a broken piece of a once grand singular super continent. For reasons unknown, it appeared inner forces fragmented the ancient super landmass into sections. Then over time, these sections somehow drifted away from each other to produce the world map we know today. Scientists named their ancient super continent "Pangaea".

As technology advanced, investigation of shallow ocean floor became possible. As exploration took place, the first underwater maps came into existence. From these, it was discovered the edges of the continents did not lie at the coastline, but instead were under the sea at varying distances from the shore. All continents ended abruptly at a cliff type edge. Broken escarpment formations continued around the perimeter of all continents

Our Expanding Earth

Fig. 4.3
The edge of the continents.

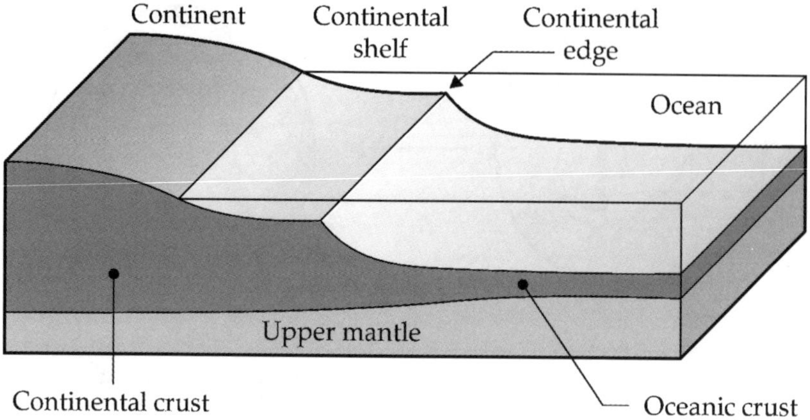

Continent   Continental   Continental
shelf   edge

Ocean

Upper mantle

Continental crust

Oceanic crust

The edge of the continents do not lie at the coastlines, but instead extend out under the sea at varying distances from the shore.

Fig. 4.4
Continental shelves of the world.

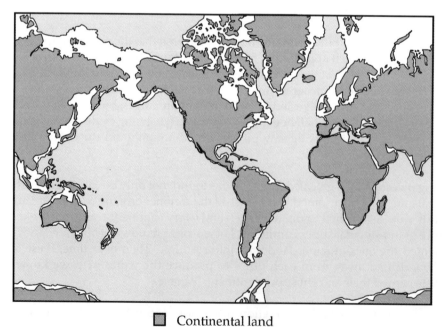

◼ Continental land
☐ Continental shelves
☐ Ocean floor

Our Expanding Earth

of the world. There were no exceptions. It is here, landmasses provided a more perfect fit when reunited. The submerged region between the ocean shore and the cliff edges became known as the "Continental Shelves". Beyond these edges, the sea bed plunged into the oceanic abyss. (Figs. 4.3, 4.4, 4.5)

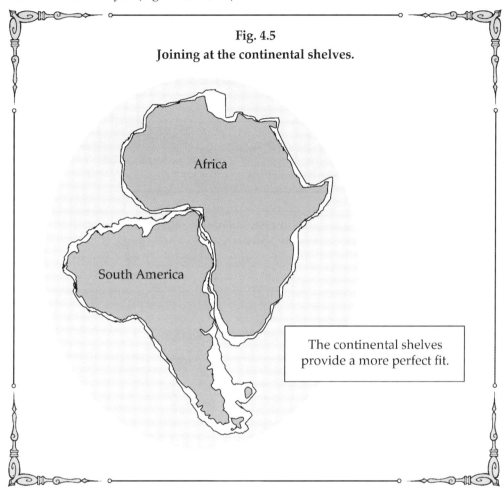

Fig. 4.5
Joining at the continental shelves.

Africa

South America

The continental shelves provide a more perfect fit.

Human thirst for knowledge pushed the boundaries of technology forward and new methods of exploration were developed. With unmanned submersibles and depth sounding advancements, we had our first look at the dark watery realm beyond the continental shelves. As the abyssal ocean floor progressively came to light, a deeper layer of understanding arose.

There had been much speculation as to what the world's oceans were concealing, but no-one could have imagined what they were about to discover. Preconceived ideas of random hills and valleys were extinguished by a repetition which surfaced. Latest equipment had unveiled new shapes forever hidden below. Scientists were now mapping one of Earth's great wonders, continuous mountain chains, running the length and breadth of the planet, never before seen. Mountains located in mid oceanic regions mimicking the outline of the surrounding land masses. Without realising it, we had become witness to the backbone of all oceanic floor creation. We had finally discovered the Earth's largest and most extensive geological structure. These formations were named "Mid Ocean Ridges". (Figs. 4.6, 4.7)

Our Expanding Earth

Fig. 4.6
Mid ocean ridges.

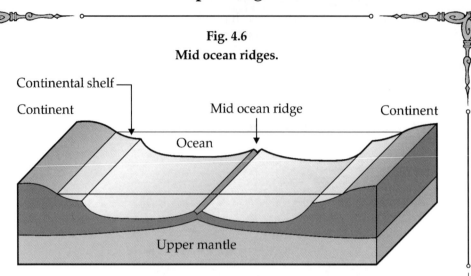

Like a huge submerged mountain range, mid ocean ridges
follow the oceans and encompass the entire globe.

Fig. 4.7
Mid ocean ridges of the world.

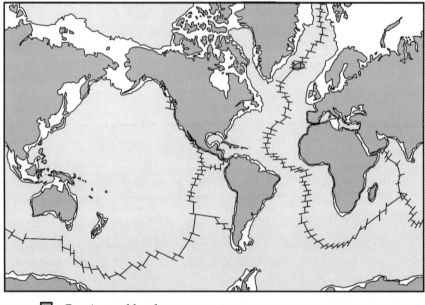

■ Continental land
☐ Continental shelves
☐ Ocean floor

Mid ocean ridge

Our Expanding Earth

Scientists became captivated in this new frontier, as a real possibility arose that the answers to continental drift could be just below the surface. Great effort and resources were put to work and a new in depth investigation of the ridges was undertaken.

They were amazed when they found these mountain ranges were volcanically active. Underwater eruptions followed the ridge's centre line bisecting the ocean floors. This bazaar submarine activity was observed through the entire mountain chain. The very existence of these unique volcanic ridges became the latest inconsistency in Earth's confusing geology. A new mystery of global proportions had appeared over the horizon.

Recently formed ocean floors

It was obvious that some unknown but natural phenomenon had created the mid ocean mountain chains, but what? And what part did they play in the evolution of Earth? Puzzled scientists searched the ocean floor for clues. Studies conducted on the mid ocean ridges found their structure was very young, formed in recent geological times. Discovering these globally extensive features was quite a shock, but, to understand that they were also geologically very young, was something totally unexpected. So further investigation of the ocean floor followed.

Studies of the sea bed crust in the near vicinity of the ridges also showed very young geology. These large areas of ocean floor had been created in recent times. As progression was made away from the ridges, the age of the ocean floor increased. Finally, deep ocean beds, next to the continental land masses, were both the oldest and furthest from the mid ocean ridges.

The oceanic crust was discovered to be different in structure from the surrounding continental landmasses. Apart from being younger, it was also thinner and more dense in its composition. It is the same throughout the world, regardless of where tests were carried out. Scientists became aware of a direct relationship between volcanic activity taking place at mid ocean ridges and the age of ocean floor geology.

Another point of interest was noticed. Whilst sedimentary rock occurs frequently over all the continents of the world, the deep oceanic floor was found to be devoid of this common geology.

With a higher degree of understanding, it was soon realised the shape shared between the chains of ridges and continental outlines had a common link. Considering the continents were fragments of a once single super landmass, scientists concluded, ocean floor had been created between the present continental pieces as the main landmass broke up and drifted apart. The mid ocean ridges are the source of ocean floor creation. They are responsible for filling in the gaps between the continents, a process still continuing today. This led to the renaming of the mid oceanic ridges to "Spreading Sites". And so, a greater comprehension of continental movement had been achieved.

By the use of scientific dating techniques it is agreed that the continental landmasses were formed up to 4,000 million years ago. It is also known, by the same dating techniques, the oldest ocean floor is found next to continental shelves, this the furthest point from oceanic spreading sites. But the calculations presented a serious discrepancy. The age of the oldest ocean floor was dated at only 200 million years, 3,800 million years short of Earth's continental beginnings. Why?

Our Expanding Earth

This equates to 200 million square kilometres of Earth's surface having been created in the last one twentieth of the planet's surface crust history. In other words, almost all the area of the Earth's surface presently covered by the oceanic expanses, didn't exist 200 million years ago, yet all the continents did. What was the Earth like then? Creation of two thirds of Earth's surface in the last 200 million years adds up to a surface space problem on the planet, a planet assumed having always been its present size, and therefore surface area, right through its 4,000 million year continental history.

Increasing surface area problem

The scientific community had found themselves confronted with a serious problem. Oceanic crust forming throughout the globe was seemingly adding new surface area to the Earth. But how could this be possible? This would be symptomatic of a planet in a state of expansion, something their understanding of gravity simply did not allow.

Gravity was the force that bound material together. It held the planet's mass, and everything on it, in a state of compression. An expanding Earth contradicted all accepted beliefs, beliefs that had become facts welded in our minds and could not be changed. Gravity was the answer in the past and no-one was going to leave its comfort zone to explore these inconsistencies. Having come this far, it was too late to turn back now. The decision was made. There had to be another answer.

So where did mankind stand now?

It was known all Earth's present oceans had been created at spreading sites over the last 200 million years. This computed to an average of one square kilometre added per year over this time period.

It was also known that no ocean floor older than 200 million years existed anywhere on Earth. As expansion was deemed impossible, it was concluded our constant diameter Earth must have supported older expansive oceanic areas, those existing prior to the present 200 million year era. But what happened to them?

A perplexed scientific community sought a solution to this, their newest bewildering mystery. With minds pooled, it was mutually agreed the ancient ocean floors must have somehow been proportionately consumed as new ocean floor was added at spreading sites. With this preconceived idea in mind, mankind interrogated the sea bed in search for evidence.

Whilst the mid oceanic ridges are the major structural formation, other less prominent geological features exist here too. Deep oceanic trenches, dwarfed by the size of the ridges, exist around the perimeter of the Pacific. In some cases, the floors of these trenches lie more than 11 kilometres below the sea surface. Being natural fault lines, earthquakes are often recorded along their network. (Figs. 4.8, 4.9)

This is where the scientific search ended. The trenches were all that was available to fulfill theory requirements. Their linear format and observed seismic activity became the centre of attention. It was concluded, the trenches were merely the surface formation of a deeper cycle of geological processes. It was proposed that this must be where old ocean floor passes down into the molten interior to counteract growth at spreading sites. Their theory of ocean floor destruction was appropriately named "Subduction".

Our Expanding Earth

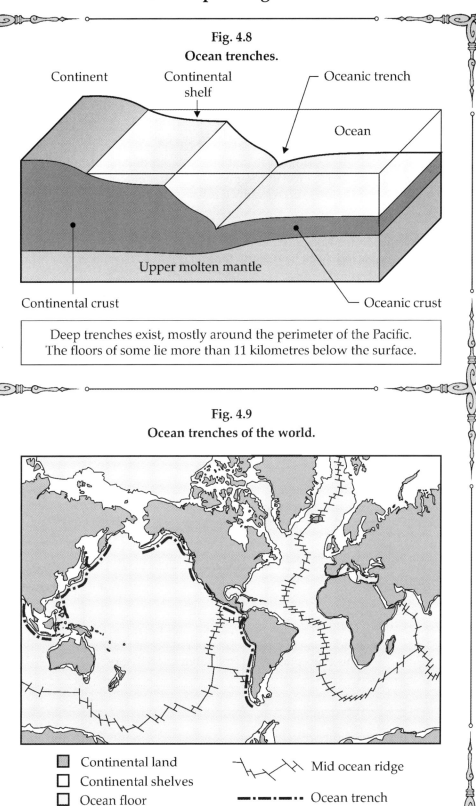

Fig. 4.8
Ocean trenches.

Continent

Continental shelf

Oceanic trench

Ocean

Upper molten mantle

Continental crust

Oceanic crust

Deep trenches exist, mostly around the perimeter of the Pacific.
The floors of some lie more than 11 kilometres below the surface.

Fig. 4.9
Ocean trenches of the world.

Continental land
Continental shelves
Ocean floor

Mid ocean ridge

Ocean trench

Our Expanding Earth

It is considered fact that all the landmasses and ocean basins making up the planet's surface are just a thin veneer or crust of solidified material. This crust, resting on the molten interior of our planet, is broken into several sections or pieces known as plates. The edges of these plates are situated almost entirely on the ocean floor. It is in close proximity to these boundaries that most of the world's earthquakes and volcanic activity occurs.

Spreading sites, which exist between some plate boundaries, add new ocean floor to both edges. As extra space is created, the sea floor and continents move laterally away from the mid ocean ridges. It is surmised that at other corresponding plate boundaries the pressure from spreading site growth progressively forces one plate beneath the other into the molten interior below. This is assumed to have produced these geological features known as trenches.

The counteractive destruction of ancient ocean floors is theorised to have maintained a constant surface area and diameter of Earth throughout its 4,000 million year continental history.

Satisfied with their concept, scientists renamed the trenches "Subduction Zones". (Fig. 4.10)

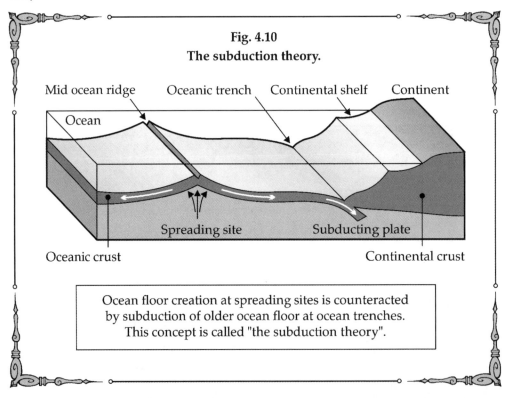

Fig. 4.10
The subduction theory.

Mid ocean ridge   Oceanic trench   Continental shelf   Continent

Ocean

Spreading site   Subducting plate

Oceanic crust   Continental crust

> Ocean floor creation at spreading sites is counteracted
> by subduction of older ocean floor at ocean trenches.
> This concept is called "the subduction theory".

Finally they had solved the creation of excess surface area on the Earth, the absence of any ancient ocean floors, and the reason for continental movement. Their new theory was prominently named "Plate Tectonics". Everyone was satisfied and content in their new comfort zone of understanding.

However, there was still one problem to be solved.

Our Expanding Earth

It was concluded that continental movement must be the reflection of far deeper inner planetary workings. But exactly how they worked was still a total mystery.

Continental movement and ocean floor growth had been observed, but their Plate Tectonics theory was incomplete without an explanation of its driving force. This would be a force that would link their subduction theories with spreading sites. To help resolve this dilemma, several proposals have been put forward.

Theory No. 1 - Pressure from below forces plates apart.

The super-heated interior gives rise to all volcanic activity on the planet. Spreading sites are believed to be a direct link with this volcanic material within. One theory proposes, molten material originating from the Mantle, rises under pressure at spreading sites and forces adjoining plates apart. (Fig. 4.11)

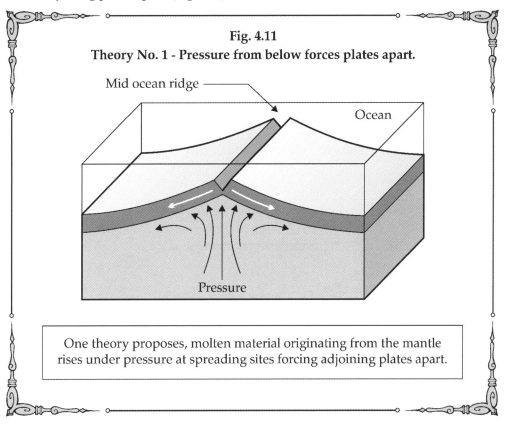

Fig. 4.11
Theory No. 1 - Pressure from below forces plates apart.

Mid ocean ridge

Ocean

Pressure

One theory proposes, molten material originating from the mantle rises under pressure at spreading sites forcing adjoining plates apart.

The feasibility of this system is considered questionable by many scientists. It is unlikely that any material, in a molten state, could supply enough force to push plates, complete with continents thousands of kilometres across and thousands of kilometres wide in a sideways movement, particularly when one takes into consideration how thin these plates are in proportion to their size. Being just a few kilometres thick, they would simply buckle and fold if pressure was applied from one edge. Because of their sheer volume together with friction over the Mantle, lateral movement originating solely from spreading site pressure is not physically plausible.

Other forces coordinated with spreading would need to be at work if whole plates are to

Our Expanding Earth

move in one singular piece.

Iceland, located in the northern Atlantic off Greenland, is bisected by the northern reaches of the Mid-Atlantic Ridge. This rare and easily accessible segment of spreading site has given scientists a first hand view of plate movement. Observations and studies conducted here indicate that rather than forcing plates apart, rising lava permissively fills gaps as they appear in the island. Sitting astride two plates, this island is gradually pulled apart by forces other than spreading site pressure, forces yet to be determined.

Theory No. 2 - Plates slide downhill from spreading sites to subduction.

A second theory suggests the action of gravity helps slide plates apart.

Pressure rising up from the Mantle has lifted the sea bed to higher elevations at spreading sites, whilst at the opposite edges of plates, subduction trenches have provided lows. The critical difference in altitude between the two, allows the action of gravity to slide the whole plate downhill from spreading to subduction. This can be somewhat likened to a tablecloth sliding off an inclined table. The theorised advantage of this suggestion is, the action producing movement is applied to the whole plate area instead of pressure at one edge as in the previous theory. (Fig. 4.12)

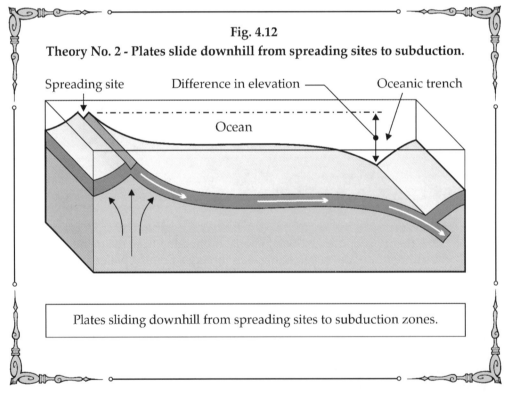

Fig. 4.12

Theory No. 2 - Plates slide downhill from spreading sites to subduction.

Spreading site   Difference in elevation   Oceanic trench

Ocean

Plates sliding downhill from spreading sites to subduction zones.

If we are to assume spreading sites and trenches are part of a synchronised cycle causing plates to slide downhill, then surely a similarity between their shapes and proximity to each other would result. Just as spreading sites mimic the outline of continental shapes, shouldn't subduction trenches do the same?

The fact is, they do not.

Our Expanding Earth

Trenches are located randomly over the globe bearing little to no relationship to the positioning and shape of spreading sites. The majority of trenches are located around the perimeter of the Pacific, thousands of kilometres from the greater percentage of spreading sites. This presents a particularly difficult problem when considering downhill gradients. Distances are too great.

One such example is the East Pacific Rise. This spreading site creates new ocean floor which, if we are to believe this theory, slides downhill to subduction trenches in excess of 12,000 kilometres away off the coast of Japan. Whilst the difference in elevation between spreading and subduction varies a few thousand metres, the amount is far too insignificant to effect any downhill gradient over this 12,000 kilometre distance. What is being suggested is the Pacific ocean floor is sliding downhill for a distance of more than one quarter the way around the world!

We should bear in mind, the theory for downhill sliding is calculated on elevations in the immediate vicinity of spreading sites and subduction trenches. The greater percentage of the remaining ocean floors, despite many undulations, averages out as roughly level and therefore unable to assist any downhill sliding process. Even if we consider other situations where subduction trenches are in closer proximity to spreading the problem still arises.

The oceanic plate on the eastern side of the same East Pacific Rise travels from this spreading site to subduction in the Peru-Chile Trench off the coast of South America some 4,000 kilometres away. This lesser distance is also too far for downhill sliding to work.

For an easier understanding of the problem let's draw a comparison.

Imagine this 4,000 kilometre distance scaled down to a one and a half metre long table. The plate is a tablecloth on the table. To represent the elevation at the spreading site we lift up one edge of the tablecloth just two millimetres. Then at the opposite end of the table, to represent the subduction trench, we overhang the tablecloth another two millimetres down over the edge. For this Plate Tectonics theory to work, the tablecloth is now expected to slide off the table under the pull of gravity. For the 12,000 kilometre distance the same model applies provided the table is now three metres longer. Unfortunately for supporters of this theory, the mathematics behind it don't add up. Some other process needs to be found to satisfy Plate Tectonic believers.

Another thing that appears to have been overlooked by the instigators of this theory is, if spreading is resultant of plates sliding downhill away from each other into subduction trenches, what process activates those spreading sites that are devoid of trenches?

The Antarctic Plate is a good example of this. Here, as sea floor is added at spreading sites, the plate's margins extend out in all directions. As the plate grows, spreading sites ridges slowly migrate away from Antarctica. The fact that no subduction trenches exist between the ridges and Antarctica means the action of spreading is taking place totally oblivious of any downhill sliding motion. Another almost identical situation exists around the African plate.

Downhill sliding does not activate the phenomenon of Plate Tectonics. Another driving force needs to be found if we are to solve this riddle.

Our Expanding Earth

Theory No. 3 - Subducted sections pulled down by gravity

The concept of gravity acting on the ocean floor is the basis of yet another theory. It is thought extended sections of old ocean floors protrude deep into subduction trenches. Assumed to have sufficient mass, these plate edges are pulled down by gravity into the Mantle below. This operation drags the entire plate behind it, which in turn opens up spreading sites at opposite edges. Here rising lava passively fills widening cracks building new sea floor replacing the old as it is destroyed in the Mantle. (Fig. 4.13)

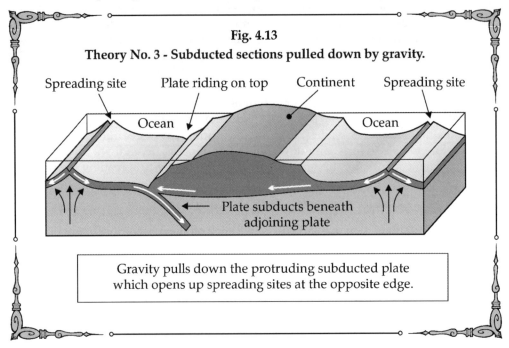

Fig. 4.13
Theory No. 3 - Subducted sections pulled down by gravity.

Spreading site   Plate riding on top   Continent   Spreading site

Ocean   Ocean

Plate subducts beneath adjoining plate

Gravity pulls down the protruding subducted plate which opens up spreading sites at the opposite edge.

Unfortunately as before, this theory fails to provide any satisfactory answers. Its concept is based on workings similar to the previous proposal where ocean floor growth at spreading sites is resultant of subduction occurring elsewhere. As already discussed, the absence of subduction zones on the Antarctic and African plates presents an exception. Here, it is not possible to explain the spreading process as simply the result of gravity pulling subducted plate edges down.

Just to add more confusion, it is not possible for both meeting plate edges to subduct simultaneously. Instead, as expanding plates come together, one supposedly rides over the other (As seen in fig 4.13). As the theory proposes, the one beneath sinks down into the Mantle dragging the rest of the plate behind it opening up the spreading site. Even if gravity was able to pull down the subducted trailing crust, what of the plate riding over the top? It cannot subduct through the other plate.

How does its spreading site expand if gravity cannot act on a downward trailing edge? As already discussed any downhill gradient over these extensive distances is too slight to aid the process.

It is expressed as doubtful by many tectonic scientists and mathematicians that these thin ocean crusts, thousands of kilometres wide, complete with continents, are strong enough to be pulled in single portions from one edge. They would simply break.

Our Expanding Earth

Several discrepancies appear with this theory.

Not only is it assessed there would be insufficient mass in subducted edges for gravity to activate the continental movement process, but how did the process begin in the first place? Initially there would not have been any subducted crust for gravity to act on. Furthermore there is totally insufficient volume of trenches to cater for the amount of ocean floor creation at spreading sites.

Trenches, as discussed, are wrongly located for any synchronised movement to take place. In many cases it would be necessary for the ocean crust to turn almost at right angles on its journey to subduction, something not evident when studying the structure of the sea floor. Twisting as well as compression would be necessary if ocean floors were to fit into trenches, this resultant friction would nullify any effect that gravity might have on the assumed subducted plate edges.

There are further problems when evaluating sinking subducted plate edges. Geological studies below the surface indicate Earth's outer crust rests upon the molten upper reaches of the Mantle. In other words, all the continents and ocean floors are thought to be buoyant on liquefied material lying beneath. If the assumption is correct and the Earth's plates do in fact float on the Mantle, what process allows this material to conveniently sink to destruction at subduction trenches? The Earth's crust either floats on or sinks into the Mantle. It cannot do both. Yet this Plate Tectonics theory requires just that. In addition, various mathematical calculations evaluate the compressed state of the Mantle as too great to allow oceanic crust to sink into it.

As tectonic understanding is advancing, further complications continue to surface. The discovery of gravity variations across the ocean floor is one such instance. The action of gravity is accepted as the prime motivating force behind Plate Tectonic theories. Yet specialised gravimeter equipment has revealed abnormal deficiencies in gravity in the depths of oceanic trenches. The greatest depletion has been recorded in trenches off Indonesia in the Western Pacific. Here and elsewhere, it is considered obvious, gravity in its reduced strength, would be insufficient to activate downward subduction of plate edge margins. Analysts agree, if subduction does actually take place here, then some force other than gravity must be at work. But as of yet, none has been found.

At this point we must ask the question as to why no satisfactory explanation has come forward to clarify the reason for these ocean floor gravity lows and thus what causes them.

The problem with this theory becomes even more obvious when examining a cross section of the Mid-Atlantic Ridge. (Fig. 4.14)

The diagram represents an approximate 30 million square kilometre area of the Earth's surface. It includes parts of South America, the Atlantic, Africa and portions of the Pacific and Indian Oceans. This region is 9,000 kilometres wide extending from the Equator to 4,500 kilometres south. Here the spreading sites of the Mid-Atlantic Ridge and Southwest Indian Ridge are continuously creating new ocean floor as the South American, African and Australian Indian plates move apart. This adding of new ocean floor is slowly increasing the overall area of the plates. As can be seen on the diagram, these sections of the South American and African plates are devoid of subduction edges. Yet spreading and consequent ocean floor creation is taking place successfully, without the aid of gravity

Our Expanding Earth

acting on any downward trailing edges.

These features, vital to support the accuracy of this theory, are missing.

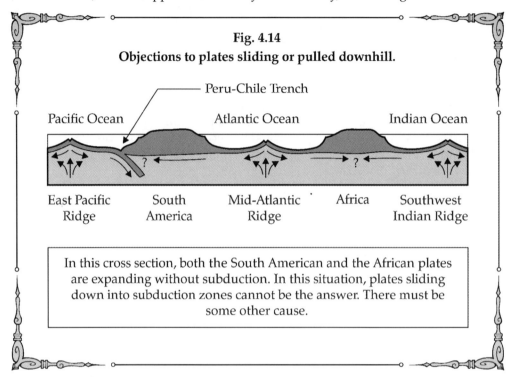

Fig. 4.14
Objections to plates sliding or pulled downhill.

Peru-Chile Trench

Pacific Ocean   Atlantic Ocean   Indian Ocean

East Pacific   South   Mid-Atlantic   Africa   Southwest
Ridge   America   Ridge   Indian Ridge

In this cross section, both the South American and the African plates
are expanding without subduction. In this situation, plates sliding
down into subduction zones cannot be the answer. There must be
some other cause.

In summary, unfortunately all these considered theories fail when evaluated against the real "in the field" situation. Calculated gravitational forces acting on the edges of Earth's immense plates are far too insignificant to complete the assigned subduction task. Models so easily presented in our text books don't align with the real situation. The scales of distances, thickness of crust and size cannot be seen or even imagined. Their illustrations only present Plate Tectonic preconceived ideas, viewed in simplistic form for ease of understanding. Regretfully, this only serves to distort the real picture.

Concerned Plate Tectonic believers, realising this, went in search for an alternative to support their subduction theory. Despite being contrary to observations at spreading sites, it had already been decided, the action of gravity pulls matter together into compression thus eliminating the remotest possibility of the Earth being in a state of expansion. Yet, new surface area is being constantly created, year by year, as plates move apart. Just a few centimetres at a time but equating to approximately one square kilometre is added per year to the Earth's surface.

All the known ocean floors worldwide have been formed over the past 200 million years by this creation action at spreading sites. Scientists knew, without subduction theories to counteracting ocean floor growth, upheld beliefs concerning gravity would have to be changed to accommodate Earth expansion. Decisions already made on gravity were indisputable. It was therefore reconfirmed, in order to maintain Earth's constant diameter throughout history, destruction of excess ocean floor by subduction must occur. To add credibility to their cause it was necessary to find a solution, a force that could move whole plates in one action, plates too thin and immense to be pushed or pulled from one edge.

Our Expanding Earth

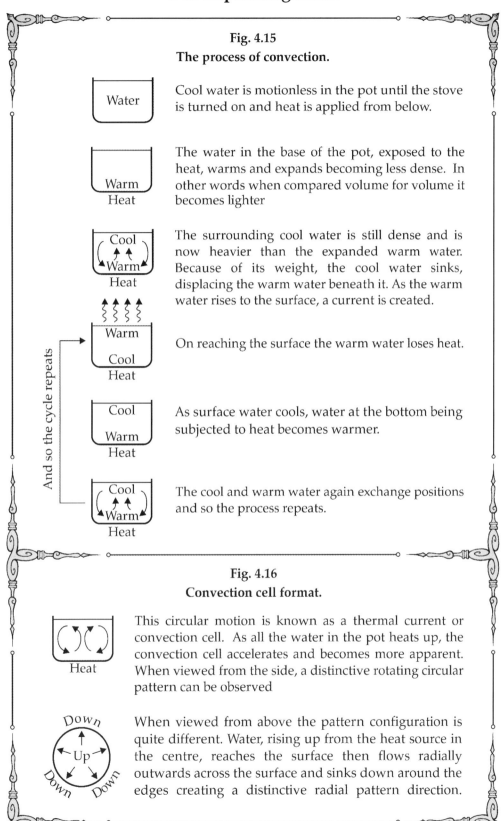

Fig. 4.15
The process of convection.

Cool water is motionless in the pot until the stove is turned on and heat is applied from below.

The water in the base of the pot, exposed to the heat, warms and expands becoming less dense. In other words when compared volume for volume it becomes lighter

The surrounding cool water is still dense and is now heavier than the expanded warm water. Because of its weight, the cool water sinks, displacing the warm water beneath it. As the warm water rises to the surface, a current is created.

On reaching the surface the warm water loses heat.

As surface water cools, water at the bottom being subjected to heat becomes warmer.

The cool and warm water again exchange positions and so the process repeats.

And so the cycle repeats

Fig. 4.16
Convection cell format.

This circular motion is known as a thermal current or convection cell. As all the water in the pot heats up, the convection cell accelerates and becomes more apparent. When viewed from the side, a distinctive rotating circular pattern can be observed

When viewed from above the pattern configuration is quite different. Water, rising up from the heat source in the centre, reaches the surface then flows radially outwards across the surface and sinks down around the edges creating a distinctive radial pattern direction.

Our Expanding Earth

Surely there must be a deeper functioning cycle that is yet to be discovered. A force powerful enough to carry these whole plates, complete with continents and ocean floors, in one single piece. Discussions were focussed on the super-heated interior of Earth. Is it possible that heat rising from within the planet generates huge thermal currents? If so, does the magma, driven by these convection cells, rotate and interchange beneath the crust? Likened to a pot of soup boiling on a stove? Surely such currents must exist when considering the magnitude of the super-heated environment existing within the planet. For scientists, implementation of this proposal presented a conceivable solution to their Plate Tectonics dilemma. Was it just possible such currents existing in the Mantle could be responsible for continental drift? Could floating plates be carried intact on thermal currents, as if on giant conveyer belts powered from within?

This was considered a real possibility and must be investigated. Several fresh theories were proposed, all based on thermal movement within convection cells. How convection cells are applied to Plate Tectonics is best understood by imagining a pot of water on a stove. (Figs. 4.15, 4.16)

It is the working mechanics operating in convection cells that are the foundation of a new selection of theories proposed in a final attempt to solve the Plate Tectonics riddle.

Theory No. 4 - Shallow convection cells

Because of the difficulty with lower sections of the Mantle being super compressed and presumed solid, the first theory focuses on convection cells functioning in the upper Mantle. (Fig. 4.17)

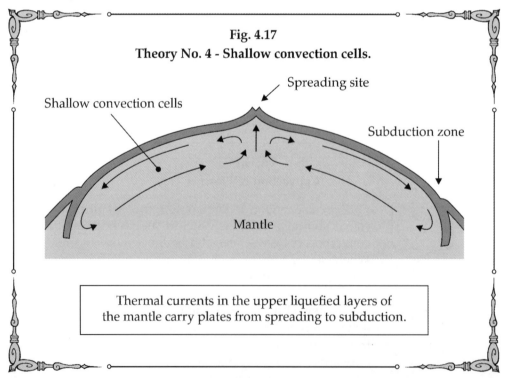

Fig. 4.17
Theory No. 4 - Shallow convection cells.

Spreading site

Shallow convection cells

Subduction zone

Mantle

Thermal currents in the upper liquefied layers of the mantle carry plates from spreading to subduction.

Tectonic investigators calculated, superheat generated from fixed hot spots within the Earth, fuels convection cells that operate in the upper liquefied levels of the Mantle. These fixed cyclic currents carry the Earth's plates, buoyant above, in complete singular sections across the Mantle thus effecting continental drift. The theory speculates, spreading sites mark the location of hot "up" currents and subduction indicates cooler "down" currents.

As with all the previous theories, this one too has its objections. Firstly; when a convection current is viewed from above as shown in fig 4.16, its cycle has a distinctive radial pattern. A pattern very different from the linear direction observed at spreading site ridges. Here we see lines of expansion running for 1,000's of kilometres, structure that is contradictory to what would be expected in a naturally occurring convection cycle.

Secondly; there is a discrepancy when considering the rotation depth needed for convection cells to operate. This theory requires there to be only one convection cell beneath each spreading site. This way, plates either side move in singular pieces, carried on the current. Unfortunately the typical singular cell required for their theory does not fit in the area proposed. The available molten area of the Mantle is believed to be only 150 kilometres deep. Gravitational pressure below this point creates a solid unworkable environment when taking convection cells into account. Because plates are thousands of kilometres across, the workable area beneath them is in the wrong proportions for a singular convection cell to form. They are all too shallow.

For example, as already mentioned, it is believed the Pacific Plate travels from the East Pacific Rise spreading site to subduction off Japan some 12,000 kilometres away. With only a workable depth in the Mantle of 150 kilometres, the proportionate area is far too flat for their rotating thermal cycle to work. The distance is 80 times the depth of the workable Mantle. In other plates, even though distances may be less, the situation is the same. If convection does occur at spreading sites, heated material would travel outwards, cool and then sink some 150 kilometres or so from its origin, 11,850 kilometres short of Japan.

Theory No. 5 - Deep convection cells

To help overcome this problem a further theory asks; is it at all possible that convection cells do in fact function normally throughout the entire Mantle? If heat expansion is indeed possible there, then larger rotating currents could be possible and perhaps sufficient in size to drive plates complete with their continents and ocean basins in single pieces as required. (Fig. 4.18)

However, whilst this may alleviate problems associated with shallow convection currents, the difficulty with flow patterns across the surface still remain. Spreading site ridges and subduction trenches are not structured in the correct format to indicate the operation of such a cycle. And of course, still to be answered is the question as to the assumed amount of pressure created by gravity in the Mantle. Is expansion of matter, required to fulfil the convection process, possible there?

If thermal currents release heat of an intensity to move whole continents around the globe, its effects radiating through the crust would be felt by all of mankind. The planet's surface would be uninhabitable and therefore unable to support us. Life would not have evolved as it has.

As with the stove, heat is generated from below, warming the water in the pot. But what generates and maintains the level of heat required for convection, if it is continuously

Our Expanding Earth

escaping from Earth at its spreading sites? No-one seems to know.

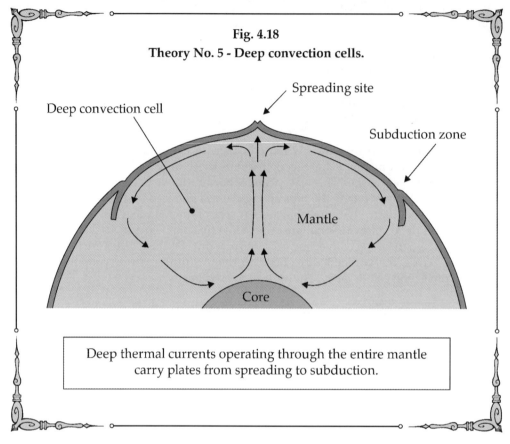

Fig. 4.18
Theory No. 5 - Deep convection cells.

Spreading site

Deep convection cell

Subduction zone

Mantle

Core

Deep thermal currents operating through the entire mantle
carry plates from spreading to subduction.

Other objections lie in the formation of proposed currents within convection cycles. Some appear to be incomplete. In many instances "up" currents are present without the necessary "down" currents. As already discussed, there are areas where subduction trenches simply don't exist, such as around Antarctica and South Africa. How does the cycle work there? In convection cells both "up" and "down" currents are essential to complete the thermal circuit. However, contrary to normal thermal requirements, this Plate Tectonics theory has "up" currents without "down" currents, spreading without subduction.

Other problems with convection cells

Originally, all the continents of the Earth were believed to be joined as one super landmass known as Pangaea. One portion of this landmass, today identified as Antarctica, was sandwiched between regions that are now Australia and South Africa. 200 million years ago, Antarctica's expanse was all that separated these two continents.

Then a cataclysmic event changed the face of Earth forever. Fractures were tearing their way through the super landmass. Pangaea was disintegrating into the continental shapes we recognise today. New surface formed as molten lava filled ever widening gaps appearing between the new landmass shapes.

Antarctica broke free from Australia and South Africa. The first spreading sites repaired

Our Expanding Earth

developing fissures around Antarctica's perimeter. When these spreading sites established themselves, Antarctica's expanse was all that separated Australia from South Africa, an average of 4,000 kilometres. Because of the creative action of spreading sites, new ocean floor was continuously added to the edges of the Antarctic Plate. As the plate increased in size so did the distance between the spreading site ridges either side of Antarctica.

Today, 200 million years later, this distance has increased from its original approximate 4,000 kilometres to a present approximate 7,000 kilometres. Spreading sites are now located in the Southern, ocean midway between Antarctica, Australia and South Africa. They have migrated 3,000 kilometres further apart over this time period. (Fig. 4.19)

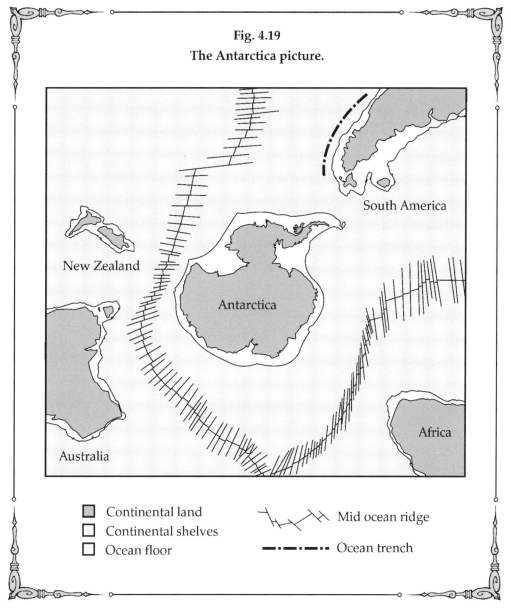

Fig. 4.19

The Antarctica picture.

☐ Continental land   Mid ocean ridge
☐ Continental shelves
☐ Ocean floor   Ocean trench

This migration projects another objection into convection cell theories. If these convection cells supposedly originate from fixed hot spots in the Mantle, how do they move to remain aligned with spreading sites drifting over the globe? How do these same hot spots being a few thousand kilometres below, line up to mimic the outline shapes of continents on the surface?

Other theories

Unyielding supporters of convection cycles in Plate Tectonics have attempted to alter and combine ideas in a last ditch effort to reach a final solution. Their theories evolve around the idea that bodies of molten lava form in the depths of the Mantle. Called "Mantle Plumes", they supposedly originate from fixed hot spots and slowly work their way upwards to eventually break the surface at spreading sites. Then somehow, shallow convection currents take over to carry plates from spreading to subduction.

Unfortunately these speculators don't seem to quite understand the real problems involved. They appear oblivious of the difficulties with convection cycles when applied to Plate Tectonics. All the same disputed points still remain. Quandaries include; problems with shallow convection cells, inappropriate shape of spreading sites compared to convection current patterns, and missing down currents. How can solid matter expand to become liquid in the lower Mantle environment? What generates the heat that operates this continuous cycle? How do hot spots remain lined up with migrating spreading sites? None of these problems are addressed in this new theory. Inventing Mantle plumes serves only to complicate the issue, offering no solution whatsoever.

All we have are failed theories. Nothing proved. We are left wondering and vacant. Not surprising though. So often, anticipated solutions end up proving nothing. So what is the truth behind continental drift? Does science really have the answers? The trouble is, the further we investigate Plate Tectonics, the more problems we encounter.

Problems with subduction

The very idea of subduction itself has its own set of inherent objections. Trenches don't align correctly with spreading ridges. All important seismic evidence, supposedly indicating plates subducting beneath, is sketchy and inconclusive. In fact many trenches are completely devoid of any seismic activity altogether.

Further problems originate from a completely different angle. The total extent of subduction trenches worldwide is far exceeded by a greater length of spreading ridges. How can ocean floor destruction keep up with ocean floor creation in this situation? Spreading sites add new floor to both plate edges. At the opposite end, subduction eliminates the edge of one plate only. The other supposedly rides over the top. This in effect means that in order to cater for the volume of spreading there has to be twice as much subduction. But there is less than half the required trenches to perform the task. This being the case, how can the volume of spreading be counteracted, particularly when the trenches we do have are wrongly placed and lacking in seismic evidence?

Sedimentary contradictions

Throughout our oceans, remnants of marine life, dust, and other matter constantly rains down on the ocean floor. Over time, the remains build up to substantial depths. The older the floor the greater the depth of sediment. Seabed beside continental landmasses, being the furthest from the spreading site ridges, is the oldest and therefore carry the

Our Expanding Earth

largest volume of sediment. Here deposits can reach depths of several hundred metres. They have slowly built up over a life span of up to 200 million years. It is theorised, this build up is finally scraped off by the overriding plate during subduction.

If so, deposits of scraped off sediment should be clearly evident in all the trenches. But they are not. On examination most of these trenches have little or no sedimentation at all. Those with sediments are naturally layered, not chaotic as would be expected if scraped off by subduction. If theories of subduction are correct what happened to the sedimentation from their 200 million square kilometre ancient ocean floor?

An alternative suggestion was made. Is it just possible these sediments have been uplifted to form the mountain ranges that surround the Pacific? Inspections that followed immediately dispelled this theory. Only small amounts of oceanic sediments were found, not enough to cater for millions of years of scraping hundreds of metres deep. Crucial evidence to support subduction by sediment scraping off, has not been found.

Today, with overwhelming geological evidence, we are aware that all the present continents were once joined as one. It was therefore assumed a single super continent existed, which they named Pangaea. Isolated on the Earth's surface, it was thought to be surrounded by a super sized oceanic expanse some 200 million square kilometres in size. No other dry land was imagined to exist. As Pangaea broke apart new ocean floors were born in opening cracks. Pressure from ocean floor creation distorted the Earth's surface producing the deep sea trenches. These have supposedly totally consumed all the ancient ocean as it was replaced by the oceanic expanses we have today.

Why can't we find any remnants of this ancient ocean anywhere? How could two thirds of the Earth's surface disappear without a trace? Not even a scrap has been left behind, 200 million square kilometres vanished, an ocean without sediments.

One thing theorists fail to explain is why this single continental landmass existed anyway. What force created an Earth with all its dry land in one place? Why isn't the same geological situation repeated on any of the other planets of the Solar System?

Pivoting gaps

Another problem with Plate Tectonics concerns the continental puzzle itself. We are all aware Earth's landmass pieces were born from the breakdown of Pangaea. But assembly of this world size jig-saw puzzle has its own set of unique complications.

Rebuilding the ancient super landmass starts by reuniting North and South America to Europe and Africa eliminating the Atlantic Ocean. We can also join Australia, Antarctica, India and Africa by removing the Indian and Southern Oceans. Suddenly just as the picture of Pangaea starts to come into view, we encounter a problem. Closer examination reveals gaps developing between the pieces. (Figs. 4.20, 4.21)

If these continents were once joined as geological evidence indicates, why do these spaces appear during reconstruction? As edges are brought together in one place, others elsewhere pivot and move apart. Why don't all the edges meet at the one time? Instead, one connection displaces another. Why does this happen? Are we missing pieces? Or are we missing something else?

Our Expanding Earth

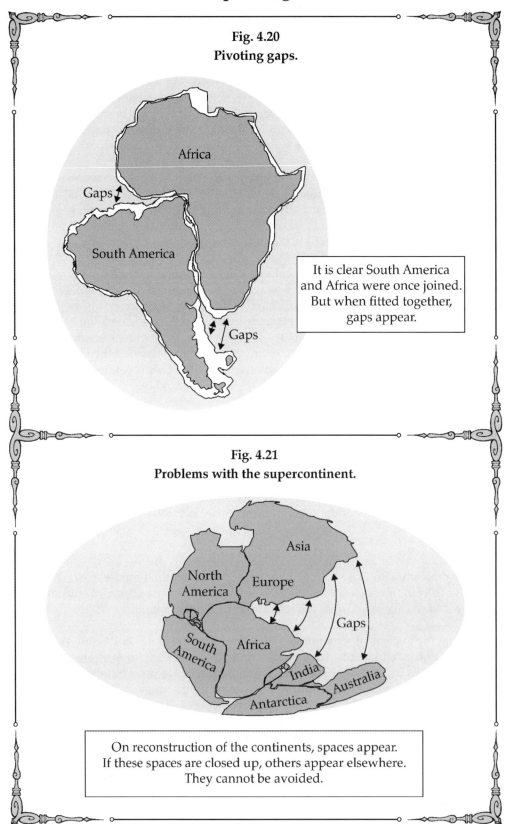

Fig. 4.20
Pivoting gaps.

Africa

Gaps

South America

Gaps

It is clear South America
and Africa were once joined.
But when fitted together,
gaps appear.

Fig. 4.21
Problems with the supercontinent.

Asia

North
America

Europe

Gaps

South
America

Africa

India

Australia

Antarctica

On reconstruction of the continents, spaces appear.
If these spaces are closed up, others appear elsewhere.
They cannot be avoided.

Our Expanding Earth

Other problems for Plate Tectonics

When reconstructing Pangaea, the task is accomplished by joining continents at continental shelf edges. This is because, these edges mark the point where the ancient landmass broke apart. The enigma is, when fully reconstructed, Pangaea itself has its own surrounding continental shelf. Why?

If this single landmass had nothing to break away from, what produced these cliff edge formations on its boundaries? Why do continents that made up the outer boarders of Pangaea have continental shelves completely around their perimeter? Is it possible these shelves are not what we think they are? Or, did Pangaea break away from some other landmass? Perhaps itself? Is this possible?

Difficulties in calculating continental movement

Over geological history the Earth's continents have migrated to new positions over the globe. The extent of movement can be determined by both glacial evidence and the study of continental rocks.

When molten, magnetic particles within lava align naturally to Earth's magnetic field, just as a compass does. This signature is locked into rocks as they solidify. Magnetic alignment is then used to calculate just how far the landmasses have drifted away from their original positions. Investigations show every continent, with the exception of Antarctica, has assumed a more northerly aspect since continental drift began. However, this is contradictory to observed activity taking place in the northern reaches of the Mid-Atlantic Ridge. Here spreading sites are slowly pushing landmasses south away from the North Pole, as the Arctic Ocean increases in size.

How can these continents assume more northerly aspects and move south away from the North Pole at the same time? How is this possible? Or is it we don't fully understand the evidence before us?

The Pacific enigma

On a constant diameter Earth, the Plate Tectonics theory supports the view that as spreading sites expand the Atlantic, Indian, Southern and Arctic oceans, continental landmasses forced apart must ultimately encroach over the Pacific. The presence of most of the subduction trenches in the Pacific, is employed to support this idea. It is believed the Pacific is shrinking at a proportionate rate to the combined expansion occurring in all the other oceans. This convergence maintains a constant surface area over the planet.

But there is a problem. If we study a world map, one thing becomes apparent. All continents surrounding the Pacific, instead of encroaching upon each other, are in fact moving apart.

North America and South America, originally joined as one, have separated and drifted away from each other, this expanding the perimeter of the Pacific. South America has drifted away from Antarctica, again expanding the perimeter of the Pacific. Australia has moved away from both Antarctica and Asia, more expansion. And finally Siberia is further from Alaska. In total the perimeter of the Pacific has increased by 50% since continental drift began. This is quite opposite to the halving in size required to compensate for expansion in all the other oceans. Despite the existence of subduction trenches, the continents around the Pacific are now further apart. As continental masses themselves are not shrinking, how can such a situation exist? It is a physical impossibility for the Pacific to decrease its size while at the same time expand its perimeter.

The unknown force building mountains

Plate Tectonics has attempted to solve many of the Earth's most difficult mysteries. But in doing so, some of the simplest and most taken for granted seem to have been forgotten and left unanswered.

Why do we have mountains?

Whilst Plate Tectonics offers reasonable theories explaining the existence of mountains on plate edges, ranges in the interior of continental land masses have remained unsolved. Many of Earth's greatest mountain chains exist thousands of kilometres from plate edges. Like all mountains, it is known these too are built by horizontal compression forces. But the source of such forces has to this point eluded tectonic investigators. We were simply left to wonder and marvel at these giant tectonic creations everywhere, mystery geology completely unsolved. With so many mountain ranges throughout the world, is it not unreasonable to ask why such a mystery still remains unsolved?

The force that generates earthquake activity

As previously mentioned, another mystery concerns earthquake activity. What is the true cause of seismic movement within the Earth's crust? As said, most people see them as natural happenings that reoccur in faulted regions throughout the world. But Plate Tectonics fails to explain the workings of the geological process behind them, or even why they occur at all?

If Plate Tectonics cannot resolve these obvious problems then one must question the very essence of the theory itself.

Gravity anomalies effecting sea level

Gravitational forces shape the surface of the sea. Tides rise and fall in unison with the moon. Just as attraction from the moon varies the sea surface, so does gravity from the mass of the ocean floor. Despite being very slight and unnoticeable to the naked eye, the ocean surface actually dips over deep sea trenches. The reason being; in the vicinity of the trenches, there is less matter beneath making up the ocean floor. Where matter is less, gravity is also less. Attraction from ocean floor either side of trenches, draws the sea to it creating the dip in the surface over the trench. Accordingly, minute rises and falls are present in the sea surface. They reflect the contours of the ocean floor.

But there are other anomalies as well. With the aid of new satellite technology, additional variations have been discovered. Other larger hills and valleys exist across the surface of the sea. Previously unknown, they are completely unrelated to the known sea floor. These undulations are again gradual and not visible to the naked eye. They remain fixed in position and maintain constant elevations. Scientists were surprised to find a worldwide altitude variation of up to 200 metres between hill tops and valley floors. The fact that both highs and lows exist on similar latitudes confirms they are not related to the spinning

Our Expanding Earth

of the Earth. In other words, the sea surface is not as level as we previously thought. We can reach a better understanding of this by comparing the ocean level around Sri Lanka which is actually 200 metres lower than the ocean level off the north-east coast of New Guinea and around Iceland.

It is thought, mass inconsistencies within the Earth produce this unusual feature. However if trenches 11 kilometres deep vary the sea surface by a mere one or two metres, how large must mass variations be to alter the surface by as much as 200 metres?

Plate Tectonics theories are incomplete

There are so many questions left unanswered. It appears we are at a dead end. Worldly observations have given rise to theories, concepts and assumptions. Developed mathematical equations, too complex for us to follow, force pieces into place. But do they really fit? How do we differentiate between what is fact and what is desired to be fact? Does Plate Tectonics give us the truth, or do we just accepted it as correct because any other "reality" is too difficult for us to comprehend? Do we too easily accept partially solved puzzles? Should we be accepting anything less than the complete picture?

The solutions given are incomplete and unsatisfactory. We should not accept them. Plate Tectonics has failed to deliver. Instead it has only served to confuse the picture further.

- If conclusive evidence points to the world's continents being once joined as one landmass why do gaps appear when they are reassembled?

- Why are Plate Tectonic scientists unable to define the origins of a force powerful enough to drive whole continents across the globe?

- Did their ancient super-ocean exist? If so, why has no evidence of it ever been found?

- If this ocean did exist where are its sedimentary deposits?

- Is it possible for drifting continents to acquire more northerly aspects at the same time as moving south away from the North Pole?

- How can the Pacific halve in size when its perimeter has increased by 50%?

- Why did Pangaea have continental shelves surrounding it if it had nothing to break away from?

- Why can't Plate Tectonics explain the force that creates all mountains and earthquake activity?

- How is it possible for Earth to remain a constant diameter if the volume of subduction is insufficient to cater for the amount of spreading?

- And what causes the sea surface to vary as much as 200 metres in altitude?

Our Expanding Earth

Plate Tectonics cannot resolve any of these questions. Why? The reason lies in the foundations of its theories. They have all been designed around fixed ideas. Beliefs on how gravity holds the Earth's matter in a state of central compression have become "fact", and are no longer open for debate. For them, the Earth cannot expand. Subduction zones are the cornerstone of Plate Tectonics. They were invented to take care of this, created to eliminate excessive space created by ocean floor spreading. But Plate Tectonics is merely a tool used to maintain human comfort zones of belief, beliefs that have been born from preconceived ideas.

The path that provides the solution

Fortunately, there is an answer. We must retrace our steps back to an incorrect turn made generations ago. Our preconceived understanding of gravity is wrong. Gravity acting on the Earth's mass, structures a very different world to the way we believe.

We must face the truth.

The evidence uncovers facts not previously considered.

The Earth's diameter has not been constant as proposed.

The planet's structure is gradually expanding.

Expansion caused the breakup of Pangaea, 200 million years ago.

And it still continues today.

Following chapters will show how the workings of gravity has produced this and so many other events through Earth's natural planetary evolution. It will be explained how ocean floor growth and continental drift are a direct result of the Earth expanding.

Realisation hands us the key to unlock the unsolved. We are entering a new age of understanding. Our world will never be viewed the same again.

Subduction inventions are no longer required on an expanding Earth. Therefore all the problems associated with them immediately disappear. This is why there is insufficient subduction trenches to cater for spreading. This is why trenches are wrongly located in conjunction with spreading ridges. And, this is why there is insufficient seismic evidence. Subduction Zones are nothing more than oceanic trenches.

On an expanding Earth the whole subduction theory becomes obsolete.

Gravity acting on the Earth is the driving force that produces continental drift.

200 million years ago the Earth was much smaller. Its surface area was only a third of that of today. Reassembling the continental puzzle on a smaller Earth presents an entirely new picture. Not only do all the pivoting gaps disappear, but the reconstructed pieces totally encompass the Earth. The puzzle is complete. The Earth's ancient crust is reborn in its original entirety, a complete and continuous surface, devoid of present day ocean basins. Pieces once parted by expansion are now separated by oceans. All fit perfectly onto an Earth one third its present size. (Fig. 4.22)

Our Expanding Earth

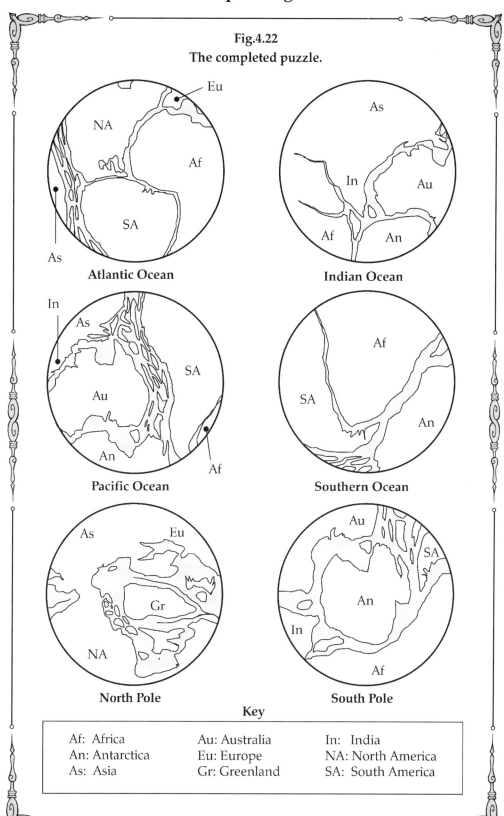

Fig.4.22
The completed puzzle.

Atlantic Ocean

Indian Ocean

Pacific Ocean

Southern Ocean

North Pole

South Pole

Key

Af: Africa	Au: Australia	In: India
An: Antarctica	Eu: Europe	NA: North America
As: Asia	Gr: Greenland	SA: South America

Our Expanding Earth

This is why all continents are fully surrounded by continental shelves. Pangaea, the super continent, was not set amid an ancient super-sized ocean. It was the whole Earth's surface, one complete crust. And through expansion, it actually did break away from itself. This is the reason why continental shelves the world over are of a similar geological age.

An ancient super-sized ocean was not subducted. This is why we find no evidence of it. This is why there are no ancient scraped off sediments. The continents we know today were once the ocean floor of a smaller world, a world almost completely submerged by one encompassing ocean. The continents emerged as the Earth's surface area increased through expansion.

On an expanding Earth the Pacific too is expanding along with all the other oceans.

The evolution of ocean basins is a direct consequence of Earth expansion. The size of each ocean tells us just how much expansion has taken place. When we study a world map, we find the oceans are not evenly distributed. The larger oceanic areas in the Southern Hemisphere confirms this part of the world has expanded at a much greater rate.

Uneven expansion is responsible for the migration of continents northward. As mentioned, all the world's continents with the exception of Antarctica have moved away from the South Pole to more northerly latitudes. In effect, it can be likened to the Earth expanding south rather than the landmasses moving north. On the other hand, expansion in the Northern Hemisphere has progressed at a slower rate. Spreading in the Arctic Ocean has moved continents south away from the North Pole. But when viewed on a constant diameter Earth, this equates to continents migrating both north and south at the same time. This is not possible. However, on an expanding Earth, like an inflating balloon, the distance between the poles increases. The result is, continental landmasses drift away from both poles at the same time, a situation that is inevitable on an expanding Earth.

As the Earth expands so does its diameter. Resultant flattening of the Earth's curvature produces horizontal compression in the outer surface of the crust. This is the force that science has been looking for. It produces mountains. (Fig. 4.23)

This same flattening causes tension and stretching in the underside of the crust. Lava fills developing splits and cracks. Volcanoes are born when such cracks reach the outer surface.

As the Earth expands it creaks into shape. The resulting vibrations are felt on the surface as earthquakes.

Uneven expansion has caused mass inconsistencies within the Earth. Gravitational forces originating from these inconsistencies produce the recently discovered and unexplained 200 metre undulations on the sea surface.

Understanding gravity is the key. Gravity has structured the Earth differently to the way we believe, it has built an Earth that is expanding.

Our Expanding Earth

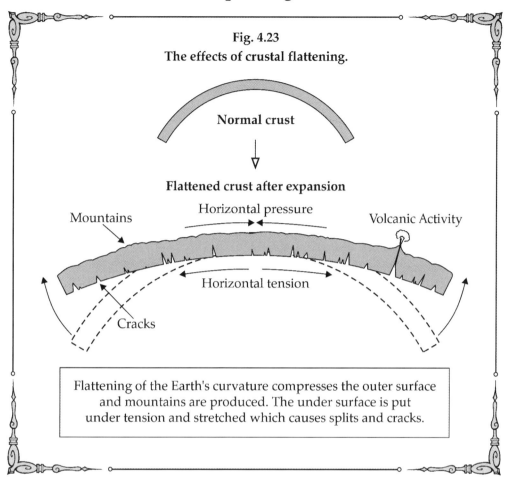

Fig. 4.23
The effects of crustal flattening.

Normal crust

Flattened crust after expansion

Mountains

Horizontal pressure

Volcanic Activity

Horizontal tension

Cracks

Flattening of the Earth's curvature compresses the outer surface and mountains are produced. The under surface is put under tension and stretched which causes splits and cracks.

Chapter 5

The Ice Age Myth

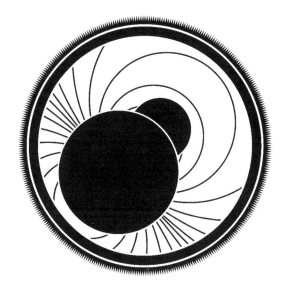

When the complexity of the solution exceeds the complexity of the problem...
it is time to take another look.

The Ice Age Myth

W e are told of great ice ages in the past, periods of time when sheets of ice advanced south from the North Pole and north from the South Pole, cold dark cycles in Earth's history when an icy grip besieged the land for hundreds of thousands of years at a time. It is proposed the last one ended as recently as 10,000 years ago.

Here again, is it just possible after examining other scientific theories, that we have all been a little too eager to accept unproven ideas as fact? Did the great ice ages really happen? Perhaps we should re-examine the evidence. Or is it too late to change minds already made up? What force caused the formation of these huge glaciers ravaging once warm lands? What factors govern decisions made by science? Why are ice ages so firmly considered as fact?

Glaciers leave their own individual footprint behind. Erosion, caused by these icy tracts is quite different from that of other eroding processes such as rivers, the sea or wind. Today, shaped valleys, characteristic of ancient glacial action, are found across North America and Europe, in areas now too warm for glaciers to exist. The reality of extensive glacial erosion confirms just how cold these lands once were. This was the primary factor governing the decision that the Earth had experienced climatic changes in the past. There is little doubt as to the prior existence of glaciers in these areas but the real question is; how could this have come about? What caused them?

Despite many proposed theories, some extreme in their complexity, no-one has come up with an even near satisfactory answer. But is a solution really necessary? After all, the glacial evidence is there for us all to see? No-one can deny it took place. But, if the North Polar ice extended over America and Europe to produce these glaciers, why is the same evidence missing in Siberia and Northern China. They too are a similar distance from the Pole? The fact is; mountain ranges in these countries are free of ancient glacial action. Why? Was the climate different in Northern America and Europe? How could this be? How could one side of the Northern Hemisphere be warm and the other cold?

The Ice Age Myth

But there is an answer. It lies with continental drift. This new geological discovery seems to have been overlooked as an aid to solve this puzzle. Continental drift has moved land masses away from the North Pole, some more than others. If we reassemble the continents back around the Pole, closing up the Arctic ocean, a new picture develops. Continents located on similar latitudes today were not located on the same latitudes in the past. North America and Europe, then much closer to the Pole than Siberia and North China, were covered with ice. This, the simple solution to the puzzle, makes a lot more sense. World climate didn't change, it was the position of the continents that did.

The same situation is repeated in the Southern Hemisphere. Geological markings suggesting ancient glacial action in South America, Africa, India and Australia all link up into one polar region when landmasses are reassembled around the Antarctic continent.

But there is other ice age evidence to be considered as well. Long groove type markings in bedrock across continental areas are called striations. These, along with erratic boulders, have also received some of the blame for ice ages in the past. But these geological features too, can be easily misread. It is thought the markings and scattered boulders were left by large ice sheets moving across continents.

When considering "continental drift" eliminates most of evidence, are the striations and scattered boulders on their own, enough to support ancient ice age concepts? As discussed, the flow patterns of erratics indicate a flooding type event rather than movement by ice. Some of the erratic boulders have been carried to higher altitudes from their origins. How can ice action produce this? Glaciers only travel downhill.

Another problem is, striations and erratic boulders exist across Siberia and Northern China, yet mountains there, support no ancient glacial evidence. How do ice age supporters explain this? To add further complications to their case, many striations, claimed to be the result of ice ages, are found across large flat areas of continental landmasses. Southern Sweden, Finland and north east Russia are such places. Here there are no mountains from which glaciers could advance. This land is flat. As already mentioned, ice only travels downhill following sloping gradients, not across flat surfaces. Studies conducted in Antarctica confirm this. Here, ice cover over flat country, actually protects the underlying surfaces rather than eroding them.

The conclusion drawn that these markings were caused by an ice age is wrong. Just as with other Great Flood erosion, striation grooves were carved into the land when the invading sea crossed the continents. Waves thick with sediment and boulders, scored and polished the dry ground, stripping it clean.

As already discussed, the sea level is deeper today than it was 5,000 to 10,000 years ago. Remnants of riverbeds, forests and ancient cities still remain beneath the surface on continental shelves worldwide. For many, the rise in sea level is attributed to the melting of glaciers and ice sheets built up over the last ice age. At first, to the uninitiated, this might seem quite feasible. As the Earth warmed, water from melting ice returned to the ocean. As a consequence the sea level rose flooding low lying dry land areas. Mystery solved.

But unfortunately, it is not as simple as that.

Many of these remains lie at considerable depths beneath the surface. For example; the

The Ice Age Myth

5,000 year old Oak forests of the North Sea stand, roots intact, on the ocean floor at 36 metres below the surface. If the ice age theory is to be correct this means the remains originally stood on dry ground just before the Earth warmed and the ice melted. Or, another way to look at it is; for the forests and other remnants to stand above sea level, 36 metres must have to be evaporated off the world's 200 million square kilometre oceanic expanse and turned to ice on continents.

This amounts to an unimaginable quantity of water particularly when considering just one third of the Earth's surface is dry land and only a portion of this received ice cover. To accommodate all the water removed from the oceans, glaciers and continental ice sheets, in a great many places, must have reached several kilometres in depth. This without taking into account ice expands as it freezes. The whole idea of 36 metres X 200 million square kilometres of ocean turning to ice on continents is in itself awe-inspiring and gives the feeling of being a little far fetched. Remember, this is just to explain why various geological remnants and other markings exist. The features themselves pale into insignificance when compared to the complexity of proposed solutions.

Evidence indicates coastal lowlands were flooded suddenly rather than a slow process as one would expect from the gradual melting of continental ice cover. To some, this offered another possible solution. Perhaps instead of a melting ice age, these remains simultaneously sank below sea level by some other event, yet to be explained. In other words the evidence may not have been caused by an ice age after all. Not surprisingly, absolutely no geological evidence to support these sinking lands has ever been found.

But with minds made up theorists pressed on. They assure us, at the commencement of each ice age, some unknown factor causes the Earth's temperature to cool. There are several theories for this. One suggests some solar process, within the Sun, periodically decreases its radiation output. Another puts forward; variations in Earth's reflectivity cuts down heat reaching the surface, possibly by a reduction of carbon dioxide in the atmosphere. Or perhaps displacement of altitudes in the Earth's crust with higher lands turning cold. Even variations of Earth's orbit away from the Sun. Another suggests the Sun's warming rays blotted out by dust from celestial impacts, volcanic activity or particle clouds in space. The theories go on. Some even propose different plants growing on the surface may, combined with other factors, help towards the cause of ice ages.

Have they lost the thread somewhere? What about the amount of heat it would take to evaporate 36 metres off all the world's oceans? Has anyone considered that? This impossible mathematical problem is the point at which the ice age theory falls apart. Falling snow is necessary for the production of glaciers and ice sheets. For snow we need clouds. Clouds result from evaporation. Evaporation requires heat. We should again ask; how much heat would it take to evaporate 36 metres off a 200 million square kilometre worldwide oceanic expanse? A lot! Where did this heat come from if the Earth was plunged into a deep freeze darkness? No-one is denying past collisions would have reduced the Sun's rays. But in such times the world would have turned cold or frozen. There would have been little heat for precipitation and consequently, any glaciation would have been minimal. Certainly not enough to reduce the ocean level as suggested. Even today, with the present Earth temperature, it would be impossible to evaporate 36 metres off the oceans.

The ice age theory is wrong.

The Ice Age Myth

As the Earth expanded, its broken continental crust drifted apart. Regions subjected to millions of years of glacial action moved away from the poles. In warmer climates, glaciers melted leaving the remnants we see today.

The Great Flood was a later event. Its erosive action scored and polished the surface scattering boulders across the lands. It changed the level of the sea forever.

The evidence has been misread. A lack of understanding is the reason. This stems from a misconception of gravity, and how it has shaped the Earth. Ice age theories fail to offer solutions. They have only served to create bigger problems that require even bigger and more complex theories to solve.

Ice ages are a myth. They never happened.

Part II

The Primary Key

There are two parts to the key...
the answer, and the reason why we don't know it.

Chapter 6

Gravity and the Earth

The key to truth is simplicity

Gravity and the Earth

ravity is responsible for all creation. Without it, the universe could not exist. All around us we are witness to the wondrous architecture built by this force. Not just mountains, rivers and oceans but other planets, stars, solar systems and galaxies beyond. Gravity is the ultimate creator. Likened to an almighty god with a power over all, it governs everything we do in every moment of our lives. Reigning throughout the universe, in an infinite empire, its never ending creation completes a cycle with destruction.

Gravity's size cannot be measured. From the smallest atom to the realms of space, it is infinite. We have all been made aware of how the force of gravity structures everything around us.

Like all other celestial bodies, both Earth's outer surface and interior dimensions are shaped by this force. The fact is, even though we might be able to view the universe for millions of kilometres into space, we are yet to witness what lies beneath our feet. But we, as gravity's prisoner on the surface, journey in our minds to the forbidden world within. Here we see lava and heat with inconceivable pressure increasing with depth to form a solid central core. The inside world is visible to us all in our thoughts. Images present and true, built by imagination, have been implanted in our minds by those who know.

But are the visions right?

Have we once again accepted ideas too readily? We should remember these images originate from formulated ideas like those given by the authorities that presented us with Plate Tectonics and ice ages. Ideas based on assumptions once accepted become "truth" and are difficult to erase. How can they prove what they say? Are beliefs concerning the internal structure of Earth correct?

Gravity and the Earth

Early presumptions

> Prehistory humans looked up and saw the Sun, the Moon and stars. They observed them circling around them. And thus it became so. The Earth was the centre of the universe. Everyone could see this, so it was right. Mankind was happy and content with their discovery.
>
> But time passed. Following generations brought forward new minds. Their studies proved beliefs from the past to be wrong. It was the Sun making up the centre, with Earth and the other planets orbiting around it. How could this be? How could everyone be wrong? The new explorers tried in vain to convince the people. But failed to change minds already made up. Upheld beliefs were not to be questioned. Their knowledgeable forefathers had put the Earth in the centre and that is where it was going to stay. Only as new generations followed, could fresh minds accept the truth. And mankind was happy once again.

Incorrect assumptions have produced a problem.

So, are current beliefs from the past, concerning the inner Earth correct? Or, is history repeating itself? Have we once again taken a wrong turn?

Unfortunately, the latter is the case. Our full understanding of the workings of gravity is wrong. Original interpretations passed down over so many generations have been accepted without question. Established theories now taken as truth, were born out of nothing more than pure speculation. Studies of gravity were based entirely from observations made on and above the surface. This, in conjunction with our limited understanding of the universe, has provided us with the wrong answers. In truth, the interior of Earth is a totally unexplored frontier. This is a territory unseen by human eye, an area 12,756 kilometres from one side to the other, a distance of which we on the surface have not penetrated any more than just a few inconsequential kilometres.

It is now time to change.

Today, our knowledge of the complexity of things around us is less than complete. It is time to enter a new era of greater understanding. Current concepts of gravity must be brought up to date. Our beliefs concerning the effects of this force on the inner Earth, are wrong. As the true workings of gravity are explained, the boundaries beneath the surface will come to light. Only then will natural solutions to the origins of humanity and other mysteries become clear. To reach the world obscured within, it is necessary to investigate deeper into that mysterious force we have named "gravity".

So, what is gravity?

To this day no-one knows. Even with all our present day technology, we are yet to break this mystery of universal proportions. Observations tell us it is an energy force relating to all substances throughout the cosmos. It is a force that brings together all matter, controlling everything right down to the smallest atom. The planets, stars and galaxies have all been created by gravity's mighty power. Their orbits continue in never ending journeys, eternally trapped in its persistent grasp. This is the force responsible for uniting

Gravity and the Earth

Earth's mass as one, and holding us together with everything else in place on the surface. Not a moment of our lives goes by without experiencing the effects of this power called gravity.

It is yet to be discovered whether gravity is a force of attraction that pulls matter together or one of pressure that pushes matter together. Today, most view gravity as a force of attraction. So for ease of understanding, and because the end resultant is considered the same, this chapter refers to gravity as a force that attracts, pulling matter together.

So how does gravity work?

Again no-one knows. At present we can only study its effects. Today, we are aware that gravity and matter function together. Neither exists without the other. They share an equal relationship, where the greater the volume of matter, the greater gravity's strength. This is the energy responsible for pulling all matter together. But an object's size or volume is not the only governing factor. The gravitational attraction one mass has over another also depends on the distance between them. Because of a multiplication factor over distance, this calculation has a crucial bearing on gravity's strength. Astronomers have come to recognise this from observing orbits of planets in space. As a result, science has now concluded; gravity's strength is influenced by two important factors; mass and distance.

Mass

"Mass" is a term used to describe a quantity of matter or material. The matter making up a whole planet may be considered as a large mass in comparison to the amount of material contained in a single rock. However, in a different perspective, the mass of the Earth is regarded as small when compared to that of the Sun.

Mass and gravity

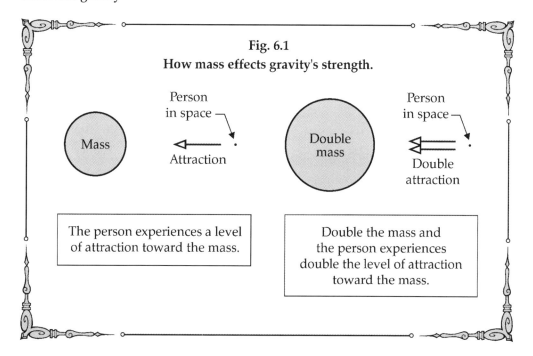

Fig. 6.1
How mass effects gravity's strength.

Person in space

Mass

Attraction

The person experiences a level of attraction toward the mass.

Person in space

Double mass

Double attraction

Double the mass and the person experiences double the level of attraction toward the mass.

Gravity and the Earth

If mass and gravity coexist, it is easy to recognise; the greater the mass the greater the force of attraction. For example, a person located in space at a fixed distance from a planet feels a certain amount of gravitational pull on their mass. If the planet's size is doubled, the amount of gravity felt is also doubled. The same process works in reverse. A person on the Moon experiences less gravity than that on Earth. This is simply because the moon's mass is less. With gravity reduced, a spaceman on the moon is able to leap his body mass much higher from the surface than when on Earth. (Fig. 6.1)

Distance and gravity

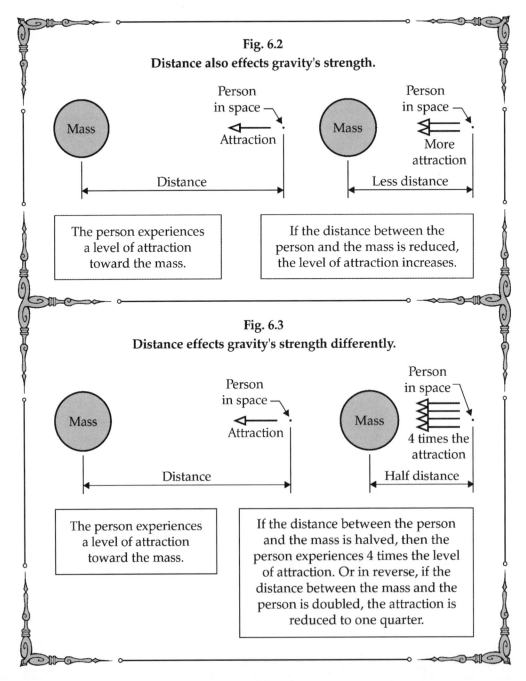

Fig. 6.2
Distance also effects gravity's strength.

Person in space
Attraction
Distance

Mass

Person in space
More attraction
Less distance

Mass

The person experiences a level of attraction toward the mass.

If the distance between the person and the mass is reduced, the level of attraction increases.

Fig. 6.3
Distance effects gravity's strength differently.

Person in space
Attraction
Distance

Mass

Person in space
4 times the attraction
Half distance

Mass

The person experiences a level of attraction toward the mass.

If the distance between the person and the mass is halved, then the person experiences 4 times the level of attraction. Or in reverse, if the distance between the mass and the person is doubled, the attraction is reduced to one quarter.

Gravity and the Earth

Gravity is also affected by distance. The greater the distance between separate masses the weaker the force of attraction between them. Or in reverse, if the distance between individual masses is reduced, the strength of attraction increases. (Fig. 6.2)

However, gravitational attraction when related to distance is different to that of mass. This is because, with distance, gravity works on a sliding mathematical scale. For example, if the distance between a person in space and a planet were halved, they will experience not double but four times the strength of attraction. Or in reverse, if the distance is doubled the person will experience one quarter the attraction not half. (Fig. 6.3)

The important point to be considered here is; the closer the mass the greater gravitational attraction it has, much more than that of any other comparable size mass that is further away. Gravity reduces increasingly with distance. An example of this can be seen with the Earth's tides. The rise and fall of the ocean is caused by gravitational pull from both the Sun and Moon. Even though the Sun's mass is 27 million times greater than that of the Moon, the Moon is the main governing element controlling the tides. This is because the Sun is further away. The multiplying factor of distance over gravity reduces the Sun's 27 million times gravitational attraction to less than that of the Moon. Just by being much closer, the Moon is the main influence ruling the world's oceanic tides.

Gravity acts in a similar way to light.

We can see this by making a simple comparison. Just as light is seen to travel out in all directions from its source, the strength of gravitational attraction is felt in all directions out from a planet. If we imagine light shining from a bulb onto a piece of paper positioned at a fixed distance, we observe a certain level of brightness on the paper. When we double the distance between the bulb and the paper, the brightness reduces to one quarter, not half. This is because the light radiates away in all directions at once, becoming ever weaker. Effectively, it is the same with gravity. As the distance from a mass increases, its attraction value is spread over an ever enlarging area. Expanding in all directions at once, its strength weakens on a multiplying scale as it travels outwards throughout the universe. This sliding scale of gravity's strength over distance is a vital part of the formula responsible for structuring the interior of the Earth. (Fig. 6.4)

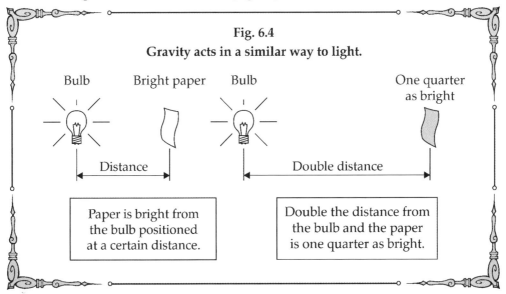

Fig. 6.4

Gravity acts in a similar way to light.

Bulb   Bright paper   Bulb   One quarter as bright

Distance   Double distance

Paper is bright from the bulb positioned at a certain distance.

Double the distance from the bulb and the paper is one quarter as bright.

Gravity and the Earth

The centrally compressed theory

In the past, it was soon realised that no matter where anyone stood on the Earth, "down" always pointed directly to the centre of the planet. They imagined how a dropped object, with nothing in the way, would naturally fall to this central point. The inner Earth was visualised as a molten place with compression increasing with depth. It was perceived the centre supported unimaginable pressure, super compacted by the total weight of Earth's mass pressing down for 6,000 kilometres from all directions simultaneously. This gave birth to the centrally compressed theory.

Today, without any solid evidence to support it, this concept is still accepted as fact.

To develop a clearer picture of this current concept, lets imagine what effects gravity would have on us if descending into a theorised "solid" and "centrally compressed" planet.

Gravity within a centrally compressed planet

Firstly, we are all aware that wherever we stand on any planet's surface, its entire mass is beneath our feet. In this position we feel the full force of the planet's mass as gravity. This action, pulling us down onto the surface, is measured as our weight. The larger our mass, the more gravitational attraction and therefore the more we weigh. (Fig. 6.5)

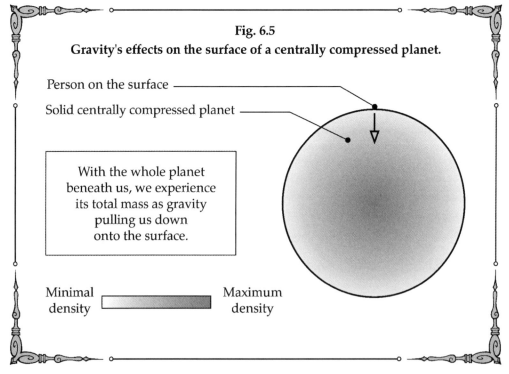

Fig. 6.5

Gravity's effects on the surface of a centrally compressed planet.

Person on the surface

Solid centrally compressed planet

With the whole planet beneath us, we experience its total mass as gravity pulling us down onto the surface.

Minimal density   Maximum density

Secondly, if it were possible to descend to a point within the planet midway between the outside surface and the centre, what would the effects of gravity be there? How would things have changed?

In our midway location, the distribution of the planet's mass around us has changed. The volume of mass beneath continues to attract us down. But its volume has reduced.

Gravity and the Earth

And so, a compensating reduction in downward attraction has taken place. Consequently we weigh less. In addition to this, a portion of the planet's mass, that was below us when on the surface, is now above us. It has gravitational attraction too and pulls on us from above. This reduces our weight further. (Fig. 6.6)

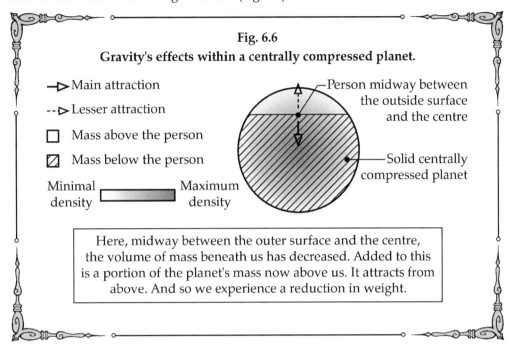

Fig. 6.6
Gravity's effects within a centrally compressed planet.

➨ Main attraction

--▷ Lesser attraction

☐ Mass above the person

☑ Mass below the person

Minimal density   Maximum density

Person midway between the outside surface and the centre

Solid centrally compressed planet

Here, midway between the outer surface and the centre, the volume of mass beneath us has decreased. Added to this is a portion of the planet's mass now above us. It attracts from above. And so we experience a reduction in weight.

As we descend further and further towards the middle of the planet. The mass below us continues to decrease as the mass above increases. Downward attraction reduces further in accordance with the changing configuration of mass around us. And so, we weigh less and less.

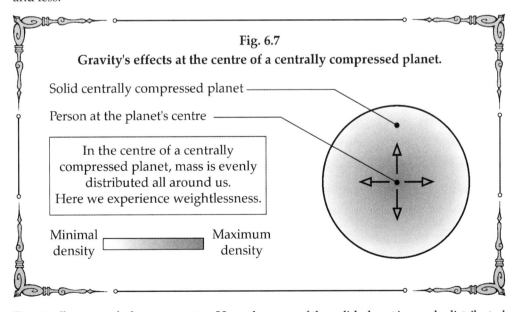

Fig. 6.7
Gravity's effects at the centre of a centrally compressed planet.

Solid centrally compressed planet

Person at the planet's centre

In the centre of a centrally compressed planet, mass is evenly distributed all around us. Here we experience weightlessness.

Minimal density   Maximum density

Eventually we reach the very centre. Here, the mass of the solid planet is evenly distributed all around us. Now, gravitational attraction acts upon us by pulling equally outward from all directions. The result of this is, the effects of gravity are neutralised. This is experienced as weightlessness. (Fig. 6.7)

At this point we can go down no further. From here, all directions are up.

Problems with the centrally compressed theory

These are the effects we would experience on an Earth solid and centrally compressed as is currently believed. But, there are definite problems with the workings behind this theory. When the idea was first developed, some crucial factors were not taken into consideration. Certain aspects were missing out of the equation. Most importantly, the force of gravity dramatically changes in value throughout the birth and development of a growing planet. This vital point has a significant bearing on the eventual format of the planet's mass. As a result, most conclusions drawn have provided us with information that unfortunately is not correct.

When these changing values of gravitation are properly analysed, we see an end result very different to that currently believed. With the correct understanding, it becomes clear where the solid, centrally compressed theory has gone wrong.

So, how do these differences take effect?

Gravitational influence as a planet is born

The answer begins with a succession of events at the time of a planet's birth and early development.

All the planets, including the Earth, started from just a few specks, to build and grow to their size today. Each began with the first two small particles drifting through space. Because of the particles mass, gravitational forces present in them attracted them towards each other. However, as they were small, attraction between them was minimal. They gradually moved closer together. As the distance between them reduced, the strength of attraction increased until they finally met. Then, as they touched, the attraction between the two particles turned to weight against each other. But due to their attraction being small, the weight between them was likewise small. The measure of weight between them created an equivalent measure of slight pressure. This measure of pressure in turn created slight compression. Again, due to their minuscule combined size, the compression created was virtually unmeasurable. Yet none the less, a level of compression was present.

Compression in a growing planet is the key

This process, whereby compression is created between any such matter attracted together, is the primary process that governs the way a planet is structured. This is the essential key. An understanding of this is crucial if we are to fully perceive the birth and progressive development of our planet. It is the combining effects of gravity causing compression that is the missing piece.

The total mass of a planet equals its total attraction. Attraction gives matter its weight which creates pressure and in turn compression. The greater the compression, the higher the density. (Fig. 6.8)

Gravity and the Earth

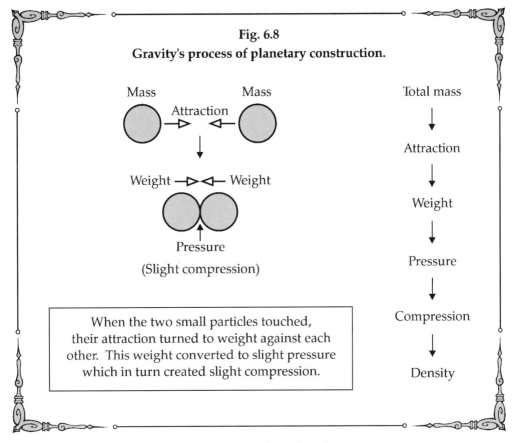

Fig. 6.8

Gravity's process of planetary construction.

When the two small particles touched, their attraction turned to weight against each other. This weight converted to slight pressure which in turn created slight compression.

So where does compression occur in a growing planet?

Compression occurs in accordance with certain related factors. We need to know these factors because they tell us where and why compression develops.

Matter only becomes compressed because of weight above it.

This is the first factor. Compression is a product of opposing forces. Whilst matter at the surface is attracted down by gravity, its direction of attraction is met with resistance from other matter further below. These opposed forces put stress on material sandwiched in between which then compacts to match the level of weight applied from above and resistance below. It is this action that causes compression within a planet's mass.

As we return to the birth of the planet, shortly after the first two particles came together, we now find their combined attraction has drawn in many more particles. As a result, a small unit has formed.

The original two particles are now in the centre. They are completely surrounded by several layers of other particles. Because each particle has mass and accordingly its own level of attraction, the centrally located particles now experience even attraction from all directions. This means they have effectively become weightless. But the situation for newly arrived particles on the outer surface is different. They are feeling the full effects of downward attraction from the total mass of the growing unit. Surrounding weight from newly arriving matter pressing down on the surface, converges in on the centre,

Gravity and the Earth

compressing particles there closer together. With that, the central region becomes more dense. At the very surface, with no downward weight from above, compression does not take place. And so, at this early stage, the matter of the new developing planet has a format of being centrally compressed.

Even though the unit has greater compression in the centre, its mass is small, and so the level of attraction holding the particles together is minimal. At this point, the matter comprising the unit is still relatively loosely packed.

The weight of surface material is a product of gravitational attraction from the total mass of the planet beneath it. When the Earth was smaller, it obviously had less mass. And so surface material, then under less gravitational attraction, weighed less.

Accordingly, the larger the planet the more attraction and the more surface matter weighs.

Now, more and more matter is attracted in to join the unit. With the passage of time, the unit's mass has grown. Things have changed. Many layers of incoming matter have completely buried the original unit. The increased volume of the unit's mass is generating more gravity. Greater gravitational attraction is being felt by other matter passing nearby. Particles similar in size to those before, are now drawn in by an increased force of attraction. As they join the unit, the extra force of attraction, converts to extra weight. This adding value of attraction, is causing increasing compression of the mass beneath. As a result, the loosely packed centre becomes more dense, and so the unit becomes more centrally compressed. (Fig. 6.9)

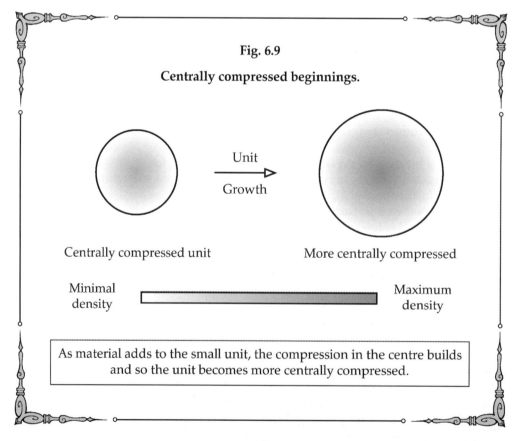

Fig. 6.9

Centrally compressed beginnings.

Unit

Growth

Centrally compressed unit

More centrally compressed

Minimal density

Maximum density

As material adds to the small unit, the compression in the centre builds and so the unit becomes more centrally compressed.

Gravity and the Earth

The surface effect

The level of density at the very surface of a celestial body is always much less than any other part of its mass. The reason for this is simple. Outer surface material has no matter above it to apply downward pressure to compress it. However, this changes immediately beneath the surface. There, the weight of successive layers of matter quickly add up with depth. The result is, as we progresses down, matter rapidly becomes more dense. This is known as the surface effect. (Fig. 6.10)

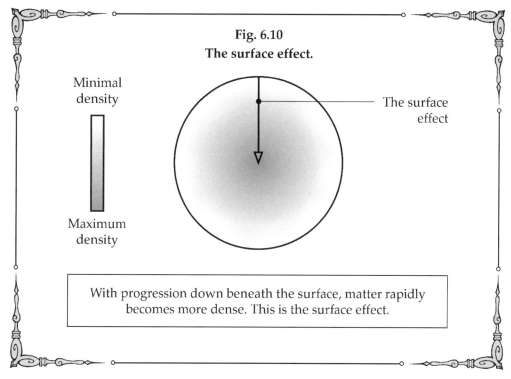

Fig. 6.10
The surface effect.

Minimal density

The surface effect

Maximum density

With progression down beneath the surface, matter rapidly becomes more dense. This is the surface effect.

At this stage, the planetary mass is small, and so the distance between the outer surface and the centre is nominal. Because of this, pressure brought about by the surface effect reaches down through the mass and converges in on matter in the middle. As a result, the greatest compression is found in the centre. But as the planet's size builds, other factors that effect compression come into play.

Downward attraction is strongest at the surface of a planet

This is the second important factor concerning compression. We have already discussed downward attraction at the surface of a planet. In this position we feel our full weight as the planet's total mass pulls us down onto its surface. Again as discussed, from here, downward attraction reduces with depth. So, in other words, the same matter becomes increasingly lighter the further down it is located in the planet. This is because a portion of its downward attraction is neutralised by attraction from other matter above and around it. And of course, in the centre all matter is weightless.

The relevant point here is; matter, when located at the surface, weighs more there than anywhere else in the planet. This means, surface matter possesses the greatest compression power.

Gravity and the Earth

As the planet grows in size, both gravity and compression increase. But compression in the centre will only continue to build if downward pressure can reach it.

Planetary growth causes inner matter to lose weight.

This is the third important factor concerning compression. Here we encounter a problem if compression in the planet's centre is to be maintained in line with increasing compression at the surface.

In a growing planet, matter at the surface is subject to full downward attraction from the total planetary mass beneath it. This gives it weight. The weight is such that it compacts other layers beneath. The amount of compression produced is equivalent to the value of weight applied by downward attraction. Over time, as incoming matter further adds to the celestial body, this surface material becomes buried deeper within the growing planet. Now, mass configuration around it has changed. No longer is all the planetary mass beneath it. Layers of new matter have built above. These layers have attraction too. But the direction of this attraction is from above. As mentioned, this opposes and thus neutralises some of the downward force originating from matter beneath. Layers of matter added on the opposite side of the planet have little effect in adding to downward attraction because of the multiplying factor distance has in reducing gravity's strength.

Because downward attraction gives matter its weight, any reduction of the force causes the matter to become lighter. This is precisely what happens as matter builds up at the surface. Planetary growth increases attraction from above and so causes matter further down to lose weight. (Fig. 6.11)

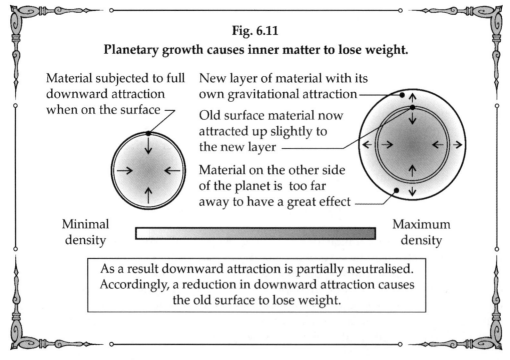

Fig. 6.11

Planetary growth causes inner matter to lose weight.

Material subjected to full downward attraction when on the surface

New layer of material with its own gravitational attraction

Old surface material now attracted up slightly to the new layer

Material on the other side of the planet is too far away to have a great effect

Minimal density

Maximum density

As a result downward attraction is partially neutralised. Accordingly, a reduction in downward attraction causes the old surface to lose weight.

This factor of how matter at the surface loses weight as it is buried, has vital significance. The crucial point here is; once matter becomes lighter, it no longer has the ability to add compression to matter beneath it.

Gravity and the Earth

A steamroller is used to compact a layer of gravel. The compression or density achieved within the gravel is directly proportioned to the machine's weight. If for some reason, the same steamroller has its weight reduced, it is not possible for it to add further compression to the layer of gravel. This same rule applies to matter in the growing planet.

As the planet continues to grow, inner matter continues to decrease in weight. Any additional compression further down and in the centre is now no longer possible. But at the same time, new material arriving at the surface is subjected to ever increasing gravity. Its extra weight compresses layers immediately beneath progressively denser than each one layed down before. And so the compression format in the evolving planet begins to change.

It becomes more externally dense.

If matter deeper within the planet cannot be further compressed by matter above it, what effects does this increasing pressure at the surface have on the developing structure of the planet?

Resistance in the mass must be overcome for compression to take place.

This is the fourth important factor concerning compression. Mass has resistance. In order for compression to take place, the value of downward attraction must be sufficient enough to overcome frictional resistance contained in the mass. If not, compression cannot occur.

How compression and resistance work in conjunction with each other is again somewhat similar to the action of a steamroller compacting a bed of gravel.

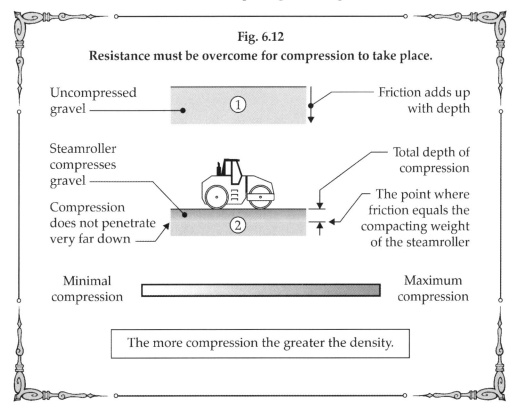

Fig. 6.12

Resistance must be overcome for compression to take place.

Uncompressed gravel ① — Friction adds up with depth

Steamroller compresses gravel — Total depth of compression

Compression does not penetrate very far down ② — The point where friction equals the compacting weight of the steamroller

Minimal compression — Maximum compression

The more compression the greater the density.

Gravity and the Earth

As with the outer layer of the planet, the mass of the steamroller has weight. It is this weight that is used to compress the gravel. But, compression requires a certain level of energy. The energy applied must be enough to overcome friction contained within the gravel. The steamroller derives this energy from its weight. But, its weight is only sufficient to overcome an equivalent value of friction.

Because friction adds up with depth, compression on the surface doesn't reach very far down. Compression stops when the added value of friction equals the compacting weight of the steamroller. Because the steamroller's compression ability depletes with depth, the amount of compression is always the highest at the surface. If the gravel is too deep, the lower layers will not be sufficiently compressed. And so the road may end up being unstable. The adding of water aids the operation by lubricating the gravel. This effectively reduces some of the friction in it. (Fig. 6.12)

It is the same with the growing planet. Weight at the surface, is transferred to the layers beneath causing a certain amount of compression. But, on its own, it is not possible for this same surface pressure to compress layers further down to an equal density. As with the steamroller, its power of compression depletes with depth. Downward pressure is produced by a certain value of gravity. There is only so much force. And so, only so much matter can be compressed before the force is spent. As said, downward attraction can only compress if it is strong enough to overcome frictional resistance present within the matter beneath. Resistance adds up with depth, and this depletes the force as it travels down. As a result, surface pressure is spent in compressing the outer layers of the planetary mass only.

This is the "Surface Effect".

Added weight of incoming matter can not compress material below the surface effect region. Here, attraction from the surface material works in reverse and the weight of matter begins to reduce.

The externally compressed format.

As the planet grows, the strength of its gravity builds. Extra gravity creates extra surface weight. This increased surface weight creates increased compression. And so its outer extremities become more and more dense. This produces a structural format that is increasingly externally compressed. (Fig. 6.13)

The measure of external compression in a planet is directly related to the size of its mass. The outer compressed regions of any planet will always be approximately twice as compressed as those of a similar planet half its mass. Or, each time a young growing planet doubles in mass, the compression of its outer layers likewise approximately doubles. The greater the planetary mass, the greater its gravity. The greater the gravity, the greater the weight of matter at the surface. The greater the weight of matter at the surface, the greater the compression beneath. It is this compression that produces density.

By the time a young planet has reached a few hundred kilometres in diameter, the strength of its gravity has increased immensely from its beginnings. Its power of attraction has become several billion times greater than that experienced by the first few particles floating in space.

Gravity and the Earth

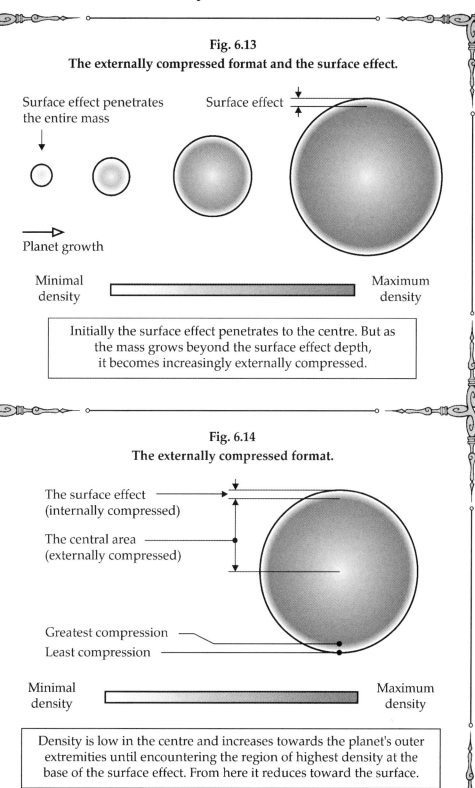

Fig. 6.13
The externally compressed format and the surface effect.

Surface effect penetrates
the entire mass

Surface effect

Planet growth

Minimal
density

Maximum
density

Initially the surface effect penetrates to the centre. But as
the mass grows beyond the surface effect depth,
it becomes increasingly externally compressed.

Fig. 6.14
The externally compressed format.

The surface effect
(internally compressed)

The central area
(externally compressed)

Greatest compression
Least compression

Minimal
density

Maximum
density

Density is low in the centre and increases towards the planet's outer
extremities until encountering the region of highest density at the
base of the surface effect. From here it reduces toward the surface.

Gravity and the Earth

The planet is still in the early stages of its evolution. Yet, a definite density configuration has developed throughout its mass. In the centre where matter is weightless, density is low, but then increases with distance outwards towards the planet's outer extremities. The greatest density is encountered at the base of the surface effect. In this location, compression is at its maximum. Ascending above this point compression noticeably starts to reduce. The depth of remaining matter overhead is beginning to decrease, and so, in line with reducing pressure from above, density rapidly depletes. Compression continues to decrease until petering out at the surface of the planet's mass. Here, with nothing above to provide downward weight, compression can not take place.

This is how the mass of the Earth was initially configured. It was not centrally compressed as has been theorised. But instead more and more compressed towards its outer extremities. (Fig. 6.14)

This is how the law of gravity works. Somewhat in reverse to the way we have always believed. This is where our understanding of the Earth's interior has gone wrong. When calculating the internal structure, this reversal of density within a developing planetary mass plays an important role. It completely changes the eventual outcome. With our wrong understanding of Earth's internal density, the correct effects of gravity have never been understood. Gravity's force has shaped an Earth that is very different to the way we believe.

So how does this reversal of density change things? How is the matter of the newly developed planet effected by its own gravity?

Gravity's effects within an externally compressed planet

Gravity's effects within an externally compressed planet are completely different from those anticipated within a planet centrally compressed. This is because, in an externally compressed planet, the most densely concentrated matter is situated a short distance below the outer surface. As already stated, the higher the concentration of matter, the stronger its gravitational attraction. In addition to this, these outer layers are a major part of the total volume of the planet.

The combination of these two factors produce the strongest force of attraction, not from the centre, but instead from the outer extremities of the planet. This is a direct contradiction to all currently accepted theories portraying the Earth as a solid centrally compressed mass. Attraction originating from the outer regions of the planet has a significantly different effect on matter deep within the planet. This understanding now dramatically changes all concepts on how the evolutionary process has structured the Earth.

In order to understand how these forces work, it is necessary to investigate within the externally compressed planet.

Firstly, as before, when standing on the outer surface, we feel the full force of the planet's mass beneath us as gravity. It gives us our weight.

Secondly, if located in the very centre of the planet, where mass is evenly distributed around us, as before, we are attracted evenly out in all directions. Accordingly, gravity is neutralised and we experience weightlessness. (Fig. 6.15)

Gravity and the Earth

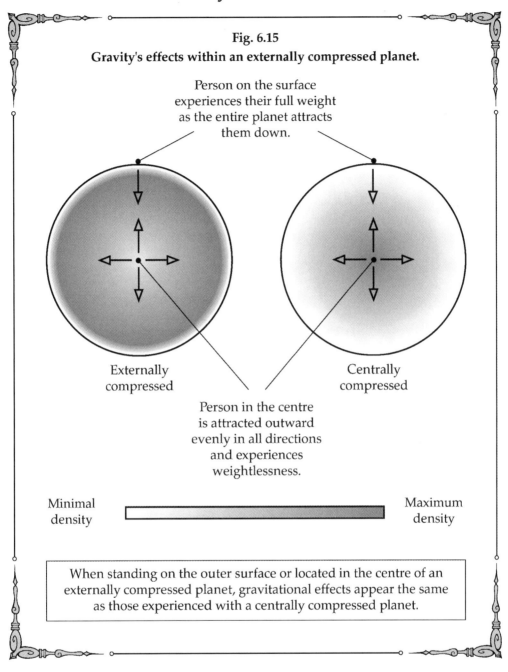

Fig. 6.15

Gravity's effects within an externally compressed planet.

Person on the surface
experiences their full weight
as the entire planet attracts
them down.

Externally
compressed

Centrally
compressed

Person in the centre
is attracted outward
evenly in all directions
and experiences
weightlessness.

Minimal
density

Maximum
density

When standing on the outer surface or located in the centre of an
externally compressed planet, gravitational effects appear the same
as those experienced with a centrally compressed planet.

Up until this point, gravitational effects appear to be the same as with a planet centrally compressed. But, this is where the similarity ends. If we were to imagine ourselves located within the planet a short distance out from the very centre, what would be the effects of gravity there?

In order to answer this, it is necessary to break down the planet's interior into two separate parts. The first part is a spherical area extending outwards from our position, large enough to reach all the way out to the surface. This area is marked as "A" in the diagram. The second is the remainder of the planet marked as "B". (Fig. 6.16)

Gravity and the Earth

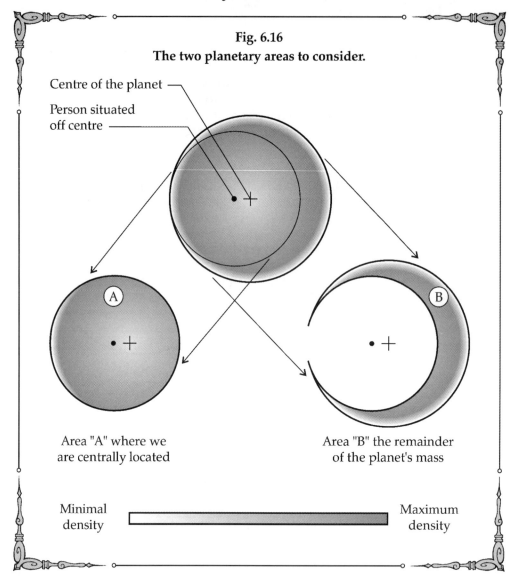

Fig. 6.16
The two planetary areas to consider.

Centre of the planet

Person situated
off centre

A

B

Area "A" where we
are centrally located

Area "B" the remainder
of the planet's mass

Minimal
density

Maximum
density

Initially, lets consider the effects of "A" on its own. Here we are centrally located. We are completely surrounded by its mass. And so, its gravity attracts us out in all directions. But in this position, the forces of gravity are different to those experienced when located in the very centre of the planet. The configuration of its attraction has changed. This is because, compression within "A" is not even. One side of the sphere is much more dense. Denser areas have more mass. And, where the mass is greater, gravity is stronger. Whilst it is true, in the centre of "A" we do experience a certain level of gravity from all directions, a much stronger force of attraction originates from the side where mass is more concentrated. Accordingly, gravity's resultant force is towards this area. And so, when in this location, we experience a direction of attraction that is outward, away from our near centre position, towards the outer surface of the planet. (Fig. 6.17)

Finally we must consider area "B". What effect does it have? The majority of its mass is on the opposite side of the planet. The direction of its attraction is back towards the planet's centre. (Fig. 6.18)

Gravity and the Earth

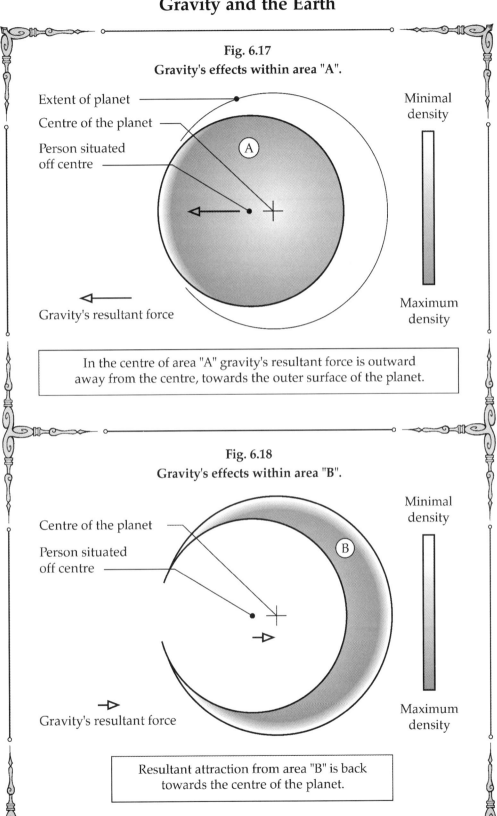

Fig. 6.17
Gravity's effects within area "A".

Extent of planet

Centre of the planet

Person situated
off centre

A

Minimal
density

Maximum
density

Gravity's resultant force

In the centre of area "A" gravity's resultant force is outward
away from the centre, towards the outer surface of the planet.

Fig. 6.18
Gravity's effects within area "B".

Centre of the planet

Person situated
off centre

B

Minimal
density

Maximum
density

Gravity's resultant force

Resultant attraction from area "B" is back
towards the centre of the planet.

Gravity and the Earth

But when considering "B" there is one important difference. All of the matter within "B" is further away than any part of "A". Due to gravity's rapidly diminishing strength over distance, "B's" effect on us in this position is minimal. As an opposing force, it is only strong enough to reduce the strength of outward attraction slightly. Accordingly, when in this location, the resultant direction of attraction on us is out towards the planet's exterior surface.

Just as with ourselves, all matter this distance from the centre of the planet is effected by the same resultant force and experiences the effects of outward attraction away from the planet's centre. (Fig. 6.19)

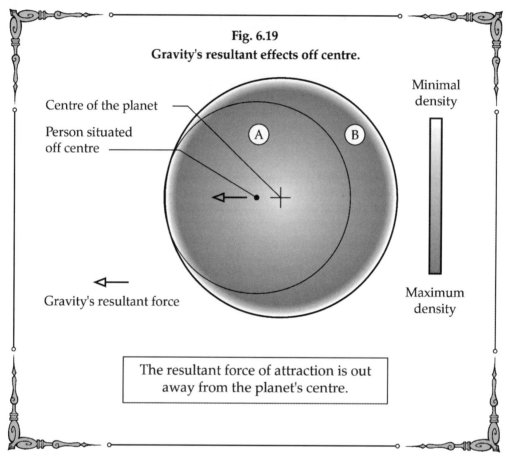

Fig. 6.19
Gravity's resultant effects off centre.

Centre of the planet

Person situated off centre

Minimal density

Maximum density

A

B

Gravity's resultant force

The resultant force of attraction is out away from the planet's centre.

So, how would things change if located further out from the centre? Lets imagine a position, midway between the planet's centre and the surface. What would the effects of gravity be there?

If we again divide the planet into the two parts "A" and "B" we can see the proportion of each area has changed. (Fig. 6.20)

Area "A" is now smaller and area "B" is proportionately larger. If we again consider the effects of "A" on its own, the same situation exists as before. Attraction is out towards the more dense portion of "A" in the direction of the planet's outer surface. Again, attraction from "B" is back towards the planet's centre. But now, the size ratio between "A" and "B" is different, and so the combined effects of their gravity has altered.

Gravity and the Earth

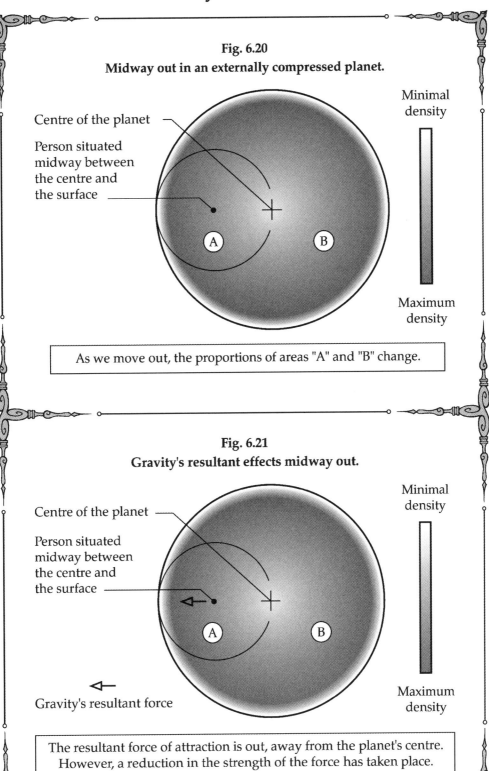

Fig. 6.20
Midway out in an externally compressed planet.

Centre of the planet

Person situated midway between the centre and the surface

Minimal density

Maximum density

A   B

As we move out, the proportions of areas "A" and "B" change.

Fig. 6.21
Gravity's resultant effects midway out.

Centre of the planet

Person situated midway between the centre and the surface

Minimal density

Maximum density

A   B

Gravity's resultant force

The resultant force of attraction is out, away from the planet's centre. However, a reduction in the strength of the force has taken place.

Gravity and the Earth

Because area "A" is smaller than before, its own outward attraction has reduced. Area "B" is larger, its opposing attraction on us has increased. However, attraction from "B" is still significantly reduced by distance. But, as the distance is now less, its ability to reduce outward attraction in this location has increased. Despite the proportional change, the resultant attraction is still out towards the planet's surface. But a reduction in the strength of the force has taken place.

Again as before, all matter this distance from the planet's center is effected by the same force and experiences outward attraction away from the centre. (Fig. 6.21)

As we consider other positions further and further out, the more the ratio between areas "A" and "B" change. As we near the outer surface, "A" becomes smaller and smaller. As a result, its outward attraction reduces. At the same time, "B" is becoming larger, and so its opposing attraction increasingly neutralises the out-pulling effects of "A". Eventually we reach a point within the planet where the two opposing forces are equal. Here outward and inward forces cancel each other out, and so we experience no attraction at all.

In this position we, and all matter around us is weightless. (Fig. 6.22)

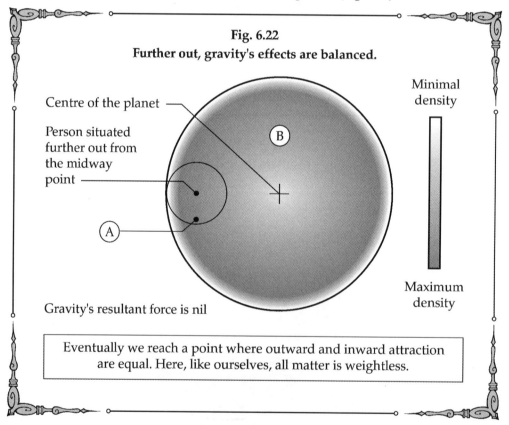

Fig. 6.22
Further out, gravity's effects are balanced.

Centre of the planet

Person situated further out from the midway point

B

A

Minimal density

Maximum density

Gravity's resultant force is nil

> Eventually we reach a point where outward and inward attraction are equal. Here, like ourselves, all matter is weightless.

If we consider another position further out again we find attraction forces have reversed. Lets imagine our position is now a short way in from the outer surface. Areas "A" and "B" are now very different. Area "A" is small and so has a small level of outward attraction. Area "B" is most of the planet and so its attraction is large. With a mass much closer than before, its gravity is now strong enough to overpower "A". As a result the balance of attraction is back towards "B" in the direction of the planet's centre. (Fig. 6.23)

Gravity and the Earth

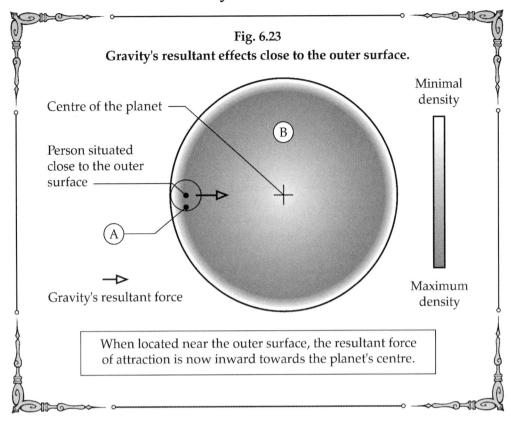

Fig. 6.23

Gravity's resultant effects close to the outer surface.

Centre of the planet

Person situated close to the outer surface

A

B

Minimal density

Maximum density

Gravity's resultant force

When located near the outer surface, the resultant force of attraction is now inward towards the planet's centre.

An important understanding is achieved from this. As we travel out from the planet's centre, the force of outward attraction decreases. This continues until we reach a point nearer the outer surface where outward and inward forces are equal. Outward from here the direction of the force of attraction is opposite. We are now attracted back towards the centre. This opposite force increases as we progress up to the outer surface. Eventually when the surface is reached we once again feel our full weight as all the planet's mass beneath attracts us down, in the one direction, onto its surface.

Attraction towards the centre of gravity

The forces of gravity, within a planet when externally compressed can be graphed. (Fig. 6.24)

Various things can be deduced from this graph. Firstly is the transition zone where inward and outward attraction meet. This is a point of balance within the planetary mass. It is known as the "Centre of Gravity". In this region of balance, the force of matter attracted out is equal to that of matter attracted in. But, although the attraction values are equal, the volume of the two areas and consistency of densities therein are not. Whilst inside matter is less dense than that of the outside, the area outside is smaller and more compressed. The combination of density and area produce equal attraction on both sides. In other words, the inside with less density and greater area is equivalent in attraction to the smaller outside area with greater density.

This can be likened to the balancing of an uneven seesaw. Whilst one side of the seesaw is shorter, it can still remain balanced provided the weight on the short side is sufficiently

Gravity and the Earth

Fig. 6.24

Gravity's graphed effects in an externally compressed planet.

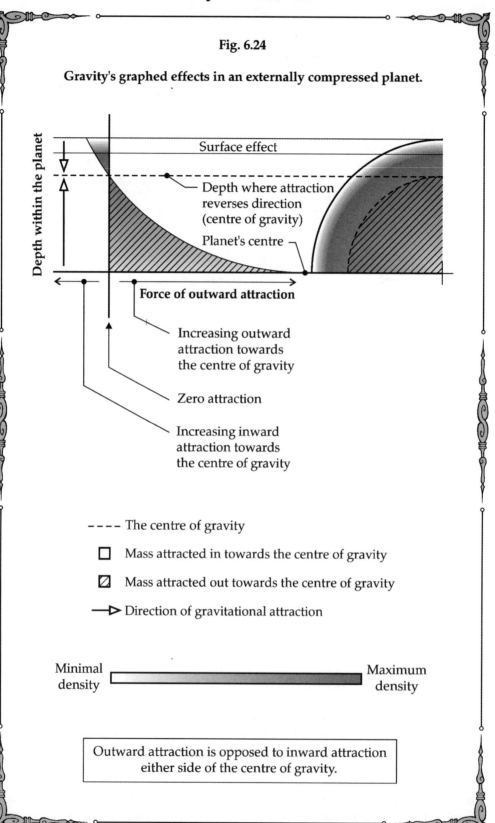

Outward attraction is opposed to inward attraction
either side of the centre of gravity.

Gravity and the Earth

heavier to compensate for the value of weight on the opposite longer side. (Fig. 6.25)

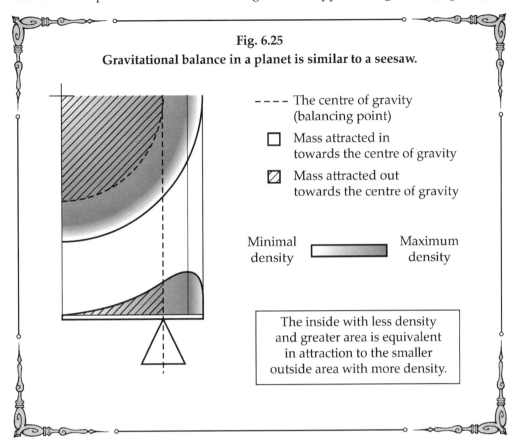

Fig. 6.25
Gravitational balance in a planet is similar to a seesaw.

- - - - The centre of gravity
(balancing point)

☐ Mass attracted in
towards the centre of gravity

▨ Mass attracted out
towards the centre of gravity

Minimal density — Maximum density

The inside with less density
and greater area is equivalent
in attraction to the smaller
outside area with more density.

When gravity acts on mass, it always takes the easiest route. This can be seen when water flows downhill. The water always follows the steepest gradient available to reach the bottom. This is the path of least resistance.

The process, where gravity always takes the path of least resistance, is this same process that operates within all planets.

The more density an area has, the more resistance present within its mass. Near the outer surface, where mass is dense, resistance is high. In the centre, where matter is loosely compressed resistance is low. Gravity acting on matter cannot move material without firstly being strong enough to overcoming frictional resistance within the mass. In the centre, where resistance is lower this task is easier.

A second important point can also be seen from the graph. The force of outward attraction on interior matter increases as we penetrate further towards the middle of the planet, reaching maximum strength at the very centre. The higher the force of attraction, the more resistance it can overcome.

The combining of low resistance and strong outward attraction in the centre of the planet has important significance. With more matter adding to the planet's outer surface, outward attraction continues to build. Eventually a point is reached when the force is powerful enough to overcome the resistance contained in the central matter.

Gravity and the Earth

Once this happens, matter there begins to move to accommodate gravity's direction of attraction. Movement is accordingly outward away from the planet's centre towards the centre of gravity further out. The bond that held the original small unit together no longer exists. It has been neutralised by the stronger attraction surrounding it.

As matter in the centre of the young planet moves away from its middle point, a small void or opening is left behind. (Fig. 6.26)

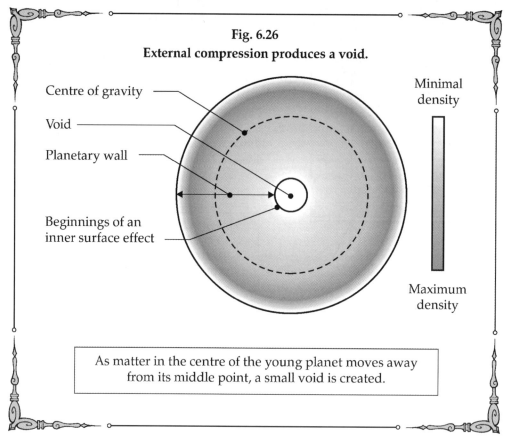

Fig. 6.26
External compression produces a void.

Centre of gravity

Void

Planetary wall

Beginnings of an
inner surface effect

Minimal
density

Maximum
density

As matter in the centre of the young planet moves away
from its middle point, a small void is created.

This is the beginnings of a new era in the evolution of the planet, the beginnings of a planet that is not solid but instead naturally hollow.

A new understanding

This immediately changes almost everything we understand about the interior of our earth. Until now, upheld beliefs have not provided us with the correct answers. Unproven assumptions have led to wrong conclusions. Such conclusions are responsible for one of the greatest miscalculations in mankind's history.

It is the working combination of low density and outward attraction in the centre of the planet that has structured our world. But, it is a structure totally different to that imagined. There are many who will find it difficult to accept. For some, beliefs are fixed and cannot be changed. In time however, the truth will be realised by all.

The matter making up the hollowing planet is now referred to as the "Planetary Wall".

Gravity and the Earth

Because density and resistance increase with distance from the planet's centre towards the outer surface, gravity, taking the path of least resistance, naturally compresses innermost areas first. Then it progressively works its way out, compressing material more and more dense towards the centre of gravity.

Compression greatly reduces the area taken up by inner matter. Consequently, the central void expands as the planetary wall concentrates and compresses. This takes place without any significant change to the outer surface area. As a result, the planet's diameter remains almost constant through this period of its evolution.

The density ratios within the planet's mass change as inside matter settles out towards the centre of gravity. (Fig. 6.27)

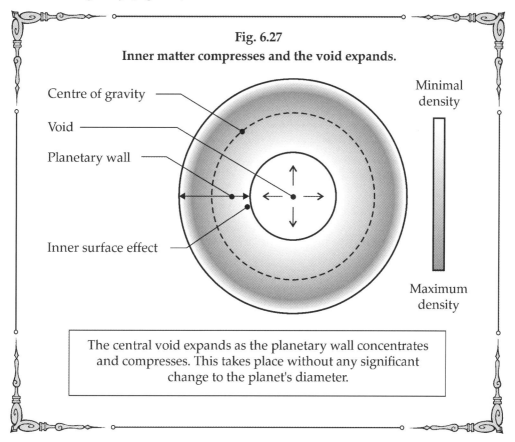

Fig. 6.27
Inner matter compresses and the void expands.

Centre of gravity

Void

Planetary wall

Inner surface effect

Minimal density

Maximum density

The central void expands as the planetary wall concentrates and compresses. This takes place without any significant change to the planet's diameter.

Compression of inner matter towards the centre of gravity continues until its density builds to comparably the same as matter on the outer side of the centre of gravity. Once this happens, the force of gravity reacts differently on the planet's mass. Matter either side of the centre of gravity now share equal resistance. And so gravity, always taking the easiest path, compresses matter both sides of the centre of gravity at the same time. This means, further compression involves all of the matter of the planetary wall, not just matter inward from the centre of gravity as before.

As density builds in the wall, so does its resistance. Because of this, further compression takes more and more force. Eventually a point is reached when The level of resistance is such that it becomes easier for gravity to rearrange matter rather than compress it.

Gravity and the Earth

Planetary expansion

The path of least resistance has changed once more. The force responsible for compression, now acts on the planet's mass differently. Gravity's force of attraction begins to spread the mass of the planetary wall out thinner. As the wall thins, its surface area increases. This expands the diameter of the planet. (Fig. 6.28)

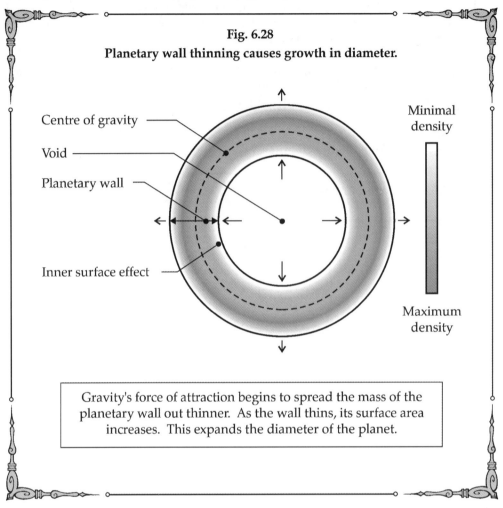

Fig. 6.28
Planetary wall thinning causes growth in diameter.

Centre of gravity

Void

Planetary wall

Inner surface effect

Minimal density

Maximum density

Gravity's force of attraction begins to spread the mass of the planetary wall out thinner. As the wall thins, its surface area increases. This expands the diameter of the planet.

The action can be paralleled to rolling out pastry. As it is rolled thinner, its area increases.

And so, only now, after many millions of years of inner planetary development, does the outer dimensions of the planet change. Expansion has finally begun.

The diameter of the planet is now growing larger. The size of the central void has increased. And the planetary wall is thinning. But because the wall is becoming thinner, any one part of it now contains less mass. Where there is less mass, there is less gravitational attraction and consequently less weight. A reduction in weight means a reduction of the thinning force on the wall. However, even though the force has weakened, it is still strong enough to overcome the resistance of the mass in the wall. And so, pressure continues the action of thinning. This further increases the diameter of the planet. And the inner void grows in size. (Fig. 6.29)

Gravity and the Earth

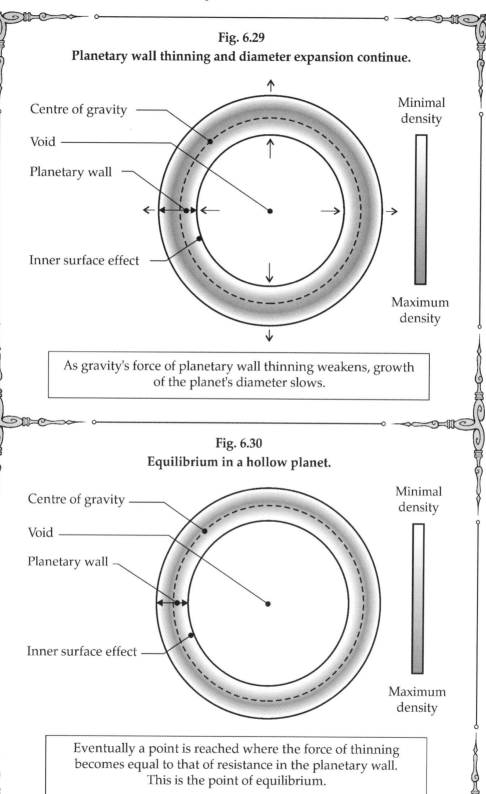

Fig. 6.29
Planetary wall thinning and diameter expansion continue.

Centre of gravity

Void

Planetary wall

Inner surface effect

Minimal density

Maximum density

As gravity's force of planetary wall thinning weakens, growth of the planet's diameter slows.

Fig. 6.30
Equilibrium in a hollow planet.

Centre of gravity

Void

Planetary wall

Inner surface effect

Minimal density

Maximum density

Eventually a point is reached where the force of thinning becomes equal to that of resistance in the planetary wall. This is the point of equilibrium.

Gravity and the Earth

Equilibrium

This is the final stage of planetary development. As wall thinning continues, the planet's diameter increases. But all the time, with expansion, the thinning force is weakening. Eventually a point is reached where the force of thinning becomes equal to that of resistance in the planetary wall. When this happens, gravitational attraction from the planet's mass is no longer strong enough to further rearrange matter in the planetary wall. This means equilibrium within the mass of the planet has been achieved and planetary expansion will cease. (Fig. 6.30)

The point of equilibrium can be seen on a graph. (Fig. 6.31)

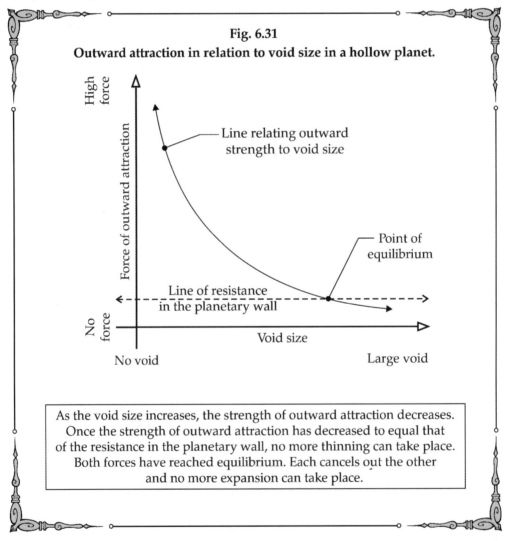

Fig. 6.31
Outward attraction in relation to void size in a hollow planet.

As the void size increases, the strength of outward attraction decreases. Once the strength of outward attraction has decreased to equal that of the resistance in the planetary wall, no more thinning can take place. Both forces have reached equilibrium. Each cancels out the other and no more expansion can take place.

This is how the Earth is formed. It is not solid and centrally compressed as is believed. It is hollow. Gravity causes the Earth to be hollow. Vital changes take place in the development of a growing planet. Because such changes have not been properly considered, we have never come to fully realise the true facts.

So, how does the gravity of a hollow planet effect us?

Gravity and the Earth

Gravity's orientation in the Earth

It makes no difference as to whether we are inside the planet or on the outer surface, gravity from the mass of the planetary wall attracts us to it. If positioned inside the Earth we are attracted onto the inner surface of the planetary wall. Or in other words, pulled away from the planet's centre. The force is the opposite direction to that when located outside the planet, where we are attracted down onto the outer surface or in other words towards the planet's centre. Both directions down, point to each other through the planetary wall towards the centre of gravity. This is the transition zone located between the inner and outer surfaces of the planetary wall.

At the centre of gravity we are neutralised by gravity's force. From here we can travel "down" no further. At this location, if we wish to reach either surface, inner or outer, it is necessary to journey "up" and resist the power of gravity. The action of travelling towards the surface breaks the balance with the centre of gravity and consequently, our weight begins to return. Weight increase continues the further we ascend through the wall of the Earth until we reach either surface.

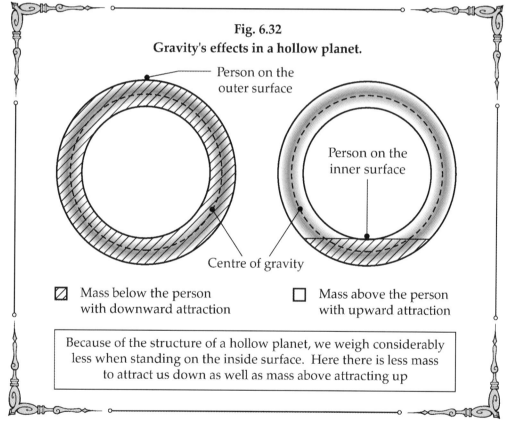

Fig. 6.32
Gravity's effects in a hollow planet.

Person on the outer surface

Person on the inner surface

Centre of gravity

☑ Mass below the person with downward attraction

☐ Mass above the person with upward attraction

Because of the structure of a hollow planet, we weigh considerably less when standing on the inside surface. Here there is less mass to attract us down as well as mass above attracting up

When standing on the outer surface, the total volume of Earth is beneath us attracting our mass down. However, the situation is different when standing on the inside surface. The mass beneath us there, is much less. Consequently we weigh less. But, added to this is gravity originating from the volume of mass over us on the opposite side of the Earth. It attracts us from above. This reduces our weight further. However, due to distance the reduction is minimal. The overall result is; we weigh considerably less when standing on the inside surface of the planet. (Fig. 6.32)

Gravity and the Earth

No matter where we are located, gravity's direction "down" is always towards the nearest point of the centre of gravity. If we are located in the very centre of the planet, "down" points in all directions. At this position there is no "up". This is opposite to when located at the centre of gravity, in the planetary wall of the Earth, where there is no "down". Here, all directions range from horizontal to "up". If standing on the outside surface, "down" always points to the centre of the planet. If standing on the inside surface, "down" always points away from the centre of the planet. If we are located in either the very middle of the Earth or on the centre of gravity, we are weightless. (Fig. 6.33)

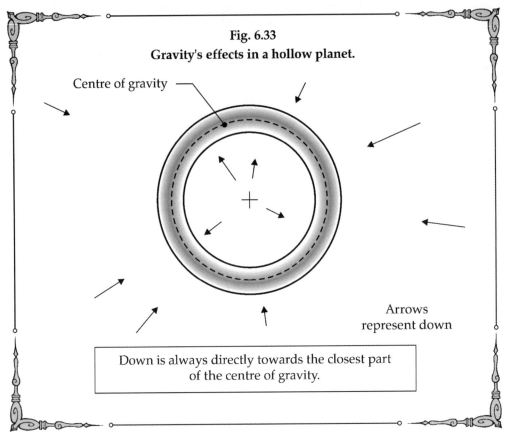

Fig. 6.33
Gravity's effects in a hollow planet.

Centre of gravity

Arrows represent down

Down is always directly towards the closest part of the centre of gravity.

Gravity effects all mass the same

The action of gravity forming a void is a natural process that takes place, not just within the Earth but, in all planets. The amount of hollowing out by gravity is relative to the resistance within the mass. In smaller bodies, pressure from the surface effect reaches the centre and so they remain solid. But once a celestial mass reaches the size where the surface effect can no longer reach its centre, it becomes externally compressed. External compression is the cause of outward attraction. Once an externally compressed planet builds to a sufficient size outward attraction overcomes resistance and a hollow forms.

Mars has two small moons. Named; "Phobos" and "Deimos", neither is spherical. They are both oddly shaped. The reason for this is because of their size. Smaller celestial bodies may not be large enough to become externally compressed. Therefore with insufficient outward attraction, the centre will never become hollow. The hollowing out of a moon or planet is the cause of its spherical form.

Gravity and the Earth

Observations of certain other moons in space indicate celestial objects of around 150 kilometres in diameter begin to take on this spherical shape. This is because the object has reached a sufficient size for its outward attraction to overcome its internal resistance. Many other celestial bodies may not reach a complete sphere if the mass is too small. This happens if the expansion force weakens to the level of resistance before a sphere is fully formed.

A parallel example of gravity overcoming structural resistance can be shown in a plank of wood. The structural strength within the plank is the same no matter what its length is. If a measured level of force is applied to the plank to bend it, the plank will only bend if the force is strong enough to overcome its structural resistance. For example, if the plank is very short, the applied force may be insufficient to perform the task. But, as the plank is increased in length it becomes more pliable and easier to bend. At the required length the applied force overcomes structural resistance and the plank bends, reshaping in accordance to the force. It is the same with gravity. Once gravity is sufficient, it overcomes structural resistance and "bends" or reshapes matter and the mass becomes hollow and accordingly spherical.

All of the planets and stars are formed into near perfect spheres. But, for some unknown reason, no-one seems to have asked why. We all accept it as normal, never considering it worthy of investigation. As a result, we have become complacent with the natural shape of our planet. But, why would celestial bodies, that are believed to be solid, assume this absolute geometric form?

With the correct understanding of gravity, the answer is straight forward. The shape of celestial bodies is caused by the action of gravity, hollowing out the centre. As planets expand they attain their near perfect spherical shape naturally. This happens as matter balances with gravity's force around the centre of gravity. Planets are spherical because they are hollow. This perfect form would not occur if planets were solid. Their shapes would be erratic and vary from planet to planet.

Gas Planets

This brings us to planets of a different structure, those not composed of rock but instead gas. Gas planets exist right throughout the universe. So how are they effected by gravity? Is their structure different?

A planet becomes externally compressed because of resistance within its mass. In gas, the level of resistance is considerably less than that found in solid matter. But this does not mean a gas planet will not become externally compressed. Density determines both the level of gravity's strength and the level of resistance in mass. Therefore in a gas planet, where density is less, the level of gravity and resistance are likewise proportionately less. Because the relationship between them always remains the same, a planet comprised solely of gas, if sufficiently sized, will become externally compressed as a rock (terrestrial) planet does. And again, if sufficiently sized, overcome the resistance of its inner mass and become hollow.

Gravity always effects mass proportionately the same. And so no matter what a planet is made of, it will become hollow. The only difference between a gas planet and a terrestrial planet is the size at which this takes place. Because a gas planet is less dense it will become hollow at a considerably larger size.

Gravity and the Earth

Fig. 6.34
Hollow planet structure.

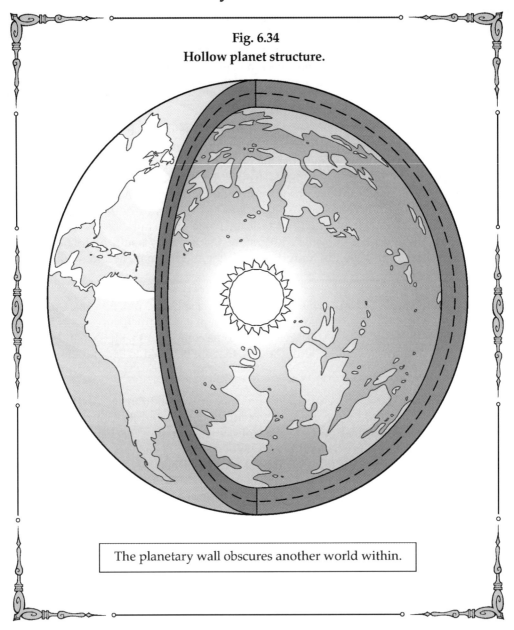

The planetary wall obscures another world within.

Misconception of gravity's strength

Earth's total mass and indeed all planets, have their own measure of gravitational attraction. The value of attraction has been used to quantify just how much gravity exists in matter. These calculations have been assessed on an Earth presumed solid and compressed. This represents an Earth containing much more matter than it actually does. Because of this, once again, gravity calculations do not add up. Earth's gravitational force is created by less matter than believed. As a result the strength of gravity in matter is greater than calculated.

As discussed in the chapter "Our Expanding Earth", the strength of gravity in deep sea trenches has been found to be less than expected. This presents a discrepancy that seriously

Gravity and the Earth

questions all currently accepted theories about the Earth's structure. Science has been unable to explain as to why gravity depletes so rapidly just eleven kilometres or so below the outside surface.

It is a commonly known fact that downward attraction reduces as one descends towards the centre of gravity. But because calculations have been based on fixed ideas that the centre of gravity is situated at the very centre of the Earth, gravitational mathematics in deep sea trenches don't add up. The rate of gravity reduction from the surface down is too great. But, the discrepancy is easily solved when the correct structure of Earth is viewed.

The centre of gravity is located a considerable distance from the planet's centre, closer to the outside surface. The closer proximity of the centre of gravity to the surface is the reason why gravity reduces at a faster than presumed rate. This feature is a normal occurrence because the Earth is hollow.

Gravity is the answer

Gravity is universal. It is responsible for all creation and provides us with simple answers.

Continental movement is caused by Earth expansion. Earth expansion is caused by gravity.

The key to the truth is simplicity.

Chapter 7

Truth Denied

The biggest step in realising the truth is not finding the answer...
but being able to change what we currently believe.

Truth Denied

W e are faced with unthinkable truth. The structure of our planet is hollow. Some may find it difficult to accept. But this is because what we currently believe is so far from the truth.

Why is this so? How could such vital information go unnoticed? Has there been a major oversight?

The human race has painted itself into a corner of false understanding for a number of different reasons.

- Human nature and conformity to beliefs within society have worked against us.

- In certain situations, scientific methods of achieving solutions appear incomplete and therefore vulnerable to error.

- Not being completely natural to the environment, makes it difficult for us to see things in their correct perspective.

- Instead of the obvious, we have been searching for solutions that are overcomplicated.

- And finally, planned cover-ups. Have they been put into place as some suggest, to purposely lead us away from the truth?

Human Nature

We as human beings are naturally inquisitive in character. As a whole, this has been beneficial for our survival and many discoveries have been made because of it. However, there have been times when this natural attribute has worked against us. It has been responsible for many impulsive decisions in the past. Our impatience to achieve the right answers to solve mysteries has so often resulted in the omission of relevant factors.

Truth Denied

This tendency to make judgment a little too hastily, sees proposed ideas prematurely becoming "fact", long before all issues within theories have been resolved.

Because we have a need to believe in something, trust in our judgments then develops into firm beliefs. Once established, such convictions are difficult to change. They provide us with essential comfort zones which are fiercely protected.

Over time, confidence in our beliefs strengthens until a point is reached when we find the need to draw further conclusions from them. These too are treated as "fact" and are likewise difficult to change.

When any new evidence contradictory to our beliefs is produced, it invariably is felt as a personal attack on our comfort zones. Whether significant or not, such information is likely to be dismissed as unbelievable or simply ignored by society. This is a normal reaction. It reflects the need to protect the credibility of our conclusions. For most, it takes a lot of strength as well as confidence to leave comfort zones for new beliefs.

Today, a mountain of evidence is required to convince us of errors in past decisions, so much more than that on which the original beliefs were built. This together with the length of time it takes for humanity to adjust to new understandings makes problem solving difficult. These are hurdles that need to be crossed. They are responsible for denying us the truth.

Problem solving using science

Science is our main source of solving problems. Because of the need to cover so many factors in any one investigation, science has been compartmentalized into multiple areas of specialty. These include divisions such as physics, mathematics, biology, chemistry, etc. Compartmentalization provides the means to analyze individual elements in greater detail. Using this method, each investigator is able to systematically achieve precise conclusions by focussing in on his/her own specific area of expertise.

Today, most of our understanding has been derived using this method. It has resulted in many new discoveries.

This system works well for smaller less complicated problems confined to just a few areas of science. However, for problems of a broader nature, solutions are more difficult. The larger the mystery the more scientific compartments covered by it. It is evident, when such problems are segregated to achieve solutions, the big picture is too easily lost. This presents an awkward predicament. Varying viewpoints between departments produce conflicting conclusions. It is these that have been responsible for the majority of the mysteries recorded in this book.

An example of a larger, more difficult problem is the origins of humanity. It sits across several areas of science from biology to paleontology through evolution to theology.

When we look into theories and conclusions developed to explain such mysteries, it seems apparent the importance of a common broad overview has not been sufficiently considered. Theories proposed by one area of science contradict discoveries made in another.

Truth Denied

In "plate tectonics" for instance, geologists may conclude continental drift results from thermal currents within the planet. But mathematicians may also conclude there is insufficient force present for this to be possible. Despite the obvious discrepancy, plate tectonics theories have been embraced throughout the community and are now treated as "fact".

This type of decision has left us vulnerable to significant error in fundamental areas of knowledge. Because there are flaws in our simplest understanding, major concepts are in error. Our belief of things around us can be likened to a jigsaw. If just one piece doesn't fit where we assume, then our concept of the entire picture must be subject to scrutiny.

Unlike normal convention, this book has been written with the big picture in mind. It has been structured using broad brushstrokes. The separated compartments of science have been brought together in a new and logical way. With all the elements of the overall picture in mind, it has shown how the mysteries we face share a common link through gravity. Whilst compartmentalization in science is an essential part, without the appropriate overview, the truth has been denied.

The human species in an unnatural environment

We, the human species, live out our lives in an environment not completely natural to us. As discussed, to overcome the difficulties we encounter, it is necessary to artificially adjust our world to suit our needs. Over time, changes such as wearing clothes, human shelter, artificial lighting and heating, transportation, medicine, etc. have become accepted as normal in everyday life. But in reality, they are not. No other life has the need to change the environment in the way we do.

There are inherent problems in thinking of our adjustments as normal. Complacency of this type clouds our conscious ability to decipher between what is natural and what isn't. Spending our entire lives in a world part alien to us, makes it difficult for us to see things in their true perspective. What most consider and assess as natural often isn't. Conclusions drawn in our attempts to solve mysteries reflect this. Our inability to apply consistent logic in problem solving comes from the confusion of living where little appears as normal. It too has provided barriers denying us the truth.

Overcomplicated solutions

The workings of gravity is an incredible find. Explanations are both logical and simple. Despite the enormity of many of our mysteries, correct understanding eliminates prolonged confusion with the obvious. Not thinking in terms of the obvious is a part of our problem. The mistaken belief that complex problems require complex solutions means the simple and logical has been overlooked. Overcomplicated proposals have not provided answers. They have only served to confuse us further. This has been a major factor in denying us the truth.

Cover-ups

For many, indisputable errors in our understanding arouses suspicion. It is thought the truth is not only already known, but has been intentionally hidden. For them, published interpretation of evidence and resulting theories have been purposely distorted to

Truth Denied

misinform society. Some even suggest the UFO phenomenon and other similar denials represent the tip of major discoveries made concerning the Earth and universe around us.

But if true, what would be the reason for this kind of world wide propaganda?

Is it a question of humanity not being ready for such drastic changes in beliefs? Is it feared the truth may unleash concern, distress and perhaps alarm throughout the community? What sort of backlash can we expect from religious organizations and other society groups? Would authorities be able to cope with anticipated aggression and opposition to such controversial understanding?

Or has the truth been withheld for other reasons. Is it simply a case of science avoiding the embarrassment of admitting error, and the consequential loss of credibility? Would those responsible bear the brunt of a displeased society believing they have been misled. Will it be judged conclusions accepted as fact obviously lacked thorough investigation. What ramifications could this have on similar studies planned by science for the future?

A great number believe however, there are more sinister reasons for concealing the truth. They claim recent discoveries have incalculable value for the purpose of defense, achieving great wealth and power. As a result, critical facts have been classified and reserved for a chosen few in high places. Here, those with exclusive preferences have the power to decide for the rest of us. Could this be true? Have authorities taken control? Is superpower status their goal?

Others subscribe to the thought the structure of the earth is known and will eventually be released. But for now the truth has been delayed allowing science time to complete its findings and assess the boundaries covered by them. This way disconcerting errors made in the past will hopefully not reoccur.

Have cover-ups been put into place as many believe? Do they play a major role in denying us the truth?

If we are to rectify our understanding and so embrace the truth we must firstly be able to overcome all obstacles before us.

Being as we are, human nature should not stand in the way to cloud our decisions.

Conclusions to problems should be based on examination of all information available. This includes everything from individual elements right up to and including the broad overview or big picture.

When making logical assessments concerning things around us, the difficulties created by our unnatural place in the environment should be kept in mind.

It is helpful to consider, solutions to mysteries are invariably simple. When proposals appear overcomplicated it is usually time for a rethink.

Whether it be past judgments in error or for other reasons, there is rarely an advantage in hiding the truth. Such action simply impedes our progress.

Truth Denied

And finally, it is recommended to examine the evidence for yourself. It is not wise to rely too heavily on decisions made by others, particularly those that are unproven. If initially, a theory is too complicated for us to fully understand, this does not automatically mean it must be correct and treated as truth. A theory is a proposed idea only. It is not proven fact.

Part III

The Understanding Beyond

The foundations of knowledge are built upon the foundations of truth.

Chapter 8

The Beginning

Reaching the truth is not the end...
It is just the beginning.

The Beginning

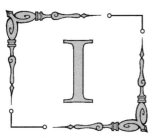n order to fully appreciate just how significant gravity is in providing solutions to so many unknowns such as the origins of humanity, it is necessary to turn back the pages of time to the very beginnings of the Earth itself. Only then can we view and scrutinise the incredible evolutionary process that created us and this wonderful planet, a world different in so many ways from what we currently believe.

The shear size of the universe cannot be comprehended. As we look up to the stars, we stand in awe at its immense size. But the true boundaries of the cosmos go on into infinity beyond our visual limitations. The further out we investigate, the more and more comes to light. As new technology grows, the extent of our knowledge grows along with it. Even in the past, we understood the dimensions of the universe extended far beyond our measurements. Because of this, a new unit of measurement had to be created. It was called a light year. A light year is the distance light travels in one year. At 300,000 kilometres per second this calculates to 9.46 million million kilometres (9,460,800,000,000 kilometres)

Earth is a minute speck in the galaxy known to us as the "Milky Way". Its dimensions, like everything else, are immense. The Milky Way's size is one hundred thousand light years from one side to the other, or 496,080,000,000,000,000 kilometres. Some sort of comprehension of this can be achieved if we were to imagine a trip across the Milky Way. Travelling at a speed of 300,000 kilometres per second, our venture would take an incredible 100,000 years. And, if that isn't enough, the Milky Way, an average sized galaxy, is just one of the known one hundred million galaxies visible from our modern day telescopes. The realms of space are truly infinite. Distances in the universe are completely beyond the range of our minds.

How the universe came into being is the ultimate question. To date there are no answers. However several theories have been proposed. At present the most widely accepted theory is known as the "Big Bang". It is surmised, the universe as we know it began with a huge celestial explosion. This was an event responsible for ejecting all universal matter,

The Beginning

superheated, out in every direction through space. Then gradually, over billions of years, gravity's force of attraction collected the mass into huge clouds. Each cloud was the beginnings of a galaxy, each galaxy building millions upon millions of solar systems. Everything from dust particles to super novas, was held captive in orbit around each other. All matter was, and still is, part of this immeasurable web of interplanetary clockwork, a balance of creation with destruction.

This is the backdrop where a few single specks spelt the beginnings of a new planet, one tiniest part in an infinite vast complexity. Out of the dust of the universe, gravity's power forged the first particles to form a new shape. It was a small celestial unit, centrally compressed by the forces of gravity within it. Growing in dimensions, it would later become the place we know as home. This is where the story of Earth's formation begins.

With an abundance of chaotic elements, the surrounding environment provided a multiple assortment of building material. Slowly, matter gravitated in to join the new growing shape, a shape destined for continual change throughout its evolutionary development.

As the young Earth increased in size, central compression gave way to higher compression towards its outer extremities. The evolving planet had become externally compressed. With that, the end of the first stage of planetary development was complete. Now, deep within the Earth, the resultant direction of gravity's force had changed. Matter there, was now under the influence of attraction that was outward towards the planet's surface.

Incoming matter added to the volume of the Earth's mass. Correspondingly, external compression and outward attraction on inner matter increased. Finally, when outward attraction reached sufficient strength, a void formed in the centre of the planet. As matter moved in accordance with gravity's force, the dimensions of the central void extended outwards.

The rate of bombardment from incoming matter had been such that the Earth's mass soon reached close to that of today. But its configuration was very different. Whilst being externally compressed, it was solid right through except for the small developing void in the centre. As a consequence, Earth's diameter was then much smaller.

Our planet wasn't the only celestial body under construction. Matter had accumulated to form many other planets and moons. Captured in gravity's grasp, each settled into its own particular orbit around a huge mass forming in the centre. This was the heart of the new Solar System, the beginnings of the Sun.

By now, bombardment from incoming matter was beginning to subside. Impacts had become less frequent. With less building material available, growth of the Earth slowed. Consequently, expansion of the void began to catch up. Gravity attracted the lower density inside matter out towards the centre of gravity first. As matter compressed outward, the size of the void increased extensively. Meanwhile, on the outside, there was no evidence to indicate the actions taking place within. Right throughout this initial period of inner mass redistribution, the Earth maintained a constant outside diameter.

Throughout Earth's evolution, many gasses including water vapour have been released

The Beginning

out of the molten material making up the planet. This action is known as "out-gassing". It is the source of the Earth's atmosphere and oceans. Without them life could not exist. Oceanic expanses cover three fifths of the Earth's surface. In places, depths exceed 11 kilometres. The atmosphere, stretching for kilometres above, encompasses the whole Earth. Most of this has been discharged from the mass of the planet throughout its evolutionary period.

When considering the effects of out-gassing, the nature of a hollow sphere, such as the Earth, has some important characteristics. If you were to travel up away from the outer surface of such a shape, the area expanse increases. This is quite opposite to when travelling up away from the inner surface towards the centre. In this situation the area expanse decreases. It can be somewhat likened to a roll of sticky tape. Each single revolution of tape taken off, gradually becomes shorter as the circumference reduces. Or, if layers were to be added, each one would need to be slightly longer to cover the next full revolution on the roll.

Over time, gasses that would later divide into atmosphere and ocean, were released from Earth's developing molten surface area. This out-gassing process involved both inner and outer surfaces simultaneously. The larger the surface area the more gas released. On the outer surface, gasses once released were able to spread out thinly into the ever increasing area above. This was different to the situation inside the planet. There, because of the physical nature of a hollow sphere, similar volumes of gasses released, built up deeper to fit into the ever decreasing area above the inside surface. As exists outside, above this inside atmosphere was a vacuum of inner space. (Fig. 8.1)

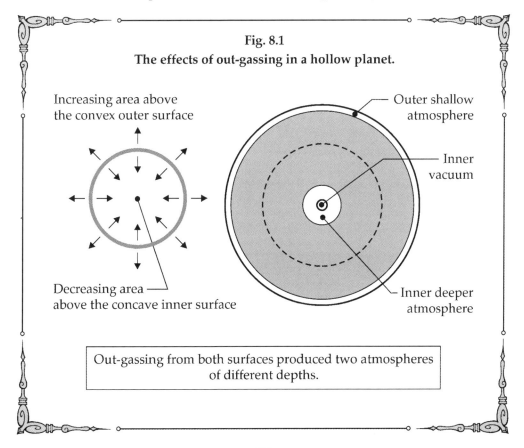

Fig. 8.1
The effects of out-gassing in a hollow planet.

Increasing area above the convex outer surface

Outer shallow atmosphere

Inner vacuum

Decreasing area above the concave inner surface

Inner deeper atmosphere

Out-gassing from both surfaces produced two atmospheres of different depths.

The Beginning

As can be seen in the diagram, extra depth of gasses occurs naturally above the inner surface of a hollow planet. This increased depth converts to added weight pressing down on the inner surface. On the outside, the depth of gasses and consequent surface pressure, always remained less. With Earth's evolutionary process continuing, there was nothing in the way to stop pressure imbalances building between the two atmospheres.

Right from Earth's beginnings, heat escaped from its molten mass. It radiated away from the outer surface into space. And now, conditions there were at last beginning to cool down. Only then, when the surface temperature had reduced sufficiently, did the first crust form. According to scientific dating techniques, solidification started approximately 4,000 million years ago. This is the calculated age of the oldest rock ever found on Earth.

Once sufficient heat had escaped from the outer crust, the atmosphere above was able to cool. Enormous quantities of water vapour contained therein then condensed into huge banks of clouds. Vapour, unable to be contained, fell as rain. Incessant torrents continued over long periods. As the waters accumulated, the Earth's first seas were born. The recently formed crust was drowning beneath a swelling ocean. When the rains finally did end, large expanses of the once dry land lay submerged. The smaller diameter Earth had less surface area to accommodate all the new ocean. As a result, there was little dry land.

And now, a very significant moment in the history of the Earth had arrived. The Sun's rays shone down and warmed the oceanic expanses. Finally, as the warmed waters combined with other essential ingredients, a great wonder of creation came into existence.

Life began on the Earth.

A whole new era had dawned upon the Earth. With most of the surface submerged, the first life forms evolved in the sea. Prehistory recorded it in stone. The earliest fossils are of marine origin only. Only later did life forms venture out to inhabit the land.

At this time in the evolutionary clock, the larger portion of incoming matter had gravitated in to form the many planets, their moons and the Sun in the Solar System. But other matter, still remained floating in space. These celestial remnants impacted upon the planets as gravity drew them in. Craters on the Moon bear testimony to the intensity of past collisions. None of the planets escaped the onslaught. The young Earth was no exception. The oceanic veneer offered little in the way of protection. Huge meteorites crashed through, pounding the crust lying beneath. Surface layers were pulverised into broken stone, sand and silts. Seas, disrupted by collisions, washed the residue far and wide.

After each catastrophe, the oceanic soup subsided in the following silence. Impact evidence was buried beneath clouds of settling sand and silt. The weight of the sea compressed the residue into sedimentary stone. But, meteorite impacts continued their assault. Sand turning to stone built deeper and deeper. Eventually almost all of the Earth's newly formed crust lay buried beneath rising multiple layers of sedimentary rock. Many of the early life forms became entrapped in the sediments from these cataclysmic events. Their images remain to this today, records sealed as fossils in stone.

The inner environment however was different, the surface there remained molten well after the outer crust had formed. This was a world enclosed and insulated. Cooling there took much longer. But, with the inner surface expanding more and more, heat was

The Beginning

able to slowly escape by radiating away into the increasing expanse above. It took many more millions of years for the inside to cool. But when it eventually did, another face of the Earth was born. A second surface started to solidify. This was another world, totally separate from the outside. A secret place, quietly taking shape, concealed within. A land out of sight and therefore non-existent to those on the outside. A world still there today. A world beneath our feet, hidden from us all.

Initially, solidification of the inner surface wasn't complete. It was a gradual process. Areas that did solidify, soon disintegrated, broken apart by the rapidly expanding surface beneath. New crust, formed over and over again. Only after further cooling did larger pieces or plates develop. Each was separated from the next by spreading sites. They added material to the edges in symmetry with surface extension. But, the geology here was different. Rapid expansion had not allowed the crust to thicken to any great extent. As a consequence the boundaries of each developing landmass were free of the familiar continental shelf structure that surrounds all present day landmasses on the outside.

As happened on the outside, rains fell inside the Earth as the atmosphere cooled. Again, because of the physical properties of a hollow sphere, the resulting ocean built to a greater depth than that on the outside. Consequently, all of the inside void surface lay submerged. It had become the floor of a deep inner sea. This world supported no dry land whatsoever. The combined extra depth of ocean and atmosphere pressed down on the inside surface of the planetary wall, considerably more than that on the outside. Earth's evolution had created a natural imbalance, an increasing imbalance capable of cataclysmic consequences later on in the planet's development. (Fig. 8.2)

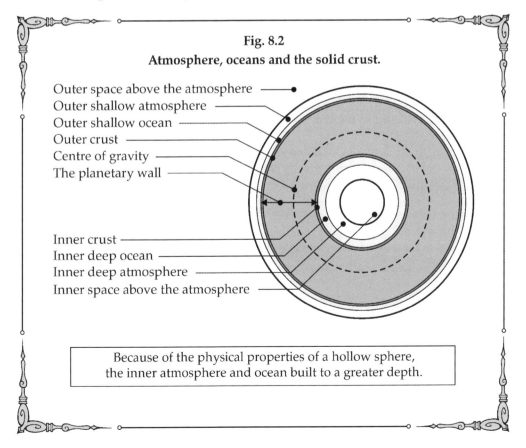

Fig. 8.2
Atmosphere, oceans and the solid crust.

Outer space above the atmosphere
Outer shallow atmosphere
Outer shallow ocean
Outer crust
Centre of gravity
The planetary wall

Inner crust
Inner deep ocean
Inner deep atmosphere
Inner space above the atmosphere

Because of the physical properties of a hollow sphere,
the inner atmosphere and ocean built to a greater depth.

155

The Beginning

After the early stages of expansion, the inner atmosphere never completely filled the central void. Just as on the outside, where outer space is encountered above the atmosphere, an inner space vacuum exists above the inside atmosphere. As the void surface expanded so did the inner space above it.

Unlike the outside, the inside surface was protected. Here, shielded from most of the effects of countless meteorite impacts, sedimentation was minimal.

The creation of Earth is recalled in the biblical book of "Genesis". This momentous event was recounted for all in its antediluvian texts. Genesis begins as the first chapter of the Bible. This book of ancient records is the cornerstone of many substantial religions throughout the world. Multitudes of people derive faith and comfort from its words. But, all too often, one very important fact is forgotten. This is not just a religious book. It is a history book as well. It seems this has been overlooked by many areas of science. The value of this ancient manuscript has not been considered in the decision making process of analysing past events. Its information has been simply ignored. It is true, most non-religious people tend to disassociate themselves from the Bible all together. But on closer examination, some interesting information comes to light.

If we look into the book of Genesis we find recollections of the creation of Earth in considerable detail. It describes Earth's structure in a way unknown to anyone at that time. The text is written in a type of riddle fashion or code, waiting to be deciphered by future advanced generations. Some of these "out of focus" messages have been artificially sharpened by self proclaimed spiritualists. Incorrect connotations have been carefully interpreted to suit desired beliefs and comfort zones of religious followers. Even today, they still do not realise the true meaning behind these words. Blind faith converts their beliefs to fact. But the Bible was describing something different. It was narrating the correct structure of our very own Earth. An Earth foretold as hollow.

The story of Genesis was composed carefully, designed for future understanding. Later generations, with hollow Earth knowledge, would come to realise the authenticity of these ancient texts. And so the Bible begins:

Genesis 1:1,2 *"In the beginning God created the heavens and the Earth; and the Earth being without form and empty, and darkness on the face of the deep, and the spirit of God moving gently on the face of the waters,"*

Here, in the very first words of the Bible, Genesis describes the Earth as empty with darkness on the face of the deep. This section of text is concurrent with the early development of the new Earth, a time when the growing inner void was still small, empty and in darkness.

Genesis continues: 1:3-5 *"then God said, Let light be - and there was light. And God saw the light, that it was good, and God separated between the light and the darkness. And God called the light Day. And He called the darkness, Night. And there was evening, and there was morning the first day."*

This passage informs us of the fact that because "light" exists, divisions are created between it and darkness. This prepares the reader for the creation of the Sun to follow.

Genesis 1:6,7 *"And God said let an expanse be in the midst of the waters, and let it divide between*

The Beginning

the waters and the waters. And God made the expanse, and He separated between the waters which were under the expanse and the waters which were above the expanse. And it was so."

In this section of text Genesis tells of two separate evolutionary developments not one. In order to achieve a better understanding, the diagram shows a cross section of the Earth as it was at the time related to by Genesis. (Fig. 8.3)

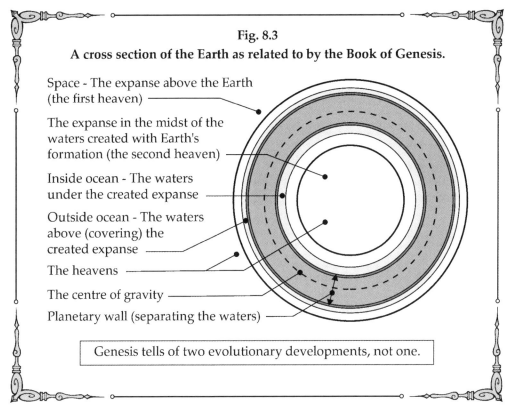

Fig. 8.3

A cross section of the Earth as related to by the Book of Genesis.

Space - The expanse above the Earth (the first heaven)

The expanse in the midst of the waters created with Earth's formation (the second heaven)

Inside ocean - The waters under the created expanse

Outside ocean - The waters above (covering) the created expanse

The heavens

The centre of gravity

Planetary wall (separating the waters)

Genesis tells of two evolutionary developments, not one.

Firstly, Genesis tells of the creation of an expanse in the midst of the waters. This is the inner void.

Then Genesis continues; "and let it divide between the waters and the waters". The creation of the Earth produced two surfaces not one, the inside and the outside. Out-gassing from both molten surfaces produced enormous amounts of moisture. This moisture condensed forming two individual oceanic bodies, one covering the inside surface and the other covering the outside surface, each separated from the other by the planetary wall of the Earth, a wall that divided between the waters and the waters.

Genesis then defines the two bodies of waters as those under the expanse and the waters above the expanse. The waters under the expanse are those on the inside surface under the created inner expanse and the waters above the expanse are those on the outside surface above and concealing the created inner expanse.

The text continues; Genesis 1:8 *"And God called the expanse, Heavens. And there was morning the second day."*

Genesis uses the plural form to describe "Heaven". This is because there are two expanses

The Beginning

not one. The first is the volume of outer space surrounding the planet and the second is the central void within the Earth.

It is easy to see why early scholars were confused. Interpretation was never clear. But, with the correct understanding of Earth's structure, not only does the true meaning of these verses become apparent but the accuracy of this amazing book of Genesis is recognised also. Passages given thousands of years ago display an advanced knowledge of the structure and evolution of Earth. Facts, that no-one then could have understood, are still not fully realised today. The puzzling text was simply written down and passed on, left for those of future generations to unravel. Peoples, being further advanced, would eventually realise the absolute authenticity of these ancient texts, texts with facts hidden from a time forgotten.

Earth's evolutionary process continued. The planetary wall compressed under the strain of mass attracting to the centre of gravity. As the void expanded, the inner crust cracked apart to accommodate the extra surface area being created. Broken crust shapes were developing into what would later become other landmasses inside the Earth. Widening gaps between each new piece formed more spreading sites. crust fragments grew as new material was added to the edges.

Eventually, as time progressed, and more heat escaped, both the inside and outside crusts began to thicken. Expansion in the void continued. Catering for the ever enlarging surface area, the thin inner crust continuously reformed into ever more numerous pieces. With each break new spreading sites formed. A broken chaotic terrain was starting to take shape.

3,800 million years had now passed since the commencement of solidification of the outside crust. The surface area of the central void had extended considerably with no effect to the outside diameter of the Earth. By now the outer crust had thickened extensively. But a point had been reached when further compression in the planetary wall was no longer possible. Resistance had built to equal gravity's force. And so, gravity again took the path of least resistance and relieved compression by spreading the matter of the planetary wall out, pressing it thinner. As the wall spread out its surface area expanded. But the thickened outer crust was unable to stretch and compensate.

As a result, just 200 million years ago, an inevitable major event took place. The power of gravitational forces found the weakest point. Unable to cope with the stress applied from within, the outside crust gave way, splitting the length of the Earth.

Bottled up pressures were released as the Earth's dimensions started to expand. The first of many spreading sites had formed on the outer surface. The split in the crust opened up as the diameter of the planet increased. Molten material from beneath filled the widening gap forming a new thinner crust. Gravity's power was on the move. It was building the first ocean basin on the outside surface of Earth, that of the Pacific.

Unlike the inside, the thickened outer crust is reflected by a considerable difference in elevation between the old surface and the new one forming. The edges of the break were marked by long unbroken cliff formations. Today, like a giant step from continents into

The Beginning

the oceanic abyss, this geology has stood the test of time. These formations, known as "continental shelves", are unique to the outside world. Reassembling of continents at continental shelf edges, reveals the intact surface of the original, once smaller world.

Gravity continued its task of balancing matter to the centre of gravity. Mounting stresses from ongoing thinning and diameter expansion focused on other weak spots in the outer crust. With nowhere to go, more splits developed. The crust fragmented into increasing numbers of pieces. Each piece "drifting" and separating from the others through the process of Earth expansion to become the familiar pattern of continental shapes we recognise throughout the world today. (Fig. 8.4)

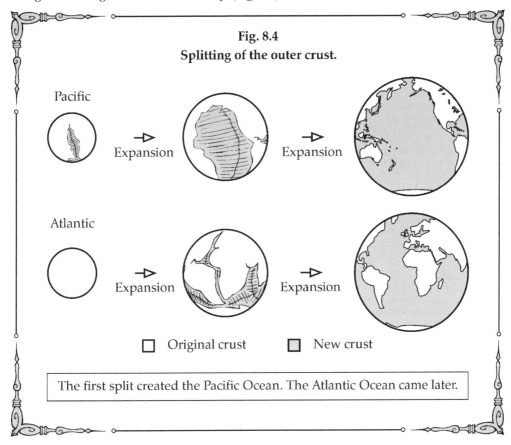

Fig. 8.4
Splitting of the outer crust.

Pacific

Expansion

Expansion

Atlantic

Expansion

Expansion

☐ Original crust ☐ New crust

The first split created the Pacific Ocean. The Atlantic Ocean came later.

Earth expansion continued. The depth of the covering ocean reduced as it spread out thinner across the ever increasing dimensions of the outer surface. The once minimal dry land broadened as it emerged from the shallowing sea. Continents were beginning to appear.

The same process was having its effects on the inside world as well. As already illustrated, because of the reducing volume of expanse above the inner surface of a hollow planet, the inside sea had built much deeper than that on the outside. But here too, surface area expansion was reducing oceanic depth. Eventually, after a relatively short period in geological time, the highest elevations of the inner crust broke through the oceanic surface. For the first time dry land had appeared in the inner world. This was the beginnings of a different group of continents, emerging in a hidden place, out of sight from the outside surface.

The Beginning

Genesis 1:9-11 *"And God said, Let the waters under the heavens be collected to one place, and let the dry land appear. And it was so. And God called the dry land, Earth. And He called the collection of waters, Seas."*

Again Genesis uses the plural form of the word "heaven" This is because the dry land appeared under both expanses, inside and out. The use of the words *"let the dry land appear"* has been interpreted by many, as describing the actual creation of land, placed above the sea by God. However, this is a misunderstanding. The land already existed. It was part of the sea floor, the higher sections of the crust lying just submerged beneath the ocean surface. These were the first areas to appear as the sea receded in response to Earth expansion.

With further expansion, outside dry land emergence continued. Most of the surfacing crust was covered with sedimentary deposits left by the eroding forces of past celestial impacts. Stone composed of compacted grains of surface crust, reached considerable depths across all continents. Today, vast mountain ranges of sedimentary stone stand throughout the world. They remain as testimony to Earth's violent past, a record of an endless succession of catastrophic collisions in the early dawn of the planet.

Now, 3,800 million years after the first crust had solidified, meteorite impacts were less frequent.

New surface created at spreading sites filled in the opening spaces between the ancient crust shapes. Growth coincided with Earth expansion. The younger crust, bearing few impact scars, remained relatively intact. Its structure was volcanic and sedimentary rock minimal. With less time to thicken, the new crust was considerably thinner than that of the older continents. Beneath the sea and out of sight, it developed along with the expanding surface area of Earth.

With the land continuing to emerge, the shore line receded further and further. Now, almost all the original crust had surfaced to be exposed high and dry above the level of the sea. The new crust developing between the fragmented pieces increased to such an extent that today, its area is large enough to support all the Earth's outside oceans. This is why the ocean shore and continental shelves share a near alignment. Sea level and continental shelves bear no actual relationship to each other. Their close alignment is purely coincidental. The new crust, with a total area of 200 million square kilometres, is now referred to as the "ocean basins". Obscured beneath the sea, it has been completely formed catering for Earth expansion. That amounts to an increase of, two thirds of the Earth's surface, since the original crust split. All this has been produced over the last 200 million years by spreading sites. 200 million years ago, the dry continental land masses of today were then the ocean floor of a smaller diameter Earth.

The seas of the world now indicate and conceal all areas of expansion. As can be seen by the positioning of the oceans over the globe, expansion has not been an evenly distributed occurrence. The majority of oceans are today located in the Southern Hemisphere. This situation exists because, it is in the south where the crust first fractured, giving way to expansion.

From its beginnings in the region of the Pacific, the fracture divided, spread, and then travelled northward, as the Earth's diameter increased. By the time the splits reached the north polar region, extensive expansion had already taken place in the south. This is

The Beginning

why distances are greater between southern continents. In effect, the South Pole has extended away from the rest of the world through greater Southern Hemisphere expansion.

This is confirmed by reading the magnetic signature locked into solidified stone. The indication is; all continents, with the exception of Antarctica, have assumed more northerly aspects since continental drift began. Similar expansion occurred later in the north, though to a lesser extent than in the south. The creation of the Arctic Ocean, put distance between the North Pole and all continents on the Earth. The illusion here is; continents appear to have drifted north from the South Pole at the same time as drifting south from the North Pole. This is an impossibility on a assumed constant diameter Earth.

It is this confusing phenomenon, that helped bring about the "ice age" dilemma. However, the anomaly is explained in the diagram (Fig. 8.5). Here it is demonstrated how uneven expansion relocated continents on more northerly latitudes further away from both polar regions at the same time.

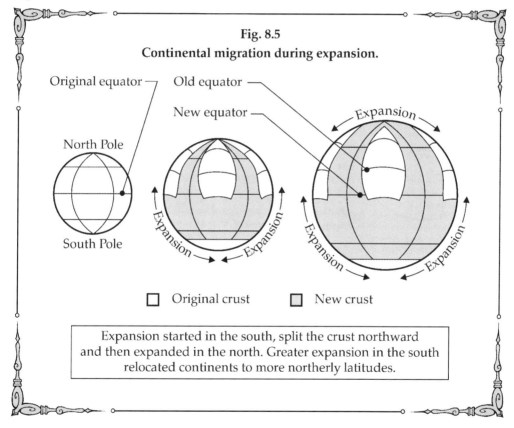

Fig. 8.5
Continental migration during expansion.

Expansion started in the south, split the crust northward and then expanded in the north. Greater expansion in the south relocated continents to more northerly latitudes.

As acknowledged in the chapter "Our Expanding Earth", whilst plate tectonic science offered some theories for the existence of mountain chains on the edges of continental plates, their constant diameter Earth assumption didn't offer any satisfactory explanation for the ranges located in the interior of continental land masses. The right answer is achieved with the correct understanding of how gravity structures our planet.

As said, mountain building and continental drift are a product of Earth expansion. With expansion increasing the diameter of the Earth, its surface curvature naturally flattened

The Beginning

out. This ongoing process has been responsible for two major restructuring features within the outer surface crust.

Firstly, increasing stresses of horizontal compression built up in outer surface matter as it flattened. This had a greater effect on the thicker and more rigid landmass plates. Oceanic plates, being thinner and therefore more flexible, offered little resistance to the Earth's reducing curvature. The thicker land mass sections, with nowhere to go, simply gave way and crumpled at weaker points in their structure. Crushing and wrinkling has produced the varying elevations we know as mountains. This is the simple solution to the mountain building phenomenon.

Secondly, to accommodate the expanding surface, the crust split radially throughout the face of the Earth. Expansion, by opening up these splits, is the singular cause of dispersal of continents across the globe, or "continental drift" as it is more commonly known. In fig. 8.6, the process of how reduced curvature produces radial splits and outer surface crumpling is demonstrated by the use of half an orange peel.

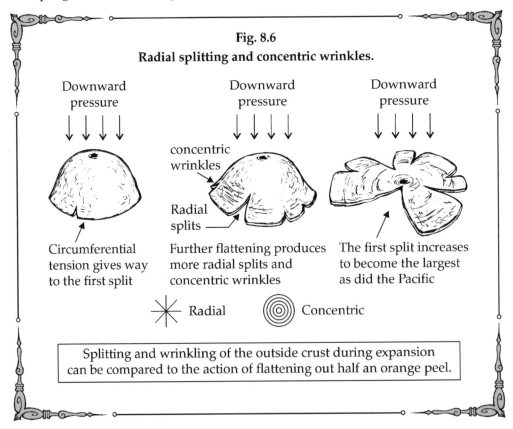

Fig. 8.6
Radial splitting and concentric wrinkles.

Downward pressure

Downward pressure

Downward pressure

concentric wrinkles

Radial splits

Circumferential tension gives way to the first split

Further flattening produces more radial splits and concentric wrinkles

The first split increases to become the largest as did the Pacific

Radial   Concentric

Splitting and wrinkling of the outside crust during expansion can be compared to the action of flattening out half an orange peel.

An easy way to reduce the curvature of the orange peel is to press it down flat onto the table. As we commence pressing down, the peel attempts to adjust by spreading itself out over a larger area. This causes tension around its circumference. If we continue pressing down, the tension gives way to radial tearing. Splits start from the outer edges and travel inwards. At the same time the action of reducing the skin's curvature foreshortens the distance covered by its outside surface. As a result, wrinkles, like miniature mountains, develop on the outside of the skin. It is the same with the Earth. Under the stress of expansion, the crust split as it was forced to spread out over the

The Beginning

increasing surface area, and at the same time, conforming to a reducing curvature, the outer surface of the crust crumpled forming mountain ranges.

Mountainous terrain is always an indication of weaker areas in the crust, areas that have succumbed to horizontal compression. This is why many mountain ranges are found on continental edges. These mark weak points where the crust originally gave way to internal pressures from an Earth wanting to expand.

Meanwhile, on the underside surface of the outer crust, the flattening process produces the opposite situation. Here the surface is stretched. Tension, from flattening, produces fractures that open up under the crust. They are immediately filled with molten matter under pressure from below. In places, splits travel right through the full depth of the weakened crust. As molten lava reaches the outer surface volcanic eruptions occur.

Both inside and outside surfaces remain separated by superheated molten material. Still in existence today, this liquefied material, between the two crusts, is the source of all Earth's volcanic matter.

With continued expansion the seas receded further and further. Lands emerged crumpled and twisted. Surfaces once level, broke under the strain of horizontal compression. The Earth shook as the ground was forced skyward to tower above the surrounding plains. Molten lava spewed out across the surface, pouring through cracks in the weakened crust. It was the same on all the continents. Mountain ranges materialised everywhere, in unison with Earth's continued expansion.

As the Earth expands and changes shape, plate edges distort and grind past each other. Elsewhere continental masses creak and rumble, adjusting to the stress of reducing curvature. Such ground trembling is familiar to most peoples across the world. Recorded throughout history, earthquakes have been responsible for mass destruction in many towns and cities.

An Earthquake is simply a series of vibrations that travel through the surface, generated either by movement within the Earth's crust or volcanic activity. Seismology is the scientific study of the earthquake phenomenon. The pathways of vibrations through the Earth's crust are determined by sensors seismologists have placed in various locations around the globe. Ongoing research, has revealed an interesting fact. Certain vibrations fail to produce expected results. A huge "shadow zone" appears on the opposite side of the Earth, as if something is blocking their path through the centre of the planet. Vibrations detected in this zone are weak and confused. Scientists can't understand why they are inhibited, particularly when considering the centre of their "solid planet" should be highly conductive.

The difficulty has arisen out of an incorrect understanding of Earth's structure. With the realisation of the Earth being hollow, the mystery is easily explained. The inner void acts as a barrier. Vibrations need matter for transmission. Each earthquake sends out vibrations that travel outwards and down simultaneously. When downward vibrations reach the inner surface they cannot bridge the gap to reach the other side. The remaining vibrations, travelling outwards, follow the path of the crust around Earth's circumference.

The Beginning

Scientists have observed another strange phenomenon unique to earthquake activity. Vibrations remain and continue to resonate through the Earth's crust for some time after each earthquake. The frequency is too low for human hearing, but none the less, likened to a huge bell, the Earth actually "rings". Again puzzled scientists have no answer. Why does a "solid" planet ring? As before, the solution lies in the hollow structure of the planet. Not unlike a huge bell, vibrations resonate around the hollow mass before gradually dissipating. With the correct knowledge of Earth's structure, both earthquake mysteries are easily resolved.

As discussed in the chapter "Our Expanding Earth", modern satellite technology has discovered elevation differences, in the form of undulations, across the surface of the sea. Not unlike hills and valleys found on dry land, their position and height remain fixed and never vary. They bear no relationship to the contours of the sea floor or spinning of the Earth. Despite a 200 metre difference between highs and lows, changes are gradual and therefore not noticeable to the naked eye. This pattern of sea surface undulations is known as the "Geoid". It is assumed mass inconsistencies within the planet must somehow produce gravity variations on the surface. Where gravity is stronger the sea is drawn in and builds to a greater depth, attracted by the force. But, on a solid and compressed Earth, sea surface contours of this size present an unsolvable problem. Mass inconsistencies would need to be of an unacceptable size to produce these effects. What could be the cause of such differences in density within a solid planet?

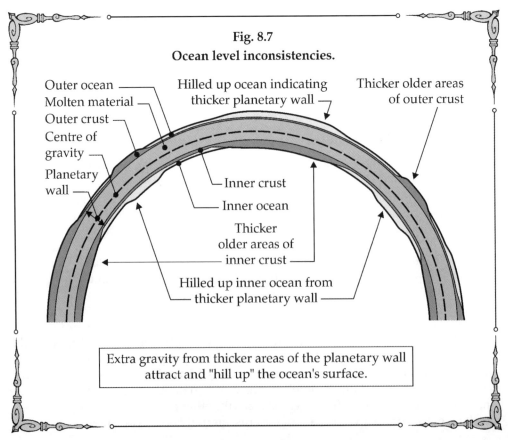

Fig. 8.7
Ocean level inconsistencies.

Outer ocean
Molten material
Outer crust
Centre of gravity
Planetary wall

Hilled up ocean indicating thicker planetary wall

Thicker older areas of outer crust

Inner crust
Inner ocean
Thicker older areas of inner crust

Hilled up inner ocean from thicker planetary wall

Extra gravity from thicker areas of the planetary wall attract and "hill up" the ocean's surface.

The Beginning

With the correct understanding of how the hollow Earth is structured, the mystery of the Geoid is easily solved. The undulations are caused by gravitational differences originating from variations in the mass of the planetary wall. This factor involves either the density of matter within the wall or the actual thickness of the planetary wall itself. Higher elevations in oceanic regions, indicate the presence of higher density mass or, greater wall thickness. Here the sea actually "hills up" as it is drawn in by the stronger levels of gravitational attraction from below. Lower contours occur in regions where the opposite situation exists.

As happens on the outside, thicker inside crust protrudes above the sea forming dry land. Quite apart from the possible indication of dense matter within the wall, higher elevations in the Geoid also provide some intriguing clues as to the location of dry land masses within. (Fig. 8.7)

With more and more matter balancing towards the centre of gravity, pressure within the planetary wall is reducing. A reduction in pressure converts to a slowing down of Earth's expansion. Future volcanic and earthquake activity will gradually diminish in accordance with slowing expansion, until reaching an eventual point of equilibrium.

Expansion has continued as has time. It is now 3,000 B.C. 200 million years have passed since the original crust split. The Earth has increased its diameter by two thirds to virtually that of today. But when viewed from the surface things are considerably different. Craters, from impacted meteorites, remain dotting the landscape. The oceans are shallower. Continental shelves the world over, are high and dry above the level of the sea. There is less atmosphere as well. Clouds are lower and rainfall is softer and different. There is less erosion. Flat lands mark the place where future great canyons will be born. This was the Earth just 5,000 years ago, a world different to the way we know it today.

However, there was an imbalance. On the inside, oceans had built deep, as had the atmosphere. Gravity's force weighed their mass heavily on the inside surface of the wall of the Earth. Inside and outside pressures were not even. With continued thinning through expansion, the distance between the two sides had become less and less. Endorsed by gravity's force, the excess ocean and atmosphere desired to escape. This would bring the planet into balance. And so the Earth was waiting, poised on the brink of disaster. If the planetary wall was to fracture, the force of nature would be unstoppable. The outside world would be ravaged and changed forever.

Potential for catastrophe was set.

Chapter 9

Inner Light

The correct understanding of gravity sheds light on the inner Earth.

Inner Light

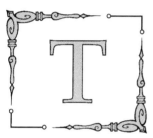

The sun holds pride of place in the centre of the Solar System. This is our own exclusive star. With a diameter of 1,392,530 kilometres, it projects energy outwards across its planetary family to reach deep space beyond. As sunlight radiates past, a tiniest fraction touches the Earth, some 150 million kilometres distant. But, as minute as it may be, the energy is enough. When these warming rays are combined with the planets essential ingredients the miracle of life is able to exist.

Today, it is said the Sun is a giant nuclear reactor. It uses the nuclear reaction process to break down its own matter into energy. This energy radiates outwards through the Solar System and beyond as light. At the same time, the process generates a vast magnetic field that surrounds the Sun. Like a huge magnet, its lines of magnetism loop outward for millions of kilometres into space. The sheer immensity of the magnetic field is a direct indication as to the size of the nuclear reaction taking place. By retracing the lines of magnetism, it has been discovered the field originates, not from the Sun's surface, but instead from its centre. This is the region where the reaction is taking place.

Similar, although less powerful magnetic fields have been detected surrounding other planets within the Solar System. The Earth is one such planet. As with the Sun, these fields originate from the centre of each planet.

Earth's magnetic field was discovered more than 300 years ago. Compasses have been used to follow its lines of magnetism for generations. The field was found to be similar in characteristics to that of a bar magnet as if located in the centre of the planet. However certain anomalies were soon discovered. The lines of magnetism are seen to be slowly drifting westward convincing scientists the source within the planet was rotating. This equated to the Earth's assumed core being somehow detached from the rest of the planet's matter enabling it to move independently. Also surprising to science was the discovery that whilst magnetic south was located as expected at the geographical South Pole, magnetic north was not aligned with the geographical North Pole. This meant the

Inner Light

magnetic field did not correlate with the Earth's rotational axis. It was tilted 11^0 out of alignment. It was also found that over time the northern magnetic pole wandered without any logical pattern. Its current location is in northwest Greenland.

To this day, the source of the Earth's magnetic field has remained a subject of conjecture. The solid Earth theory didn't allow generation of the field by magnetized ores in the centre of the planet. This type of magnetism could not be sustained in the extremes of heat and pressure thought to exist there. This created a definite need to find something else that could explain the source of this enigma emanating from within the planet.

Scientific investigation gave rise to the currently accepted concept known as the "dynamo theory". It was the only possibility left after all other avenues had been exhausted. It was a concept with the least number of flaws. The theory claims movement between materials within the core produces electrical currents which in turn generate the field. From this it was concluded such movement is likely to be in the form of thermal currents flowing over the core.

Unfortunately, the existence of so many flaws in the theory is its downfall. As discussed in "The Expanding Earth" chapter, how do thermal currents operate in the assumed enormous pressure environment of the their inner Earth? How can thermal currents, relying on gravity, operate successfully in virtual weightlessness so close to the centre of the planet? And of course, there remains the question of the westward rotation of the core independently of the rest of the planet. The same problem of assumed pressures not allowing the operation of thermal currents would also apply insurmountable weight and in turn friction on the core. In this situation, how is it possible for the central portion of the Earth to rotate freely, independent from the rest of the planet?

Alignment of magnetic north independently from the geographical North Pole presents another problem when considering rotation of the core within the Earth. To produce the 11^0 alignment anomaly, the core's rotation axis must be different to that of the Earth. Or in other words, the core must somehow travel on a circular path around the planet's centre. How does science explain this? The problem becomes more apparent when observing other planets in the Solar System. Whilst the Earth's magnetic field is 11^0 out of alignment, Neptune's is tilted at 47^0, Uranus 60^0.

The dynamo theory is clearly wrong. Science persists with it for one reason. To maintain their solid planet theory.

For those without knowledge of hollow planet structure, the cause of the Earth's magnetic field may seem unsolvable. However again, with the correct understanding of how gravity operates within a planet, the lines of magnetism are easily explained.

All matter, regardless of what it is, emits radiation. Everything, even our own bodies, discharge a share of this force. The energy is lost in space as it transmits away harmlessly from matter on each planet's surface. But, what about radiation originating from surfaces within planets? What happens to it?

As discussed, all hollow celestial bodies have a natural inner facing surface. Matter making up these surfaces emits the same energy. Here, as it radiates away, it cannot escape into the openness of outer space as happens on the outside. Instead, because of the physical properties of a hollow sphere, emitted energy converges in on itself within the planet. In

Inner Light

other words, radiation from millions of square kilometres of inside surface, focuses upwards into an ever decreasing area towards the centre of the planet. At the smallest middle point, discharged energy naturally converges into a super focussed state. This concentration of energy in the vacuum of inner space is responsible for kindling the same nuclear reaction process as that powering the Sun. This is known as the "Solar Reaction". The solar reaction manifests itself as a central sun. Isolated by the vacuum of inner space surrounding it, it rotates freely independent from the rest of the planet's matter. There it provides inner planetary surfaces with light and heat. (Fig. 9.1)

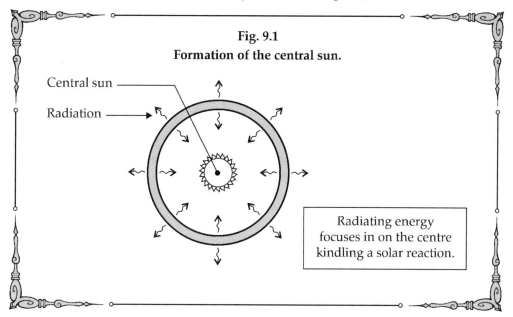

Fig. 9.1

Formation of the central sun.

Central sun

Radiation

Radiating energy focuses in on the centre kindling a solar reaction.

The extent of the solar reaction within any celestial body is dependent upon the area of the inner facing surface and the content of its matter. As a planet's void expands its inner surface increases in size. As more surface area becomes exposed, added energy radiates inwards further feeding the solar reaction. The strength of the reaction increases at a faster rate than void diameter expansion. This is because each time the void doubles in diameter, its surface area multiplies by four times. As a result, with ongoing expansion, heat at ground level gradually increases. The larger the celestial body, the larger the solar reaction and the greater the heat at ground level. This is caused as the inner sun intensifies at double the rate of diameter expansion in the void.

Due to the immense size of the Sun along with its composition, its central solar reaction is so vast that heat from it vaporises the matter structuring the Sun. When the total celestial mass is consumed in this way, the planet becomes a star. (Fig. 9.2)

Jupiter is the largest planet in the Solar System. It is gaseous and of course hollow. The solar reaction in its centre is large. Heat radiating from its surface has been measured by passing space probes. It is estimated, if Jupiter had been approximately one hundred times larger, it too would have become a star, the second in the Solar system.

Because the Earth is so much smaller than Jupiter and the Sun, its magnetic field is not as powerful. It is generated by a solar reaction taking place in the centre of the planet. Radiation from nearly 300 million square kilometres of inside surface is focused into the middle point of the planet. The resulting solar reaction provides the inner world with its

Inner Light

own small sun. Its size is such that it is able to supply enough energy to light and heat the inside world. Despite being less intense than the familiar outside Sun, its light and warmth are constant. It produces an even, single climate right throughout the inner world. Here, there is no night, just one endless day and constant warmth.

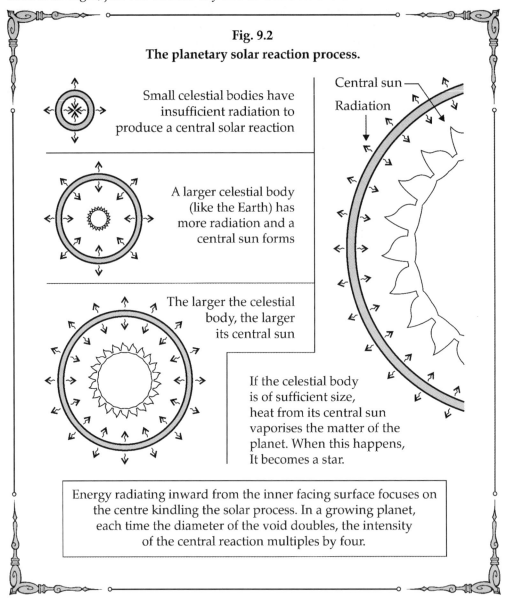

Fig. 9.2
The planetary solar reaction process.

Small celestial bodies have insufficient radiation to produce a central solar reaction

A larger celestial body (like the Earth) has more radiation and a central sun forms

The larger the celestial body, the larger its central sun

Central sun

Radiation

If the celestial body is of sufficient size, heat from its central sun vaporises the matter of the planet. When this happens, It becomes a star.

Energy radiating inward from the inner facing surface focuses on the centre kindling the solar process. In a growing planet, each time the diameter of the void doubles, the intensity of the central reaction multiples by four.

Here too, as happens on the outside, when warming rays combine with Earth's essential ingredients, the miracle of life is able to exist.

The creation of a sun within the Earth has been recorded for all in Biblical texts.

Genesis 1:14 -19 *"And God said, Let luminaries be in the expanse of the heavens, to divide between the day and the night. And let them be for signs and for seasons, and for days and years. And let them be for luminaries in the expanse of the heavens, to give light on the earth. and it was so. And god made the two great luminaries; the great luminary to rule the day, and the small luminary and*

Inner Light

the stars to rule the night. And God set them in the expanse of the heavens, to give light on the earth, and to rule over the day and over the night, and to divide between the light and the darkness. And God saw that it was good. And there was evening, and there was morning the fourth day".

If we break down the passage, facts can be clarified for ease of understanding. But before we do this, we firstly need to establish what Genesis is referring to by the use of the word "luminary".

It has been assumed by most religious interpretations that the two great luminaries are in fact the Sun and the Moon. Consequently today, in most dictionaries, this is the meaning communicated to us. But, this is not what Genesis actually meant. Generations of assumptions have changed the word's original meaning. At the time a "luminary" referred to a body that possessed its own light source such as the Sun and stars. They give off light. The Moon does not do this. It can't, because it does not have its own light source. It merely reflects light from the Sun. When this section of text tells of two great luminaries, Genesis was not referring to one of them being the Moon. He is referring to a second light source, independent from the Sun, being set in the heavens.

In the passage Genesis makes reference to the outside Sun, the inner sun and the stars.

The passage begins; "And God said, Let luminaries be in the expanse of the heavens, to divide between the day and the night." Here Genesis is referring to the stars. They only appear at .night.

"And let them be for signs and for seasons, and for days and years." This is the outside luminary; our familiar Sun in the centre of the Solar System. As the Earth spins in its orbit around the Sun, day follows night and seasons follow seasons.

Immediately after these words Genesis continues; *"And let them be for luminaries in the expanse of the heavens, to give light on the earth, and it was so."* Here there is no mention of night or seasons, just light on the earth. This the second luminary, is the inner sun. Its light shines constantly on the inside surface, giving one endless day of even warmth.

Genesis then tells of God making these two light sources; *"And God made the two great luminaries; the great luminary to rule the day";* (the outside Sun) *"and the small luminary";* (the inside sun) *"and the stars to rule the night".* The passage continues; *"And God set them in the expanse of the heavens,"* (plural - luminaries were set in both expanses) *"to give light on the earth,"* (inside sun) *"and to rule over the day and over the night,"* (Sun on the outside) *"and to divide between the light and the darkness."* (the stars) *"And God saw that it was good. And there was evening, and there was morning the fourth day."*

This passage was written in an out of focus fashion so that, temporarily, the Moon would be assumed as one of the light sources. In this manner, the words provided a simplified understanding for the people of the time. No-one knew of the amazing secrets hidden within. Once again the texts reveal an advanced understanding of the structure of the Earth.

Inner Light

Chapter 10

Life on Earth

Life evolved on the Earth not once...
but twice

Life on Earth

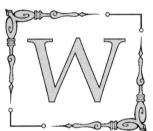 hen compared to the universe, our Earth is totally insignificant. It is just one of endless billions of tiny specks in the vast emptiness of infinite space. Yet here, on this special and unique refuge, life fills the thin veneer of air, sea, and land that extends across the outer expanse of the globe.

Combinations of elements to support other life forms throughout the cosmos are endless. Other intelligent life must exist somewhere out there. But distances are great. So vast are the realms of space our minds cannot comprehend it. Any other life is simply too far away. Here on the isolated Earth we are truly alone, separated by distance. There is no escape from the actuality of this.

UFO visitations are not from other worlds as believed. They are part of the complex picture of evolution right here on Earth. Life on our planet is precious. It is all we have. Every single life form known to us has evolved on this special lonely planet. But it wasn't always this way. This blue water world itself, evolved from a superheated molten past. For the miracle of life to be achieved, all essential ingredients and conditions needed to be in play at the same time.

Nature patiently waited for Earth's outer surface to cool. Oceanic expanses formed as released moisture rained down from the cooler atmosphere. The smaller outside surface of the Earth was largely submerged beneath new oceanic expanses. But now the stage was finally set. The Sun's rays penetrated through to warm the surface layers of the seas, and life began. Nature's first creations were uncomplicated, just simple single cells. But soon, evolution took hold and life became more complex. Newer species outclassed their less advanced predecessors. Only the fittest and best adapted survived to rule their new world. Successful species then divided into multitudes of similar designs as nature strived for perfection. This progressive development by way of natural selection is known to us as evolution. As a consequence, it wasn't long before life multiplied and filled the new outside oceanic expanses.

Life on Earth

Despite the new habitat progressing forward on the outside, the forbidding environment inside remained unchanged. The expanding inner surface was still molten. Heat was slow to escape from a world as insulated as this. There was still insufficient volume, in the small developing void, to accommodate enough of the heat radiating from the molten surface. As a consequence, the inside environment maintained its volcanic temperature. Life's essential ingredients existed here too, but it would take many more millions of years before this domain would cool sufficiently for nature to begin.

Meanwhile, life on the outside continued to advance. But the barren dry lands remained uninhabited. Nature's inventive talents took advantage of this. Using unquantifiable combinations, thousands of new species evolved. Soon vegetable and animal life had emerged from the sea to exploit the vacant landmass areas. Species multiplied, populating from horizon to horizon.

But, evolution on the outside had to overcome many difficulties. Progress was held back by inherent fluctuating factors. The Sun's warming rays were not constant as would be ideal for optimum development. At the end of each day, when vital rays sank below the horizon, life had to contend with transition from warm day to cold night. This was a time when eyes needed the ability to see into the dark and avoid its hidden perils. The night time factor slowed evolution's progress to almost half. With the dawning of each new day, warming rays replenished life to continue forward in its evolutionary task. In many regions the midday sun was hot. And life once again slowed to rest.

There were other inconsistencies as well. Long winters also took their toll on the evolutionary time clock. In a great many places much of life lay dormant for a quarter of each year. In areas closer to the poles it was longer. Life there, had to contend with strict limitations within confined climatic regions. These were places where critical temperatures ruled the day. At times, the way of life on the outside was forced to face what seemed insurmountable odds. Evolution was slow because nature's creations needed to be properly equipped to cope with the difficult changes confronting them. Despite all this, life ceaselessly continued to develop.

Then just when evolution seemed to be making some sort of headway, there was always another cataclysmic meteor impact. Nature's careful designs were again and again brought close to extinction, almost wiped out by displaced oceans that swept the lands bare. Fortunately some groups survived to continue life's struggle.

However, there was one final challenge for developing life on the outside surface of the planet. Each species had to face an unseen change, a hidden transformation brought about by Earth expansion. As the planets dimensions began to expand, fundamental forces effecting the value of gravity began to shift. This had varying repercussions for life already adapted to gravitational conditions present since the very beginning of life on the Earth. Until now, its value had always remained relatively the same. All of life had evolved in accordance with it. Those most effected by the changing conditions were the largest animals of all, the dinosaurs.

Dinosaurs belong to a group of the largest animals ever known to inhabit the outer surface of the planet. Fossilised bones reveal incredible life that no longer exists. Many species of dinosaur grew to more than 20 metres in length and thought to weigh in excess of 50 tonnes. One specimen discovered in East Africa was huge. Known as a "Brachiosaurus", it was over 22 metres long, 12 metres high, with an estimated weight of around 77 tonnes.

Life on Earth

To give an idea of this specimen's size, it had a mass equivalent to the combined weight of 12 of the largest species of elephant alive on the Earth today. But now, all that is left is fossilised bones. They remain as testimony to unbelievable animals that once reigned on our Earth.

The major question confronting science today is; why would such magnificent animals, obviously adapted through evolution, suddenly disappear after inhabiting the Earth for more than 100 million years? What changes took place to eliminate them? And then, the second perplexing question is, if such huge land creatures lived in the past, why don't similar sized creatures exist today?

Extensive investigations have been made in an attempt to solve this riddle. Studies on the massive skeletal remains reveal an immediate problem. Under the current level of gravity on the Earth today, the strength of bone structures of the larger dinosaurs were shown to be inadequate. They would fail. Skeletons are not strong enough to support the estimated weight of these prehistoric animals in present conditions. Gravity is too great. Bones would be inclined to fracture under the stresses created by the mass of their bodies. This led to the confusing question as to why? The conclusion drawn was, gravity must have somehow been less in the past. If so, how could this be? Unfortunately for those searching for answers, without the correct understanding of Earth's evolution, a solution to this problem is not easily achieved.

Throughout evolution, the structural strength of each species is governed by the level of gravity within the environment. For example, a four legged animal has an evolved strength within its bones to function and support the weight of its mass. If a species were to develop into a larger form, its skeletal structure would have to increase in strength to compensate. However, each time evolution increases the size of an animal, certain important factors come into play.

If the length of the animal doubles, so does its width. In other words, the size of its footprint doubles in both length and width at the same time making it four times bigger. And of course, the same is true for the diameter of each bone in the supporting skeleton. But then, there is an inherent problem governing structural strength when an object increases in size. The problem is, when the animal doubles in length and in turn doubles in width, it also doubles in height. This computes to a mass multiplying by twice its length, twice its width and twice its height ($2 \times 2 \times 2 = 8$) which equals a total of eight times the original mass weight. In other words, if an animal were simply scaled up to double its size, its bones, four times stronger, would need to support a body mass eight times heavier. Because of this, evolution has to compensate by additionally increasing the structural strength of the species' frame. And of course there comes a point when structural requirements to overcome the power of gravity to achieve further increases in size becomes no longer practicable.

The fact is, the physical workings of gravity do not allow nature to simply scale up a smaller species into larger varieties. This is why insects are different and can survive with their delicate structures and fine hair like legs. At the opposite end of the scale, rhinoceros and elephant, in the same gravitational environment, require huge solid frames. Both types of life are perfectly tuned with the forces of gravity. An ant scaled up to the size of an elephant would simply collapse. When observing birds and other animals we find adapted structures proportionately in-between. Nature's creations are perfectly designed for optimum strength and functionalism to suit the niche it fills in the

Life on Earth

environment. If for some reason the environment changes in any way, evolution adjusts its creatures to compensate.

In prehistoric times, not only the great dinosaurs, but all of life was vastly different to the plants and animals on the Earth today. Yet they too evolved specifically designed for optimum strength and functionalism to suit the environment. Obviously, in the time of the dinosaurs, the world was very different. This was an evolutionary period when the effect of gravity was less. It is reflected in the size of plants, insects and skeletal structures of magnificent beasts then inhabiting the Earth. The obvious question is, why? What factors were in play to alter the weight of matter? In the search for an answer, it is necessary to realise, the dinosaurs arrived on the planet prior to Earth expansion. This point has definite significance. Because this is where the solution lies. It was the action of Earth expansion that forever changed the gravitational environment of the prehistoric world.

It should be noted that our weight is determined not by gravity alone. It is determined by a combination of two factors, gravity and centrifugal force. Centrifugal force is produced by the rotating action of the Earth. It is a force in opposition to gravity. It effectively tries to spin us off the planet's surface and counteracts some of the pulling down force of gravity's strength. But gravity, the stronger of the two, overrides the opposing force and maintains us in contact on the surface. None the less, the action of centrifugal force has the effect of reducing the weight of matter. The rate at which the Earth spins governs the amount of weight reduction. The faster the rate of rotation the less surface matter weighs. This counteraction of weight is naturally strongest at the equator in line with the spinning of the Earth and reduces to zero at the poles.

Prior to expansion, when the Earth's mass was confined in a smaller diameter configuration, its rate of rotation was much faster. Under the effects of centrifugal force, life on the surface survived in an environment of less gravity. This was the environment that supported larger vegetation, insects and the great dinosaurs. All had evolved in nature's optimum design to suit the conditions present. But then, as pressures built up from within, the crust suddenly cracked apart. From that point on, the diameter of the planet started to expand and gravity slowly began to change.

Under the law of physics, the rotation of a spinning object naturally slows as its mass expands and moves outward. This can be observed with a spinning ice skater. As the skater extends her arms outward, she expands the diameter of her rotation, and so her spinning rate slows down. Or in reverse, the same skater can increase her speed of rotation by bringing her extended arms in. As happens with the skater, the Earth's rotation slowed as its mass expanded outward. This in turn reduced the level of centrifugal force. Accordingly, all regions away from the poles experienced increasing effects of gravity.

Matter on the surface weighed more. In line with ongoing expansion, downward attraction further increased. Huge dinosaurs found the changing conditions more and more difficult. The largest of all the Earth's species could no longer survive under the increased effects of gravity. Evolution responded by eliminating its now impracticable creations and reducing the size of others. Vegetation changed. Huge dragonflies along with other insects evolved smaller. The larger and heavier of the birds became flightless. Under the increased effects of gravity, developed wings no longer served their designed purpose. This is why so many species of flightless birds such as Ostrich and Emu exist in the world today. It should be remembered, wings would never have evolved if they were not intended to be used. These birds serve as reminders of gravitational changes that took

Life on Earth

place through Earth expansion.

Dinosaurs disappeared forever, not because of cataclysmic impacts, flooding oceans or ice ages, but from the drastic effects of Earth expansion.

Today, with the Earth's present rate of rotation, the difference in the effect of gravity between the equator and the poles is minimal. And so huge animals the size of the great dinosaurs can no longer exist on the outer surface. Unable to function, their cumbersome structures could not survive the crushing effects of present day gravity.

In their time, the larger of the dinosaurs inhabited equatorial regions where the effect of gravity was less. Smaller species were able to live closer to the poles. Contrary to opinion, fossilised remains found in polar regions do not pinpoint the actual areas where such species lived. Like the coals of Antarctica, remains were swept from afar by past cataclysmic events. Their amazing bones are all that now survive, left for us to wonder at the awesome size of magnificent extinct beasts that once roamed the Earth, life not extinguished by a single sudden event, but slowly eliminated by the effects of Earth expansion.

Despite the difficulties, life's determination carried through. And many species survived to continue the creation of life on Earth's exterior surface.

At the same time, right through these early pages of evolution, other major developments, of a geological nature, had been taking place inside the Earth. Conditions there had slowly improved. During the time when the dinosaurs were coming to the end of their great era, the interior structure had experienced a dramatic turnaround. This was evidenced by extensive drift between the fragmented pieces of the once original outer crust. Growth in the interior void had significantly increased Earth's diameter. The inside surface was no longer molten. Heat had escaped into the increasing expanse above. The cooled atmosphere had already released its watery load. But now, in accordance with Earth expansion, the vast enveloping ocean of the inner world was becoming shallower. Dry land began to appear as higher portions of the inner crust emerged through the oceanic surface. Increasing amounts of energy radiated upwards from the extending interior. Then, when forces in the centre of the planet were sufficient, the inside sun came to life. The new world awoke, bathed in soft dusky light.

The interior of the planet was now ruled by brand new forces, those of the waves of the oceanic expanse, the emerging land and the energy radiating from the sun above.

Finally, all was set. For the second time in the history of the Earth, warming rays combined with elements in the sea and land and the miracle of life was once again fulfilled.

Life on the outside had received a natural head start lasting for millions of years. But fluctuating conditions there had slowed evolution's progress right down, and life was still primitive. However, for those first single cells developing in the interior world, conditions were different.

The outside Sun is vast. Our planet's exterior is flooded with unimaginable measures of radiation. After each day, heat generated at the surface, escapes as the Earth turns away into the night. The rotating motion of the planet ensures all outside life is protected from certain over exposure to the Sun. If for any reason the Sun were to remain overhead, the heat build up would be such that life as we know it today could not exist.

Life on Earth

But on the inside things are very different. Life there is not reliant on Earth's rotation for survival. The internal sun remains motionless overhead, positioned directly in the very centre of the planet. Despite being formed by the same process, this sun is only a fraction the size of its counterpart in the centre of the Solar System. Because radiant energy reaching the inside surface is proportionately less, the inner world is illuminated by soft light. The sunlight experience can be compared to that of a partial midday eclipse. Yet, the rays were sufficient and life evolved to be nurtured and warmed in the everlasting glow. This is an extraordinary world. A world without night. A place of one endless day. The constant light produces a land without seasons. There was little in the hidden world to upset nature's balance of even temperature. This was a vast improvement on conditions experienced outside. As a result, life advanced swiftly.

Eyesight developed to cope with the low unchanging light. These were eyes not designed to see in the dark. There was no need in this timeless land without night. In the gentle sunlight, eyes evolved without protection from ultra violet light. It was not necessary. This situation had a considerable effect on developing animal skin. Pigmentation, important for protection on the outside, was virtually not required. Sunburn damage is not an occurrence inside the Earth. This is a place without the difficulties experienced by midday heat. There is no need for fur, hair or fat layers to protect from the cold. This is a land free of cold nights and icy winters. The warm environment is consistent right throughout the inner world. Accordingly, species had no need to specialise to cope with different temperature regions. Evolved life could migrate anywhere. Vegetation didn't have to wait for the passing of winter to fruit. Animal life too, was not limited to certain times of the year for reproduction. Species multiplied rapidly, further speeding up the evolutionary process. Life in the new world encountered few problems on its path forward. This significantly reduced the complexity of evolution's development.

Gravity inside the Earth is less. As previously discussed, the phenomenon is caused by the natural configuration of mass within a hollow sphere. Any object, no matter what its size or composition, weighs considerably less when situated inside the planet. Here, low gravity has had beneficial consequences for the ease of life. Species are able to move about with less effort. This important feature reduced the complexity of developing body structures. With less weight to support, bones are finer, muscle volume less and, without the destructive stresses of strong down pulling forces, skin tissue developed thinner. A great many life forms rapidly progressed towards flight, another task made much easier in this low gravity world. Soon small wings, driven by meagre but adequate muscles, powered larger species seemingly without effort into the air.

Weather conditions vary greatly on the outside surface of Earth. Fluctuating heat from unevenly distributed sunlight combines with the effect of gravity to stimulate the atmosphere into motion. Certain factors such as the strength of gravity, the strength of sunlight and regional climatic extremes, are all responsible for the type and extent of weather conditions experienced. As a result, outside surface conditions are turbulent. Violent storms occur from the tropics to the poles at any time. Adverse weather conditions have played an important role in the evolution of life on the outer surface. Vegetation has developed to cope. Trees have acquired strength. Solid trunks and limbs support gravity laden foliage through frequent gale force winds. Many have achieved the ability to shed their leaves and hibernate through long winters. All over the world, evolution has gradually resolved its difficulties for survival in often adverse conditions.

However, inside the Earth the weather conditions are different. The strength of both gravity and sunlight are less. Because of this, the range of extremes familiar to us on the outside are not experienced within. Interior thermal currents are not as active. With weather conditions considerably more stable, storms are fewer and rain is softer. This is reflected in the inherent vegetation. Like the bones of the animals, trees do not require the lofty strength of those inhabiting the outside. Plant life inside the Earth is softer, simpler and more fragile.

Despite life advancing at terrific speed, evolution in the hidden world, wasn't totally free of interruptions or setbacks. Earth expansion took its own share of the toll. Destruction, brought about by crustal extension and spontaneous volcanism, intermittently slowed life's progress down. But these disruptions were insignificant when compared to the meteorite devastation taking place on the outside. Life inside the Earth was comparatively safe, cushioned behind the wall of the Earth from such impact events. Evolution was able to accelerate silently forward in relative unrestricted comfort. Conditions were ideal. Progress was simpler, constant and fast. Life advanced many times faster than that on the outside. Numbers and varieties of species multiplied. And so it wasn't long before the inner world caught up. New life forms took shape, hidden out of sight, and completely unknown to those struggling for their very survival outside.

Some groups started to think and reason. Suddenly thousands of life forms were reaching out towards intelligence. Life within the Earth had reached its greatest achievement. Simple intelligence became more and more common amongst the different species. Thought and decisions became the latest rule governing the new world. Stronger species suppressed those less intelligent. Natural selection chose a few. They prospered. At the same time, as meteor impacts continued to obstruct life on the outside, the more powerful races inside grew mentally stronger. Those surviving learned to adapt and live together. Through the millions of years that followed, right to the present time, intelligent life has advanced forward. Today they have attained incredible levels of accomplishment for the betterment of life on Earth. Meanwhile, handicapped by adverse conditions, life on the outside never developed beyond basic primitive intelligence. Mankind's advanced understanding was not achieved by evolution alone.

So, where did our intelligence originate from? How do we fit into the grand picture of life on Earth? Naturally, there is an answer. But like so many others, it lies concealed in the world within. This is where the missing pieces will be found. In order to obtain them we must firstly achieve one final goal, one that will lead us to inner intelligence and ultimately the beginnings of humanity.

Chapter 11

The Land of No Horizon

The truth has its rewards.

The Land of No Horizon

The time has come to embark on a journey, an imaginary voyage that will take us beyond the Earth's great wall, to the hidden land within. We will enter a new world, the place that holds the key to both our future and so many secrets from our past.

And suddenly we are standing there...

We feel the ease of lightweight freedom in this beautiful imaginary land. Visions of tranquillity pass before our eyes. With heads raised, we now watch as the entire world covers us, a world that is wonderfully distorted.

The sun is dim. Its flare consumes the land above. The whole world is bathed in soft filtered light. In the haze of humidity, the outlines of grand forests stand. But their shapes somehow do not conform. Life is everywhere. Eerie calls echo from the shadows. But they are sounds we do not recognise. The scene around us is one of allure and mystique. Senses seeking things familiar, become strained in a place where normality does not apply.

We stand in awe, captive and lost in a world unknown. Questioning eyes have found no answers. With growing apprehension consuming our thoughts, the wonders around us are quickly forgotten. Where are we? What is this strange place? Nothing looks as it should. As minds begin to focus, anxiety closes in. What are we doing here? And, who are these strange people with us? We try desperately to understand. Then all of a sudden a fearful grip takes hold as we realise...

this is not a dream...

The inside world is quite opposed to what we perceive as normal. But as bizarre as it

The Land of No Horizon

might seem, this hidden place is perfectly natural. Here lies a special land with its own unique environment, an environment governed by the physical nature of the hollow structure within. This is a place ruled by its permanent central sun and lower gravity. It is a world with many features different to those experienced outside.

In the environment of lower gravity, there is a light and airy sensation about everything. Movement here is surprisingly easy. The relaxed grasp of gravity's hand is evident right throughout the inner world.

> **We watch as the rain drifts down through the forest. The sight is one of unexpected surprise. We marvel as it slowly descends, almost like that of snow. We feel the warmth of the humid atmosphere, as raindrops, larger than normal, gently touch our skin. We barely hear the silent drops as they land all about us. It is as if our hearing has been muffled. But the cries of unseen life come through loud and clear. Both ourselves and the forest are softly drenched with hardly a sound. We become mesmerised in the peace and tranquillity of the low gravity and misty rain enveloping us...**

The lands of the world within are tortured and broken. Images of its volcanic beginnings and tectonic past dominate throughout. This is a place of contrast. Its geology does not match the typical structure encountered on the outer surface. Tectonic forces shaped this land differently.

Forged from volcanic stone, the land is splintered and shattered as far as the eye can see. Inside the Earth the consequences of expansion are boldly apparent. Fragmented portions of original crust still remain. Linking features of the surface of the once smaller inner world lie shattered, broken apart and transported thousands of kilometres by inner planetary extension. Subjected to the ongoing stresses of expansion and reducing surface curvature, the growing crust split continuously and rifted apart throughout its evolution. This reoccurring geological action has broken the ground into chaos. The extent of scarring, proclaims the trauma in a land of turbulent history. Abundant fissure lines now criss-cross almost the entire surface. Crevassed lands are repeated everywhere. This is a world of geological tension, a place where tectonic fractures define weakness in the crust. The faulted surface resembles that of a dried out clay pan where mud has shrunk and cracked into endless geometric shapes. Like a giant complex web, crevasses encompass all.

Fault lines of the inner world vary greatly. Whilst some are small and not terribly significant, most are extensive. Lines of broken terrain span all landmasses. They divide great continents from shore to shore then continue beneath the sea. Some are the result of recent tectonic movements. Others reflect events from times long ago. Newly formed chasms cut through those from before, creating a grand complexity of ravines and gorges that interconnect throughout the inside world. And now, a new environment exists to occupy the depths of these faulted systems. It is the wonderment of an intricate network of lowlands, rivers and lakes.

Many fault lines sever the ground to below the level of the sea. Ocean, following clefts, frequently penetrates inland often for considerable distances. It is normal to see bodies of saltwater in the heart of continental landmasses. Here, the sea forms a multiple series of waterways and lakes. The few that are barren are fringed with salt encrusted shores.

The Land of No Horizon

But this is only one aspect of the fault line geology that exists inside the Earth. This is a world of numerous islands. In most coastal areas, crossing crevasses fragment the edge where landmasses meet the sea. Isolated sections of high ground form endless numbers of islands, as the invading ocean floods deep fissures that surround them. Most coastlines are broken and rugged. This is a place of steep cliffs that forever greet the sea with angular blocks of stone.

In some areas, fractures are so numerous that whole continental landmasses are divided into thousands of separate islands. Then again, in other regions, where the seas are not as deep, multiple island blocks continue, spanning the complete expanse of oceans, linking continent to continent, like groups of giant stepping stones.

There are places within the inner world where complete sections have dropped. Referred to as "Sunken Lands", these structures, whilst different to the more common crevasses, are also caused by horizontal stretching. They usually take the form of wide valleys with floors of undulating ground surrounded by steep cliffs. Some valleys cover areas of hundreds of square kilometres. Many are landlocked and support large lakes.

Ranges of mountains and hills are a common sight on the outside surface of the Earth. Most of these features exist because of built up compression in the crust. They reflect the process of Earth curvature flattening during expansion. Contrary to the outside, this type of mountain structure rarely occurs inside the planet. The energy forces at work within are different. The land is shaped, not by compression but instead, by the opposite force of tectonic stretching. Yet despite this, other mountain ranges do exist. The symmetry in their appearance gives their identity away. Rather than compression, these mountains are sourced by volcanism. In the absence of surface compression forces, volcanic ranges fail to reach the elevations of the many alpine highlands existing on the outer surface of the planet. But what they lack in height, they make up for in numbers. Volcanic mountains proliferate everywhere throughout the inner world. Many of them are still active. They are seen towering above the crevassed terrain, extending right across the inner face of the planet. Volcanic ranges have been born as the inner crust split and rifted apart, releasing molten rock from below. Active volcanism is more widespread throughout the land within. This is a place where numbers of volcanic mountains far exceed those on the outside surface. Many crevasses and sunken lands have disappeared forever, buried beneath ancient lava flows that consumed all.

Little of the land is flat. All that remains are those regions situated above the crevasses, between the volcanic peaks and lava flows. The nature of the terrain confirms the igneous origins, of a land built from volcanic stone.

Over time, the molten world has calmed. And now, more and more volcanic giants stand silent. They serve as reminders of the evolutionary past of this mysterious world.

Another significant point concerns the inner sun and its effects on the inner world environment. Besides serving as a continual light source, the sun is also a provider of even warmth throughout the land. Over most of the inner surface, the temperature varies only a few degrees at any one time. In higher elevations, amongst the volcanic peaks, it is cooler. However, this is a domain free of the familiar frozen lands and polar ice caps of the outer world.

Despite the absence of regular seasons, rainfall patterns do differ from place to place.

The Land of No Horizon

This is caused by the uneven distribution of dry land areas, volcanic high country and oceanic expanses. While most regions do receive ample rainfall, a few areas are dry, receiving little rain at all.

The combination of low gravity and gentle warmth has a direct effect on the weather. Inside the Earth the rules of meteorology are different. They are less severe. Here, thermal currents move much slower. And so, winds are usually little more than breezes. Thunderstorms do occur, but only on rare occasions. Under normal conditions, rain forms into larger droplets that fall at a decreased rate. Low gravity also has a changed effect on the sea. Lightweight waves are slower in their action and break softer onto the rocky shore.

In this low gravity world, erosion is less. The elements of constant sunlight and lesser gravity have combined to contribute to a placid environment throughout the inside world. But gentle weather patterns produce little in the way of soil. This is a place without meteorite impacts and so has largely escaped the consequential eroding action of displaced oceans. Such catastrophes, responsible for breaking down hard volcanic stone into sands and soils on the outside, are rare here. This world is protected and shielded by the cushioning effect of the planetary wall. Oceanic upheavals inside the Earth have been less frequent and considerably less destructive.

This is a land almost totally free of the fossilised coal and oil reserves so prevalent throughout the outer world. With little to aid the sedimentation process, mountains or canyons built from sedimentary stone are rare. Nearly all rock is volcanic. Some sections of ancient geology have remained virtually unchanged since their very beginnings, retaining much of their original form. In an environment without trauma, essential soils are sparse and precious. Much of what has been produced has collected in the crevasses and sunken lands, washed there over eons of time by persistent gentle rains. It is these lands that are by far the most fertile. Elsewhere soil is superficial. Above the lowlands a hard volcanic surface protrudes through shallow layers of coarse sands and gravely ground. The general scene here is one environmentally harsh.

This is a land of one endless day, a place where night never falls. The clockwork precision of time, familiar to all on the outside, does not exist inside the Earth. The inner sun is motionless, remaining fixed in its central position overhead. No cooling evenings follow to break the warmth of day. There is no night or morning after. Precious little is present to measure the passing of time. All is locked into one endless day. In a world without chronology, time seems irrelevant. Familiar expressions like "yesterday", "tomorrow" or even "today", no longer have any meaning. How does one recognise "daytime" if night-time doesn't exist? It is easy to become time disorientated in a land of endless sunlight.

In this world, shadows never move. Their boundaries can be seen, imprinted upon the bleached ground, left by continuous streams of sunlight from a sun permanently fixed in the centre of the world.

The inner sun's appearance is different to that normally experienced on the outside. Its light is muted, likened somewhat to a partial eclipse. With a centre intensely bright, there seems no edge to define its boundary. From the interior outward its image diffuses away in a flawless blend with the surrounding sky. No clear division can be seen between the sun, the sky and the ground. Unlike the outside, the soft sun illuminates the inner world with an air of placidity and harmony.

The Land of No Horizon

But beyond the sun, there stands an even more incredible sight, that of other lands far away.

We can hardly believe our eyes. The absence of time is immediately forgotten as minds are distracted by an implausible sight. It is a vision that extends in every direction above us.

A marvellous panorama is formed by the land. It is both eerie and beautiful. Somehow, the perspective of the world is wonderfully distorted. Its lands do not follow the normal lines of Earth curvature. Instead, they are strangely reversed. All around, in every direction, the land rises with distance before disappearing in an atmospheric haze. It is like being in a world size shallow depression. But then, most startling of all, is the reappearance of the land, behind and above the clouds.

The higher we look the more we can see. Faint shapes of distant places and oceanic expanses, are distinguishable where there should only be sky. The whole surface of the land is concaved inwards, continuing in all directions. Normal land dimensions are lost in the overwhelming sight. They do not exist here. From where we stand it is easy to appreciate the grand size of this world. We liken it to a hazy view of the Earth from space.

Words cannot describe its immensity or mystique. The whole vision fades away as it nears the flare of the sun, only to reappear on the other side. The panorama is completed as our eyes follow the view back down to the very ground where we stand. The mysterious world totally encompasses us, the sun, and everything within it. There is no possible way to explain the feelings of emotion as we gaze upward at the great map suspended above. This is something you have to experience for yourself. There is no separation between the land and the sky. There is no separation between the sky and the sun. And, there is no separation within time. Everything continues without division. It is truly the most unique place.

This is the land of no horizon...

Great lands encroach on all sides. There is no hiding place at all. Everything can be seen from everywhere. This is a world free of secrets. There is no horizon to hide behind. It is a land unlike the world outside, where troubles in places beyond the horizon are so easily forgotten. Here there is no "out of sight out of mind". This is a world visible to all. A world in which all appears as one, complete and whole.

Clouds everywhere follow the lie of the land. In the distance, they create a horizon of their own as they curve upwards over the inner concaved surface.

The Earth as we know it, never ceases to fulfil our inquisitiveness with its amazing beauty and geological wonders. Yet the territory we share and care for, is only part of the Earth's total picture. As incredible as it might be, through our ignorance we have been left totally unaware of the magnificent world that lies beneath. Until now, nearly 300 million square

The Land of No Horizon

kilometres of the Earth's surface has not been known to exist.

The even global climate provides ideal conditions for the ease of life. Because of this, abundant vegetation flourishes throughout the inner world. In this land there are no deciduous trees or other cold climate species. Vegetation has evolved specifically suited for survival in an environment of even warmth. Dense growth of a tropical nature predominates over the floors of ravines, gorges and sunken lands. This is where the best soils are found. The number of varieties seem almost endless. Whilst just a few are recognisable, most are not familiar at all. Impressive trees are inter-dispersed with new palm varieties and cloaked in masses of vines and other lush vegetation. The tangle of jungle blanketing most lowland regions, is virtually impenetrable.

Again, the vegetation of the inner world has evolved for optimum strength and functionalism to suit the low gravity environment. As occurred in the reduced gravitational conditions of the prehistoric outer world, the proportions of plant structures are generally larger. This is more noticeable when comparing actual species to similar type plants living on the outer surface. The dimensions of some individual leaves are remarkable. The magnification of life is apparent when standing amid the inner world vegetation. For us, it is a feeling of being somehow miniaturised in a world of giants.

A myriad of magnificent leaf shapes combine to from dark canopies of deep green. Imposing designs, somewhat intricate yet flimsy in appearance, take advantage of the gentle conditions. All growth responds to the singular direction of the sunlight. It is strange to see so many enormous leaves face directly upward in layers. Resembling large dinner plates, they stretch outwards on fine slender stems. As if defiant of gravity, they appear to float in their quest for sunlight. Some varieties are grouped around single stems. In a way they produce unusual umbrella type images that repeat throughout the forest. Others, not unlike oversized Banana leaves, drift in time with breezes passing through the forest. Despite the existence of many other smaller leaf designs, the largest leaves on Earth are found here. Leaves, in varieties, shapes and colours too numerous to describe, clothe the branches of the magnificent inner world forests.

Many trees are tall and spidery in appearance. Their unearthly designs haunt the pristine landscape everywhere. Long thin trunks branch into even thinner limbs supporting dense clusters of foliage. Other trees spread for incredible distances from single central trunks. Whilst some extended limbs are supported by curtains of aerial roots, others are not supported at all. Unseen varieties of palm reach to great heights on pencil thin trunks. Flimsy structures look as if they should fail. But contrary to logic, each species stands with obvious ease. In normal gravity this could not be. But in this world gravity is less. The vision of the forests appears unusual, giving the impression of fragility.

Inside the Earth, growth of vegetation is rapid. In this land, free from the delay of a night-time period and seasonal interruptions, plants are able to increase and multiply at a much faster rate than their counterparts outside. With little in the way to slow down their progress, competition between species is intense. Clinging vines out challenge others as they climb upward towards a share of the meagre sunlight. Many species, increase their chances by reaching to great heights. There they stand in full light above the canopy of the forest. Some trees defy the odds by sheer size alone. Their tangled masses are a spectacular sight. When viewed from a distance, their heights are seen to alter the uniform elevation of the forest canopy into what appears to be a series of undulating hills. Their spreading masses are seemingly endless. Other plants and even trees make their home

The Land of No Horizon

in the immensity of the branches above. Like multistory cities of the plant kingdom, they create their own individual environment within the extent of their dimensions.

Fallen timber does not disclose its age. In a land without seasons, trees are free from the familiar growth rings common to similar vegetation outside. One can only stand in wonder and question the life period of such majestic giants that reach ever skyward through the forest.

On the higher ground, soils have less depth. Vegetation growing there is hardier and drier than that below. Here, the numbers of species are less. Each however, is again perfectly adapted in these different conditions. As happens below, almost all of the leaves on all plants are perfectly aligned in the one direction. They face directly upwards. It is a curious sight. Even isolated plants do the same. Only when a leaf dies does it face away from above. The flat leaf arrangement is common everywhere, giving an all round artificial look to the vegetation.

Lowlands of fertility cross the terrain and continue upward following the distant curvature of the inner world. They are seen to form complex Linear patterns, spanning dark landmass shapes, dominating the sky. They show the true power and extent of how evolved life has consumed the fractured lands of the world hidden within.

In the land of no horizon shadows do not move. They remain stationery, reflecting the motionless sun above. Shaded ground, particularly that under rocky overhangs and within cliff walls, never receives direct sunlight. It is not possible for the rays of the sun to cross its defined edge and reach into the shadows. Many species of plants have evolved to take advantage of this. Delicate mosses, ferns and other vegetation types colonise these parts screened from sunlight. They grow right to the edge of their domain to meet the sun and then stop as if trimmed by a gardener's secateurs. Normal species continue growing where the shade plants leave off. It is a strange sight to observe the very same vegetation following the lines of branches across the ground, thriving in the confines of narrow shadows that never move. Their different colour adds a delicate illusionary effect to the places where the sun never shines.

In the rapid growth environment, flowers bloom in great profusion. Wherever sunlight shines, blossoms are invariably found. Not only flowering plants, but often trees too are adorned with intense measures of floral cover. Their brilliance of colour creates an imposing vision seen across distances of the inner world. Again, varieties are extensive varying in size, shape, colour and perfume. Most are amazingly colourful, others equally delicate. Once again, as discovered with the leaves, the largest and by far the most magnificent floral specimens are to be found living amongst those of the inner world. There is nothing near them existing on the outside surface. They have to be seen to be believed. In the delicate light of the inside sun, blooms last for a considerable time before giving way to seed. Without seasons to follow, vegetation species flower in line with an equivalent monthly cycle. Flowering plants are seen covering dry ground, capping tropical trees or cascading on vines down cliff walls. Numerous Orchid varieties inhabit high branches and clefts in steep rock faces. The largest of all Lilies inhabit quiet corners of lakes and ponds breaking mirrored surfaces with a diffused floral hue.

Again, whilst some flowering plants appear to have definite similarities to species outside, most are vastly different.

The Land of No Horizon

In the ideal conditions, floral sequences rapidly progress to fruit and seed. Not restricted by difficult seasons, endless numbers of often large and succulent fruits are always plentiful. Their seeds are easily dispersed on the breezes of the low gravity environment.

In the land on no horizon, countless numbers of plants and trees have flowered, fruited and produced seed, for millions of revolutions around the Sun. All proceeding quietly, locked away in the unseen pristine world within, completely unknown to life's struggle on the outer surface.

> **We are confronted by a large chasm. Like some sort of huge tectonic flaw, it divides the land in two. A cliff face drops for a hundred metres or so below us. The ground at the bottom is hidden beneath a cover of dense, tropical like jungle. It looks incredibly thick and quite impenetrable. The height of the forest cannot be determined because the ground supporting it is completely obscured. Some parts are very steep while other areas appear relatively flat. The jungle is full of life. Creatures fill the air above the trees. Strange calls of unknown animals can be heard all the way to the cliff top.**

> **Beyond the jungle an identical cliff rises to the same height, level with where we stand. In the diminished light, we trace lines of bare cliff faces as far as our eyes can distinguish. The lush forest below looks much greener than other vegetation growing above. Broken sections of higher ground can be seen extending out, still connected to the walls of the chasm. Separated from the surrounding high ground, they form grand columns built of stone. Behind them, waterfalls are seen cascading out of smaller ravines into the depths below. Here, the chasm is several kilometres wide. Elsewhere it is much narrower. Beyond, a large river can be seen flowing through the middle. In one direction complete sections of the terrain look as though they have dropped. Like a long wide valley, its inner undulations are different from the land above. The geological fracture we have encountered seems totally impassable.**

> **We stand in the warm light and marvel at the sights before us. But in a world never before seen, curious thoughts of familiarity continually invade our minds. As absurd as it may seem, there is no escaping the strange feeling that somehow we belong...**

In the land of no horizon, life is everywhere. Its forms exist in all shapes and sizes. Animal life inhabits the land, rivers, lakes, and thrives in the sea. The shear number of different species is so great, it would seem impossible to list them all. Like the flora, each creature reflects that part of the environment in which it evolved. Each perfectly adapted, fills its own particular niche within the elements of the inside world.

In the constant warmth, evolution has always been easier. Individual life forms have not been specifically required to survive extremes of heat and cold. Temperature variations present across the outer surface do not occur within the Earth. For this reason alone, there is less need for the diversity of life that exists on the outer surface. Yet despite this, the numbers of different species are still astronomic. However, because conditions are different, the majority of inside animals are quite unlike those familiar to us on the outer

The Land of No Horizon

surface.

Many have distinguished large eyes. These eyes are non-functional in the dark, yet perfectly adapted for vision in the dim light of the inner sun. There are no nocturnal animals in this land without night. Neither coats of fur nor insulating layers of fat are required in the permanent warmth. Skin pigment, vital for sun protection outside is not seen. Most species are totally naked with pale skin.

In the lightweight environment of the inner world, not only vegetation, but all of life from tiny insect varieties to large beasts benefit from the lesser burden of gravity. This is reflected in the individual structure of each and every species. Life forms, equivalent in size to animals outside, look fragile. Fine boned limbs support life of slight stature. With the lack of heavy weighted encumbrance, the gravitational environment of this world is not unlike that of the prehistoric outer world as it was at the time of the dinosaurs. As expansion extinguished the dinosaurs, here inside the Earth, the reduction of centrifugal force decreased the weight of matter further. Because species are not restricted to the same bulky strength as now required on the outer surface, great creatures the size of dinosaurs have evolved. These magnificent animals are perfectly adapted and live in ease and harmony with the lower gravity environment of the inner Earth.

To take advantage of the lightweight inside world, many more of its species have progressed to flight. Large animals, somewhat hulking and ungainly in appearance, take to the air in successful flight. Large leathery creatures, with a look of being almost fictitious, drift above on the rising currents, supported by the sound of slowly beating wings. Oversized birds, expected to be flightless, rise from the ground in surprisingly adequate flight. Tiny fanciful creatures are seen persistently flying everywhere. Some, almost human in appearance, flit from place to place on delicate wings within the forest. The sight is the same all over. Vast numbers of wonderful and yet at the same time strange creatures crowd the skies of the inner world, carried on wings somehow undersized.

The vision of so many new and amazing creatures awakens a myriad of mental pictures from the past. Questioning thoughts probe forgotten childhood memories, tales and legends of mythical beasts, dragons, fairies and even angels. Standing in the presence of the most incredible life on Earth, one is left to wonder at the true origins of such wonderful and unusual stories, fantasies and fables retold for all, passed on from one generation to the next.

In the ideal conditions, inside species are far more advanced. Many are upright in stature and have achieved varying levels of intelligence. At the same time, contending with the difficulties of the harsh environment, life on the outside has not yet reached these higher levels. Its stage of evolution is still fairly primitive, particularly when compared to those life forms within.

The complexity of life continues beneath the sea. In a climate of even global warmth, coral reefs prosper throughout, fringing all landmasses. Extensive coral banks define oceanic areas that are shallow and mirror the pattern of crevassed land submerged beneath the tropical inner sea. Occasionally coral is found short distances inland, surviving beneath the surface of the invading sea in deep faulted ravines.

In this land there is no horizon upon the sea. The margin of coral can be traced skyward as the ocean follows the contour of the inner world. With an iridescent line of blue, its

The Land of No Horizon

profile is seen as a division separating the land from the sea.

But the seas once flowed around a different coastline, one further inland, above the present level of the sea. Remnants of coral reefs mark the edges of then smaller dry land areas. Beaches, coastal erosion, and river deltas join the boarders of a stranded shoreline. This was a place where seas washed in recent times. But then, everything changed when the ocean dropped dramatically. The older shoreline is obvious everywhere. It is even identifiable in some landmasses above.

The timelessness of the land seems absolute. But there is one rhythmic motion to be found. It is the tide. As subtle as it might appear, it is none the less very significant. Its repetitive movement represents the sole timekeeper of the inner world. It is a link with the outside, a force controlled by the Moon, a moon out of sight from here but still having an effect.

The rhythm of the tide provides the only visible measure of time in an otherwise ageless land. But the Moon's gravity effects more than just the oceans. Its attraction acts on all the matter of the planet. Because of this, the atmosphere too responds in a tidal rhythm. Like the ocean it rises and falls in unison with the lunar orbit. This cyclic motion is one of the major contributing factors influencing the inner world's weather.

On the outside, it is the Sun that is the major force. Extremes of heat and cold dominate over any effects caused by atmospheric tides. This contrasts with the even warmth of the inner Earth's environment where lunar tides are left to play the prominent roll. They help produce cyclic movement within the atmosphere and resulting changing weather patterns. As with the outside, the highest tides always occur either side of equatorial regions. These areas under the path of the orbiting Moon are most effected by its gravitational force. Accordingly, atmospheric currents and corresponding weather conditions are normally more turbulent in these regions, becoming calmer towards the poles.

The rhythm of the tides is the singular clockwork motion of the inner world. With no other measure of time, life's sequence is governed by the unseen lunar cycle. This has become the ruling rhythm over the environment. Plants flower and fruit in unison with it. Animals too, cycle in equivalent 28 day intervals in line with the lunar month. Basked in the endless light of an otherwise timeless world, life has ticked along with the lunar phenomenon ever since its beginnings within the Earth.

On the outer surface, mankind is truly alone. No other species has acquired our intelligence. The reason why this situation exists has never been properly understood. The origins of humanity is not known. We are an orphaned race, a race lost without heritage. The link that connects us through evolution is missing. Today, the source of our beginnings is a paramount question to be answered. Some have chosen the easy path and accept we will never know. But for the rest, there remains a single burning desire, to meet others like ourselves, other intelligence, with perhaps just a few of the answers. There is a desperate need to know we are not the only ones. Surely there must be others. Our simple question deserves an answer. The time has come for our modest wish to be granted. It is our inherent right. But there again, as usual, the solution is straightforward. The missing pieces to mankind's great quest are close at hand. They lie concealed in the land within.

The Land of No Horizon

The land of no horizon is a complete entity within itself. It is a place where over millions of years of uninterrupted evolution, life has quietly moved forward. And now today, this world is filled with nature's ultimate creations. Many of its unique life forms are equipped with the ability to think and reason. Some are highly advanced, having reached elevated levels of intelligence. In the land of no horizon mankind's enlightened mind is not alone. This is a place where thoughts can be shared with others of different species.

The life of this world is in complete harmony with the environment. Thousands upon thousands of generations of evolutionary development has created this balance. The value of the environment is of paramount importance. Accordingly, the life blood of their world is naturally preserved for all generations to follow.

The importance of finite resources is reflected in all their cities. Stone structures are built to last for all time. Their distinctive appearance is somehow reminiscent of others elsewhere. Advanced methods mirror monolithic structures and ancient walls from forgotten times, great wonders of the outer world, built by the same hands of previously unknown peoples. An intricate diversity of technology supports the way of life for intelligent races within. One day, we too may benefit from these things beyond our present understanding.

The suitability of the environment for life inhabiting the land of no horizon is obvious. They evolved here. But even more remarkable is the fact that the same environment is also kind to ourselves. So many of the difficulties we frequently encounter outside don't exist here. Our eyes are better suited to the softer light from the inner sun. There is no need to see in the dark. Protective clothes serve no purpose. It is not necessary to defend from extremes of heat and cold in a land of even warmth. In an environment of inescapable humidity, protective layers of fur, hair or fat only serve as an extra burden producing unavoidable discomfort. In the soft sunlight, naked and low pigmented skin is not only unharmed but also better suited to the climatic conditions. Our joints and thin skin suffer less in the low gravity. The aging process is much slower here. But then, even more amazing is our reproduction pattern. Whilst our cycle is unique in the outer world, here it is perfectly aligned. We too cycle in 28 day intervals following the same rhythm as does life throughout the inner world. Like them, our biological clock is timed in unison with the orbiting Moon.

It is not surprising to observe we bear striking similarities to much of life within. We not only share some of their characteristics, but we also share a part of their intelligence. It is as if we have returned home.

> **Traumatised minds finally succumb to panic and disbelief. We stand face to face with intelligence never before witnessed. But soon as thoughts calm, fear is replaced with a sense of great privilege. Contact has been made. Large eyes focus as if investigating the very essence of our souls. The power of their intelligence is felt by all. There is no need to speak. The moment is complete. Another giant leap has been made for mankind.**

> **The species before us seem somehow out of proportion with normality. Large heads are supported by long slender bodies. Like the rest of life in this strange world, their build is somewhat delicate and fragile in appearance. Skin is greyish white and naked with a look of being almost**

The Land of No Horizon

translucent. Long limbs support large hands with equally long dextrous fingers.

The sight before us recalls images reported in encounters and abductions elsewhere.

We see the reflection of our seed in their form and realise the connection. Our ancestors have been found. The missing link is here. At last, our greatest question has been answered. The origins of humanity has been concealed with the inhabitants of the inner Earth. They are the narrators of the ancient texts, those assumed as gods in ancient times and still today.

We stand in awe and stare into penetrating eyes and wonder at the knowledge we have gained.

And then they speak and tell us their story...

Chapter 12

Intelligence From Within

The masterpiece of evolution created the canvas of humanity.

Intelligence From Within

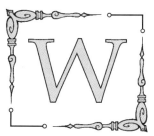e are told of the past, the very beginnings of the Earth itself, an Earth different to the way we have always known, An Earth which contains two separate worlds, each independent from the other, worlds where life evolved, divided and individual. They speak of their origins connected to life within, and their rising from it. They tell of a great time when the two worlds came together, a time when mankind was born and the important role they played. We are told about ourselves, our connection with both worlds, our link with them, and our purpose here on Earth...

Life slowly evolved. Then it came to pass that somewhere forgotten in a distant past, minds became aware. Eyes stopped to look up towards the land rising over them. Enlightened thoughts were stirred by reason, and with that each and everyone had earned the wisdom of their existence. They saw this was their world, a singular place sealed by the universe, a world enclosed. Everyone could see it was true, and thus, it was so. There was nothing for them to compare. No-one knew of anything else. There was just the one world, a world balanced by harmony, a world normal to all within its boundaries, a place of isolation locked inside a molten universe stretching to infinity, a place without fear of others. There was no questioning of its surroundings. All things were accepted without a need of understanding. This was their land, a place somehow permanent, a place theirs for all time as it had always been in the past. This was all they had and all they had ever known.

Developing races recorded their own territory. But, what lay beyond? What things were waiting for them there? Each was driven by curiosity and a desire to explore. All could see other places at a distance, places across seas and across the sky. Everyone wanted to travel to foreign lands within the expanse.

Intelligence From Within

Intelligence everywhere set out across the surface on voyages of discovery. They crossed the seas and found the lands beyond. But when they arrived, they found they were already inhabited by others. And so, life met life. Explorers stood face to face with those of other intelligence. This wasn't as they had imagined. Most species appeared strange. A lack of familiarity meant communication was misunderstood, and soon conflicts arose from their differences. Rivalry became the order of the times. Species competed with species for supremacy over others. A great many were extinguished in wars that followed. There was much destruction. The displaced were driven out, away from their lands. The stronger species survived on the spoils of greed. It became the rule of the time. Some acquired high places and great wealth, at the expense of the multitudes beneath. No-one understood the value of their world. There was nothing to compare it with. It had always been there, a place thought to be permanent and indestructible.

Ongoing conflicts, waste and pollution spoilt the once pristine environment. Technology advanced. Powerful weapons ruined the land forever. Images once visible across the expanse, slowly disappeared behind a building brown veneer. Following generations never experienced their world as it once was. Those before spoke of times now gone. But no-one wanted to listen. Instead, they accepted what they saw as normal. Everyone had forgotten. There were no victors. All life suffered. Even the rich and greedy were affected. Many species were lost into extinction. Whilst some continued their quest of trying to find new lands to conquer, others imagined a better place. But there was no escape. They were all locked together in the one enclosed expanse, sealed by the molten universe assumed to exist to infinity.

But then there came about a great dream, a dream shared by many, a dream of hope that would save them all. Its visions contained other worlds similar to theirs, places with lands unspoilt, and intelligence able to help. If their world existed so must others. They would be lying somewhere behind the wall of lava, hidden in the molten domain beyond, a domain understood to extend forever. And so the common belief was upheld by all. Assumptions were supported by hope rather than evidence. Unproven ideas somehow became fact, facts so welded in minds that no-one thought to question. Faith alone was enough. There was no longer any doubt. Their world was one of endless others, like that of bubbles suspended in an infinite mass. But it was difficult to perceive the dimensions of infinity. No-one had seen further than across the width of the expanse. Distances beyond that could only be imagined.

Great dreams continued amongst the peoples. Many fantasised as to what other worlds would be like. Others were more cautious. None the less, all agreed, to find just one expanse would be their greatest achievement. A way must be found, a way past the molten mass of the cosmos. This was their only escape from the pollution, destruction and greed. All the mistakes of the past had been learnt. They would never happen again. It was time to start anew, a new world of peace and harmony. And so, the task was finally set. A way to other expanses had to be found.

Resources were pooled for an attempt to break down the impenetrable wall, that separated their world from other worlds beyond.

Solutions were needed for seemingly insurmountable problems. All early experiments showed little in the way of promise. But the people were driven by need, and continued relentlessly with the assigned task. Determination and expectation was high across the land. Huge amounts of resources were swallowed up.

Intelligence From Within

Then, with advancing technological developments, a way was found. Excitement gave way to speculation. What would they encounter in the new worlds? Would they be habitable or not? Would they be large or small? What would their atmospheres be like? Would they be suitable for life in their world? And, what of the pressure? Was it possible to lose their atmosphere into a world of vacuum? Or could drowning seas flood from another expanse? And then, what of other life? Would they be friendly or hostile? If their world was lost, life as they knew it would cease. All things had to be carefully considered. There was a need for caution. There would be no second chance. Their world must be protected at all costs.

The grand project began. This was the greatest adventure in the history of the inner world. Excitement grew as the beginnings of a passageway took shape. Excavating down, they constructed seals behind them. This would serve to protect from potential hazards, and the unknowns of other worlds. Work was slow and complex. No-one knew how long it would take.

The further they went the lighter they felt. Eventually they were weightless. But then, gravity reversed. Their digging became upward. With that came a realisation that the tides had turned. They were nearing a new world. Anticipation built. No-one had gone this far before. Gravity increased to the level of their world, then increased more. Soundings indicated an expanse ahead. Full precautions were put into place. Everything was prepared. All of life awaited the final moment, the news of the new world ahead.

Machines broke through. A passage that for the first time joined two separate worlds as one, was finally complete.

And so it came to pass, they were freed of the boundaries of their world, free to enter the expanse beyond. The time had arrived, exploration of a new world was at hand, a giant step for life from within, the greatest moment in recorded history. Rejoicing overwhelmed the inner land. Their ultimate dream had at last become reality. Upheld beliefs had always been right.

And suddenly they were standing there...

The sight before them was one embraced by both excitement and bewilderment. Eyes from a separate world beheld the surreal environment of a strange land, a land so different to their own. Standing amid the two worlds, they were pulled between the commitment of predictions sourced by great expectations and a land of darkness before them. This was a world without a sun. How could this be? It was not as they imagined...

The way ahead was dark and cold. The new world's light was faint and scattered, like endless pinpoints across the expanse overhead. A mysterious sphere could be seen, somehow suspended above. Without a light source of its own, it simply reflected light from somewhere else. But, from where the light came, none could see.

This was a world of mystery, a world cold and dark. Blackness enveloped all throughout the land. Those there, were unable to detect the extent of its boundaries. Everything was strange and unfamiliar.

Intelligence From Within

They needed garments to insulate their bodies from the cold, and required light to find a way through the dark. Vegetation and life could be seen everywhere, amazingly surviving in a world without light. Calls of animals arrived from all directions, echoing through the barrier of darkness.

It was not as they had imagined. They couldn't understand the meaning of what they were seeing. Things here seemed out of order. How did life survive in a world without the essential support of light? Somehow nothing seem to fit. They felt strangely at odds, and out of place in a land unknown, a land with an extra burden, one of stronger gravity that drained bodies and slowly weighed them down.

They observed the strange sphere above them for some time. Rough texture was visible across its illuminated face. At first it appeared a long way off. But then, it had moved, and was now higher than before. They were mystified by its sight, something unexplainable like never before seen. None understood the significance, as it silently circled the land, that of the celestial body at the helm of all the world's tides, the hands of the rhythmic clock ruling life's cycles within, the direct link to their world from an endless voyage above, that of the Moon orbiting the Earth.

They watched as it passed over, crossing the expanse above. Its cool light reflected down, softening the land beneath. But, the source of its illumination still could not be detected. No-one knew the reason why. If in their world, it surely would be seen. But here, it was somehow obscured. This confused those standing there, alone in a land unfamiliar, a world different to that expected.

Then suddenly, there was a soft glow. It appeared in the distance level with where they stood. An edge could be seen. Defined by the growing light, it marked the place where the land divided from the sky. Nervous eyes watched as the distant glow increased. Now brighter than before, it slowly lightened the atmosphere upwards, over and above. Pinpoints across the expanse faded away, hidden behind the increasing light of the atmosphere turning blue. The sphere too had changed to become a softer tone. Forms around them gradually took shape, lightened by first light. Those of the inner world stood in awe, witness to the wonder of the ever brightening dawn. As they looked on, the cool morning sky quickly filled with colour. Soft hues of pink and cream intensified into oranges and yellows. The newly discovered land had slowly come to life, fully transformed by the touch of early morning light. It was a world of colour, unlike anything they had ever seen before.

The silhouette of life wakened. Trees appeared strangely distorted with shapes grotesque and solid. Stout bodied animals everywhere, with new and unfamiliar calls, were unusually cloaked with heavy pelts, and looking fiercely strong. Birds flew across increasing light, working hard with oversized wings, to break the weight of gravity.

A pristine landscape had come into full view. But the sight before them was somehow incomplete. Their discovered world looked strangely small. Nothing of any land or sea was visible beyond a line in the near distance. Anticipated inward surface curvature could not be seen at all. There was nothing of the lands above to complete the path of the enclosing world around them. Why was this so? Are the lands too far away to see? Is the void so large that vision is unable to span its width? No-one could be sure. Was this the reason for gravity's increased strength?

Intelligence From Within

Theories rapidly evolved out of the many questions that followed. But these only raised other questions even more complex than those before. Unexplained sights were everywhere, with no solutions for now. No matter where or how high they observed, the view was the same. Clear skies revealed no trace of any surface on the other side. Places across the width of the expanse just didn't seem to be there. To the contrary, it looked almost as if the world didn't go very far at all. Only the landscape in the immediate area could be observed. Confusion stunned the minds of those from within, lost in a place without important answers.

But, they were viewing a world very different to their own. This was a world of outside curvature, a land with its contours reversed. Outside surface curvature creates a natural horizon, acting as a visual barrier to all the lands beyond. Form here most of the land is out of sight. The structure was reverse to that familiar within. This, their first encounter, was met with utter confusion and not properly understood. It would have been easier to imagine how the world ended, like an edge behind the nearby horizon, a world with the appearance of being flat and nothing else beyond. The distorted perspective was difficult to comprehend. Everyone stared as if waiting for an answer to unfold.

Then suddenly an edge of brilliance appeared. With an energy of blinding glare, it divided the horizon in two. Driven by an unknown force it ascended from the ground beneath, emerging out of the very depths below. Blank faces glowed gold, illuminated by rays of first sunlight. The vital life support for all the environment around them had appeared. This was the light from the new world's sun. Its arrival signalled the completion of a never ending cycle, that of darkness transforming into day. The Sun slowly rose from the distance. Eyes had to be shielded from a brightness so intense. They were unaccustomed to such light, particularly at this low angle. Their sun was always fixed overhead.

Uninitiated minds conceived from a world of consistency, were unable to comprehend the magnitude of visual changes taking place. Like a fantastic dream, they were witness to the transformation of a whole world right before their eyes. A land of darkness had suddenly become a place of life and warmth.

Minds lagged behind in disbelief at a world of rotating movement, a land never at rest. This was the strangest world. Its sun somehow travelled like the suspended sphere now passed, a sun now in view but out of sight before. This was an unexplainable world, so different to theirs. It was a place where rules do not conform, with lands at odds with normal lines of curvature, a world wonderfully distorted, a make believe place that seemed somehow like a vision from the imagination. But everyone knew what they were seeing was not a dream...

this was reality...

Warming sunlight gradually dissolved the coolness of the night. But soon the land was hot and difficult for them to cope. They had no protective layers to defend from temperature extremes. Bodies insulated from the cold now required cooling from the heat. Exposed skin burnt under the intense ultra violet light. Stressed joints ached with the strain of extra gravity. There was little defence at all for those from within. This was a land of harsh extremes, a land of heat and cold. They viewed the world with eyes evolved from another place, a land where light and heat were constant throughout, the place responsible for the their development, a separate world, their world within.

Intelligence From Within

But in the new world, life had evolved differently to cope in the harsh environment. They were adapted in conditions that had slowed the evolutionary process down. And now, as a result of limited development, life was still distinctively primitive.

And so it came to pass, the truth was realised of the place where they stood. This was not a new expanse but the outside surface of their own world, that of a spherical body in orbit around its Sun. It was the Earth, a single celestial planet with their world enclosed inside. It was a world of two surfaces, each independent from the other, a world in clockwork synchrony with the solar system around.

They observed the repeating periods of light and dark and were fascinated by the Sun and Moon. Their paths were studied circling above the newly discovered world. They came to understand gravity, a power supreme over all that exists. They could see how it shaped the Earth. With a new realisation, all things became surprisingly clear. The universe wasn't solid after all, quite the opposite was true. Upheld beliefs were not as thought, a fact yet to be faced. Their assumptions had been wrong as well, just as it has been with us. An error made in their past proved to be the greatest miscalculation in their history.

But now they had to face the cold hard truth. A bitter chill was felt by all those there. Their world was all they had, that of a single minute refuge, in the vast emptiness of space. After many generations of work and hope there came that final defeat, they were now truly alone.

Unfortunately they could not live on the outside surface of Earth. The environment was too hostile for any of them to survive. Regardless of that, the new land was still another part of their world, the same Earth, and rightfully belonged to them. The previously unknown surface was actually larger than their own. A place of fresh resources and endless discoveries waited, new lands, new oceans and life never before seen. Ways to make use of the outside had to be found. So they developed a system to protect themselves and the great exploration began.

> **They saw the Moon move the tide, the rhythm of life's cycles within, the hands of a mystery clock never understood, a clock unseen until now. It was the answer to a question unresolved for all time, an answer from outside reaching in. The simple solution was easily seen, resolved by the vision from above, that of the Moon orbiting the Earth. And so it was for us, from outside looking in. We saw the inner sun, the source of the Earth's magnetic field, its lines of magnetism never properly understood, lines from inner light reaching out, guiding navigators across the Earth. A solution simple and easily seen, was resolved by a vision from above, that of the inside sun, a sun unseen till now...**

They saw a diversity of climates across the face of Earth, regions from frozen highlands and polar ice caps to warmer parts of the tropics. They observed the changing seasons and recorded weather patterns circulating throughout the atmosphere. They noted storms of a severity previously unknown. The environment was one of varying difficulties, one that somehow was endured by all. Every member of every species was seen perfectly adapted, fitting its own particular niche, each individual from the rest. There were creatures of all types, some suited for life at night, others living in the snow or deserts and life inhabiting the sea. But the environment was one in constant change. So life's essential

Intelligence From Within

reproduction cycles had evolved in time with those seasons most suitable. This was a land pitted with craters marking the place of past celestial impacts, cataclysmic events that damaged evolution's progress. And now as a result, intelligence had not yet been achieved. Life outside was completely different to that on the inside. With no seasonal changes to disrupt the consistency of the climate, life inside had adapted in time with the cycle of the Moon.

They discovered the outside ocean and atmosphere were shallower, and realised the significance of pressure differences between the inside and outside worlds. They understood the potential of great flooding if the wall of the Earth were to breach beneath the oceans, this its thinnest and potentially weakest point. The ensuing disaster would certainly damage both worlds in and out. With the added knowledge of Earth expansion and wall thinning, they were aware of the inevitability of this catastrophic event. This unavoidable occurrence would irreversibly change the face of their Earth sometime in its near evolutionary future.

Fortunately, they had discovered the outside world in time. They still had time to prepare for the catastrophic event ahead.

They were fascinated by the vast distances contained within the universe around them. Being limited by the size of the expanse of their world, they had never viewed into the realms of endless space before.

Secrets unfolded, as an infinity of perpetual clockwork focused before their eyes. They viewed a universe never at rest, a place of rotating rule with matter orbiting matter. This was a universe in existence by rotation motion alone. Born with minds from a world of perpetual consistency, they were not equipped to understand. It took time to adjust before they could accept the amazing discoveries before them. They built great observatories to study the planets of the Solar System and other systems beyond. They studied the galaxy band crossing the night-time sky and calculated the immensity of its dimensions. There would be other worlds with life, throughout the reaches of the galaxy, other worlds like theirs in the vast emptiness of space. But how could contact ever be possible? Distances were so incredibly great, so much more than ever before seen or imagined, much too far to travel.

Remnants of their ancient cities, observatories and other structures stand to this day as reminders of their fascination with the stars.

The existence of the "gravity free zone" at the centre of gravity presented great benefits for those of the inner world. Extensive development and exploitation of these regions continues to this day, silently hidden within the planetary wall beneath us.

But with the astonishing discoveries there came an ultimate price. A disappointing fact difficult for all to comprehend. They had reached a final dead end. There was nowhere left to go. They were all confined on the Earth forever, alone in the emptiness of space.

Reports of great discoveries reached the peoples waiting within. But with generations of expectation failed, disenchantment reigned throughout the land. They realised their polluted and damaged world was all they had. The imagined new worlds would never be. Previous generations were blamed for the disappointment taking place now. Everyone was forced to face the truth. There was only one thing left to do. They must repair the

Intelligence From Within

environment in order to assure their survival. There was no other way. This was the only answer. Their world must be saved at all costs.

New values were put into place. There was a new resurgence of interest. A collective effort was made by all. After generations of conflict, all the species worked together. Times of despair turned to times of fulfilment. There was a new way of life in the inner world, a new appreciation. And so the wars and pollution stopped. The destruction ceased. The land of old was rediscovered anew. Everyone learnt by caring for others. No-one benefited from greed and war. People only benefit from peace and harmony. And so there came a great calm over the land of no horizon. The value of their unique environment had been realised, an environment evolved over millions of revolutions around the Sun, an environment so precious it must be preserved for all time.

And so all the species of intelligence came together, joined by a sharing of knowledge, they combined as one, that of a single race unified to rule the inside world forever.

Chapter 13

The Origins of Humanity

When we know where we are from...
we will know why we are here.

The Origins of Humanity

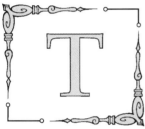he inner races had discovered a whole new world, a world completely different to their own. The outside world was a place with fresh resources, unique life, expansive lands and other mysteries, all waiting further study and use. It was surrounded by space, an endless frontier to new exciting secrets beyond. This was their world, a world they had discovered, a world they wanted to use.

But exploration of the new world had always been difficult. They had to contend with its environment, an environment to which they were poorly suited. Protection was essential. Even with protection, they could not remain on the outside for long. Unavoidable difficulties were endured for many generations.

Was there a better way, an alternative to the shielding of bodies from the extremes of the outside world? Were there new methods that could replace those so difficult and cumbersome in the past, ways to overcome the ever persistent problems?

The peoples of the inner world sought fresh thoughts. There were many suggestions and ideas and soon a new way of thinking began to surface. Was it possible to solve the difficulties encountered living against nature's rule, by instead living in harmony with it? Could they genetically change themselves in some way to do this? Would it be possible to produce a race specially adapted for conditions outside, a race with all the protection needed to survive the harsh environment, new people able to move about freely and study the outside surface, a new race designed as an extension of themselves?

There were many obstacles before them. A race able to survive outside would need certain qualities. They had already carefully studied the outer species and had seen how they were protected. Coats of fur and fat layers insulated from the heat and cold and sunlight. Heavy bones and muscle coped with gravity, and eyes were adaptable to see in the dark. These attributes combined with their intelligence would achieve the goal. This would be a race of themselves, peoples specially designed to live and travel between both worlds.

The Origins of Humanity

A decision was made. There would be experimentation. They would take the qualities of life outside and cross it with themselves. Cross matching was the key.

Genesis 1 : 26 *"And God said, Let Us make man in Our image, according to Our likeness; and let them rule over the fish of the sea, and over the birds of the heavens and over the cattle, and over all the earth, and over all the creepers creeping on the earth."*

Two important things can be learnt from this biblical passage.

Firstly, the words "us" and "our" are used in conjunction with "God". This shows God as not a single entity but many. Genesis's words tell of God as those making the decision to create Man, a decision made by the multitudes of the inner race.

Secondly, "Man" was to be created in the likeness of God, in his image. From this we are shown mankind was planned not too different from the inside race. And today we still retain many of their inherent qualities.

Certain species from the outside were selected and trials began. But early developments were poor. Outer primitive species had evolved in a harsh environment. Their genes were much stronger and dominated the experiments. This presented a problem. Results produced species with adequate protection but little in the way of intelligence. There was a need to either reduce the potency of the outer genes or build up the genes of the inner intelligence.

As experiments continued, there came a realisation of the difficulty of the task. Many generations had passed with little success.

Some early results were released to the outside before the time of modern Man. But they were immature and did not survive for long. They lacked sufficient intelligence to adequately protect themselves. And eventually became extinct, leaving their bones behind for those of modern times to ponder.

Despite their demise much was learnt from those early trials. Over time techniques improved. But they still encountered the same problem. Both levels of required intelligence and protection could not be achieved simultaneously. Species with adequate protection did not have the required intelligence. Species with required intelligence did not have adequate protection. One had to be sacrificed for the other. This presented what seemed an unsolvable situation. Their goal could not be achieved as planned.

Their imagined race of improved beings, travelling between the two worlds, was judged not attainable. This ended their hopes to inhabit the outside world by themselves. But, there had to be another way, a compromise. Could the outside be populated by others, by a different race, a substitute for themselves, a developed species between them and outside life? It was thought; a race with a lower level of intelligence but still retaining adequate outside protection would have the best chance for survival. Such a race could be taught to protect themselves. And over time future generations would adapt, using intelligence to survive in the meantime.

There was great enthusiasm behind the fresh idea and a decision was soon at hand. This would be the new framework for the creation of mankind, a species evolved from both worlds, part inside race and part outside species. A compromise was the only answer, the

The Origins of Humanity

ideal race sacrificing full protection for required intelligence, a cross match between the two worlds. They would be in the middle, not as intelligent as their creators and not as protected as the outside species. This way, by guiding their new race along the way, the inside race would then have control over the outer primitive world.

Many great plans were put into place. It was decided to compose extensive scriptures to instruct humanity and tell of the past. Its texts, containing words describing their wondrous creation, would recall another land, a distant land which following generations would not have seen, a land they will know as "Heaven", that of the inner expanse, ruled by their superior God, the ultimate being above all others. They would be taught many things. Their creators had given them the gifts of life and intelligence, the greatest gifts of all. They would be thankful for their existence and honour their God by obeying his rule. Humankind will govern over the world and care for fellow humans. They will be convinced by signs from their powerful God. Humanity will not be allowed to degrade into conflict as did the inside race. They will be shown the correct path, a path of peace and harmony, a path without greed, one to develop the outside world, harvest its resources and map the universe. And, over time, their intelligence will mature as they become aware of the purpose of their existence.

Their future will unravel hidden messages written into the ancient texts, and by this, they will realise the wisdom of their creators, those of the people within the Earth. Then there will come a time when humanity will be ready to seek out and reconcile with the inner race. When this time comes to pass, both will reunite, and bond as one again, to rule over all the lands of the Earth, together in harmony for eternity.

The new framework for the creation of humanity and their intended life on Earth was set. It was the alternative solution that best suited their needs. Once again species were collected from the outer Earth and a new set of experiments began. Finally there was success.

And so came a wondrous event, the fulfilment of generations of hope, the beginnings of our distant past, our heritage, the birth of mankind.

Genesis 1 : 27 *"And God created the man in His own image; in the image of God He created him. He created them male and female."*

The words; "He created them male and female." tell of the forming of a complete race, a race of many not one, a species containing both sexes, male and female. Despite the new race being referred to as "the man", it is not a single male as assumed by certain interpreters of these biblical texts but a singular complete race, the race of "Adam".

Furthermore, "Man" created in God's image and created male and female informs us the inside race, like ourselves, is comprised of peoples male and female.

A place was chosen, an isolated area on the inside set aside for the new race, an environment specifically designed for the development and perfection of "Man", a special place to prepare them for their existence in the outer world. Likened to a great garden, it was stocked with plants and animals selected from the outside.

Genesis 2 : 8, 9 *"And Jehovah God planted a garden in Eden, to the east; and He put the man whom He had formed there. And out of the ground Jehovah God made to spring up every tree that is*

The Origins of Humanity

pleasant to the sight, and good for food. The Tree of Life was also in the middle of the garden; also the Tree of Knowledge of Good and Evil."

"The tree of life" and "the tree of knowledge of good and evil" are symbolic. They are metaphors of life's evolutionary development. "The tree of life" is a symbol of the living. Its placement in the middle of the garden represents its importance as the heart of all life, branching out in many directions. "The tree of knowledge of good and evil" represents the inner race with their knowledge and intelligence, nature's ultimate creation. It too is in the centre of the garden with "the tree of life". By these symbols, life's growth and development is compared to that of a growing tree.

The new race of Adam was placed in the garden and the progress of their development closely monitored.

Genesis 2 : 15 to 17 *"And Jehovah God took the man and put him into the garden of Eden, to work it and to keep it. And Jehovah God commanded the man, saying, You may freely eat of every tree in the garden; but of the tree of Knowledge of Good and Evil you may not eat, for in the day that you eat of it, you shall surely die."*

The words in this text have a concealed meaning. By "Man" eating of "the tree of life" we see them as one of the living, consuming the fruit of life. "Man" not being allowed to eat of "the tree of knowledge of good and evil" has definite significance. This represents humanity had not yet reached intelligence and therefore could not consume the tree's "fruit". We are told when "Man" does finally eat of this tree they will surely die. The symbolism of this is; eating the fruit of "the tree of knowledge of good and evil" represents "Man" reaching the point of intelligence, feeding on its knowledge. "Man's" death is represented by the passing from pre-intelligent life to be reborn into intelligence.

Humanity was the end product of a cross between the inside race and certain species from the outside. Despite being well suited for the outer world conditions, "Man" as a species, was still unintelligent and somewhat primitive. To achieve their goal of required intelligence and retain adequate protection, it was realised necessary to produce a further higher race that could be introduced to "Man" and combine with them. The task would be accomplished by a second cross matching. This time between themselves and their created "Man".

Genesis 2 : 18 *"And Jehovah God said, It is not good, the man being alone. I will make a helper suited to him."*

Genesis 2 : 21, 22 *"And Jehovah God caused a deep sleep to fall on the man, and he slept. And He took one of his ribs, and closed up the flesh underneath. And Jehovah God formed the rib which He had taken from the man into a woman, and brought her to the man."*

This was the creation of the second race, the race called "woman" (Eve), a race between "Man" (Adam) and themselves (God), a new species created from the seed of "Man" (Adam's rib) joined with the seed of themselves. This was not a single female, as assumed by some interpreters of the texts, but a complete race named "Woman", made in their image both male and female. Genesis describing the new race as a woman is symbolic. It represents the joining of the two races like that of a man and a woman coming together forming a marriage.

The Origins of Humanity

Genesis 2 : 23 *"And the man said, This now at last is bone of my bones, and flesh of my flesh. For this shall be called Woman, because this has been taken out of the man."*

This tells of the race of Adam accepting the race of Eve.

Genesis 2 : 24 *"Therefore, a man shall leave his father and his mother, and shall cleave to his wife; and they shall become one flesh."*

With Adam accepting Eve they joined and became one race. Their forefathers from the past were left behind. This was paralleled to the union of two people, like that of a boy and girl coming of age, leaving their parents, and marrying to become one unit to propagate the future.

Genesis 2 : 25 *"And they were both naked, the man and his wife, and they were not ashamed."*

In this passage, we see both Adam and Eve were not yet intelligent. This is seen by them not being ashamed of being naked, such as a young child. However the intellectual level of the "Eve" race was naturally higher being situated between Adam and the inner race (God). In other words, despite neither race yet being intelligent, the "Eve" race was closer to reaching this higher state. But this had been achieved by sacrificing much of the protection essential for life outside.

Genesis 3 : 1 to 5 *"And the serpent was cunning above every animal of the field which Jehovah God had made. And he said to the woman, is it true that God has said, You shall not eat from any tree of the garden? And the woman said to the serpent, We may eat of the fruit of the trees of the garden, but of the fruit of the tree which is in the middle of the garden, God has said, You shall not eat of it, nor shall you touch it, lest you die. And the serpent said to the woman, You shall not surely die, for God knows that in the day you eat of it, your eyes shall be opened, and you shall be as God, knowing good and evil."*

The serpent was a symbol of "Eve's" internal inquisitive nature. The implanted seed of knowledge was beginning to grow. And so the race felt an urge to question all things before them. This is shown by the serpent questioning God's word. The serpent communicating with Eve and not Adam indicates the race of "Man" had not yet acquired this level of inquisitiveness. They were still primitive. In this text we see the race of "Eve" reaching out towards the wisdom of their existence, questioning their surroundings and progressing to the brink of intelligence.

Genesis 3 : 6, 7 *"And the woman saw that the tree was good for food, and that it was pleasant to the eyes, and the tree desirable to make one wise. And she took of its fruit and ate. And she gave to her husband with her, and he ate. And the eyes of both of them were opened and they knew that they were naked. And they sewed leaves of the Fig-tree and made girdles for themselves."*

This passage recalls a particular sequence of events. Firstly; as mentioned before, "the tree of knowledge of good and evil" represents intelligent life. The act of Eve eating of the fruit of the tree represents Eve reaching intelligence. The symbolism of this is; the fruit being taken from this tree shows the intelligence was received from the inside race. The "Eve" race was able to achieve this because they were closer to the inside race being the product of crossbreeding between them and "Man". Then, because of the union between Adam and Eve, the intelligence gained by Eve was gradually passed on to the "Adam" race through the generations that followed. This development is symbolised by

The Origins of Humanity

Adam taking the fruit from Eve instead of directly from the tree. The intermediate "Eve" race had fulfilled its task. This was the intention of the inside people. Adam had now received an adequate measure of inside intelligence yet retained sufficient levels of protection for life outside. The opening of their eyes symbolises the realisation of their existence, likened to a child reaching a higher state of mind where being naked now becomes shameful.

Genesis 3 : 11, 12 *"And He (God) said, Who told you that you were naked? Have you eaten of the tree of which I commanded you not to eat? And the man said, The woman whom You gave to be with me, she has given to me of the tree, and I ate."*

Genesis 3 : 21 to 24 *"And Jehovah made coats of skin for the man and his wife, and clothed them. And Jehovah God said, Behold! The Man has become as one of Us, to know good and evil. And now, lest he put forth his hand and also take from the Tree of Life, and eat, and live forever. And Jehovah God sent him out of the garden of Eden to till the ground out of which he was taken. And He drove the man out. And He caused to dwell the cherubs at the east of the Garden of Eden, and the flaming sword whirling around, to guard the way of the Tree of Life."*

The inside race looked into the eyes of "Man" and beheld the essence of their intelligence. They saw the fruit of generations of work. "Man" had become one of them, part of the same family sharing knowledge, knowing good from evil. The race was now able to survive and rule the world forever. "Man" was ready. It was time for the final test, to enter the world they had been created for. And now, there was great affection for the created race of "Man", an affection shared by all, of the inside race. They would guide and protect their future generations on the outside surface of Earth. They taught them to make clothes to protect from the harsh conditions to come and showed the way to farm the ground for food, the ground from which they partly came. And "Man" was taken from the garden of Eden and led to the world outside. The flaming sword is the barrier of lava locked within the wall of the Earth that separates the two worlds. "Man" was unable to return.

And suddenly we were standing there...

We looked up at the stars and the moon, our faces reflecting insecurity and fear of this strange place. But with generations of work now complete, the moment was finally here. By the time the sunset dimmed and faded away, those who brought us had long since disappeared beyond the horizon. But even though we were now alone, our creators would never be forgotten. Wondrous memories had been left behind, miracles and writings serving as a reminder. A bond with their world and ours. A bond with themselves and us.

They left us mysteries, mysteries which our future would unlock.

They gave us life, something we must cherish forever.

They gave us their world, a place we must protect and care for.

And they gave us intelligence, intelligence which would enable us to survive in this different world, a world of day and night, where somehow we didn't belong. We fought back the tears and pain and

The Origins of Humanity

learned to live alone. We would adapt. But, through all our hardships our eyes would never leave the horizon, for it was during that final sunset they had promised...

"One day we will return"...

Today, we still suffer the anguish of not understanding why we are different from all the other species around us. This is because we acquired our unique physical characteristics from the inner world. And now, because of this, we experience certain hardships living on the outer surface. Our bodies are not completely in tune with the adversities and harshness of the environment here. No matter where each of us reside, we have to protect ourselves from inhospitable elements outside. Everyday, mankind finds it necessary to perform an essential ritual. We dress ourselves with clothes that protect. Our part alien bodies offer virtually no insulation from the cold experienced here. Unlike all the naturally evolved species with their thick coats of fur, hair or fat layers, we have precious little. Our hair is virtually non-existent and fat layers insufficient to offer adequate insulation. In our natural state our naked bodies would perish. In many areas the outside sun burns exposed skin. The same ultra violet light damages eyes that are not adapted. Strong gravity wears out our fine bone joints and pulls down on our thin skin. Evolved from a world without night, our eyes cannot see in the dark.

But as the new race, we had an advantage. We were unique and alone with our ability to think, reason and adjust. With these inherent qualities, we would rule and manipulate the outside world. With the passing of time, future generations would gain great knowledge. They would learn the value of the environment around them and live in harmony with it. This was our world, precious and worth preserving at all costs.

Chapter 14

The Source of the Flood

When the waters were joined, the two worlds became one...
They would never be the same again.

The Source of the Flood

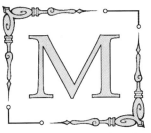ankind was at last on the outer surface. Intelligence had finally arrived. The new rule of humanity would govern over all in the primitive world. The outside Earth was about to change forever. This was now their world, the land that had been promised. But the outer world was very different to that within. The human race looked on as the Sun travelled, crossing a sky of clear blue, above a world appearing flat. The cool night air touched all. But they knew the importance of protecting themselves from the elements. They had been told of the endless struggle for life here. And how they would need to adjust. They had been taught to shelter from cold winter snows and till the ground for food. For this was their land, a land they must keep, a land to protect and rule over. The new era prophesied, was upon them. And now it was up to them to survive. They must increase their numbers over the Earth.

During the creation of humanity several variations had been produced. The race of Adam symbolises the culmination of all the types selected for the outside world. It was not known which of the varieties would survive the best so individual groups were isolated to different regions on the Earth. This way, they would learn and evolve unaided by outsiders from other races. And so as mankind developed, each race was unaware of the rest.

Success varied from race to race. Whilst a few were unsuccessful, most did well and prospered. It wasn't long before mankind began to multiply. New generations ventured out populating new lands. Humanity was increasing on the face of the Earth.

The generations that followed Adam are recalled in Biblical texts. Each was given a name together with the duration of their lives. It is stated many lived for periods of 800 to 1,000 years. However, this presented a problem for those following the texts. It had always been assumed Adam and Eve and those following were individuals, people who for some reason lived for a very long time. How could any one person live for up to 1,000 years?

The Source of the Flood

But, as already shown, Adam and Eve were not singular people. They were complete races. Accordingly, those named following Adam, represented complete races too. It is the duration of these races that is recorded in the Bible. A single person cannot live for 1,000 years but a race can.

This is another example of texts written with a symbolic meaning.

As civilisations continued to expand, humanity's hold on the Earth began to grow. The harsh environment and distances involved had made it difficult for all to be continually monitored. The inner races had always been aware of this.

As a result, many civilisations evolved in their own particular way. Related stories of their wondrous creators began to change. Legends depicting almighty Gods unfolded. Those following heard tales of unbelievable improbability. Stories passed down from generation to generation told of supernatural Gods with powers over all the universe. Fearful legends became the source of a multitude of religions. Many such beliefs and rituals still survive, carried through countless generations to the present time. Ideology varied from civilisation to civilisation, each reflecting their own unique beliefs and individuality. Not only were the types of mankind different but their customs, religions and language had evolved differently also.

Eventually race met race. The meeting of unknown peoples was something unexpected. No-one had ever encountered such a situation before. Some found it difficult to accept the others. They were strangely different. Their customs and beliefs were unusual, something they couldn't accept. Misunderstandings led to conflict.

Conflicts between the races of early humans are depicted in the Bible, related in the story of Adam's two sons, Cain and Abel. We are told how the race of Cain killed the brother race of Abel in jealous conflict.

Mankind degraded into wars. History was repeating itself. This wasn't the intended path. The knowledge of their origins and generations of development was at risk of being lost. Only with greater intelligence would humanity realise the error of their ways. If the species was to succeed, further improvements to the strain must take place.

Genesis 6 : 1 to 3 *"And it came about that man began to multiply on the face of the earth, and daughters were born to them. The sons of God saw the daughters of man, that they were good. And they took wives for themselves from all those whom they chose. And Jehovah said, My Spirit shall not always strive with man; in their erring he is flesh. And his days shall be a hundred and twenty years."*

In this section of biblical text we are informed of two separate facts. Firstly; the taking place of a further cross matching between the inside race and "Man" to improve the strain. And secondly; it is their goal for the race of "Man" to eventually stand and develop on their own without the need for constant guidance. By the use of the words, "in their erring he is flesh", "Man" is shown as human and not yet sufficiently perfected.

Those in the better developed branches of humanity were chosen for further perfection. Unfortunately, this meant the rest had to be left behind to fend for themselves. No longer guided by their creators, they degraded further into greed and conflict. The inside race knowing the consequences of this were greatly saddened by what had to be done. These

The Source of the Flood

were the peoples they had created, peoples derived partly from themselves.

The existence of multitudes of less favourable races threatened the survival of the new strains of "Man". They were at risk of being destroyed. If the strains were to become contaminated by the seed of others, generations of work would be lost. And so they were closely protected by the inside race. To ensure continued survival for the future, it would be necessary to remove the others from the environment. Only then could the new strains rule the outside world unopposed. With their survival guaranteed, the goal of those inside would be achieved.

The perfected race was named "Noah". This was a race of many, not just one man.

Genesis 6 : 5 to 9 *"And Jehovah saw that the evil of man was great on the earth, and every imagination of the thought of his heart was only evil all the day long. And Jehovah repented that He had made man on the earth, and He was grieved to His heart. And Jehovah said, I will wipe off man whom I have created from the face of the earth, from man to beast, to the creeping thing and to the bird of the heavens; for I repent that I made them. And Noah found grace in the eyes of Jehovah. These are the generations of Noah. Noah, a righteous man, had been perfected among his family - Noah walked with God."*

This section of text contains an important point. Here we see Jehovah (God) regretting his actions. It is stated he repented making "Man" on the Earth.

By the use of these words we see an admission from a God with imperfections. This is not a God without fault, but instead, one vulnerable to error like ourselves. This is contrary to what is believed by most followers of the Biblical texts. Their assumed God has always been one that is all powerful and perfect. But in this passage his perfection is refuted. Here, by the use of these words, the Bible clearly tells us such beliefs are not correct.

Another important point to be noted here is; by the use of the words; "these are the generations of Noah", Genesis further confirms that Noah was in fact a race of several generations, not just a single man.

Noah was the perfected race, the righteous ones that walked with God. This was the race that would be saved. All the rest were to be erased from the Earth. And so it came to pass that a great decision was finally made, a decision that would change the face of Earth for all time. The Earth would be cleansed by a great flood. They would use their accumulated knowledge of the structure of the Earth to achieve the task.

They were aware of the pressure imbalance between the two worlds, an imbalance that had built up naturally over Earth's evolutionary time period. They knew the depth of the inside ocean and atmosphere was greater than that on the outside. And of the pressure this exerted on the inner surface of the wall of the Earth, a wall experiencing continual thinning through Earth expansion. Once the inevitable happens and the wall fractures, inside pressures would force out the inner ocean to flood the outside world. Because Earth expansion was progressively weakening the wall of the Earth, this threat of catastrophic proportions, had always been present in the minds of the inside race. There was no way of avoiding this inundation event and no-one could be sure as to just when it might happen.

The consequences of the entire inside ocean being forced out onto the exterior surface

The Source of the Flood

would be catastrophic. The outside world would be extensively inundated. The resulting mass destruction would destroy life. Their created "Man" would be lost forever, along with most of the evolved species inhabiting the outer surface. There would be losses inside as well. For a time the inner sea would drain away, destroying most of their oceanic species. There was no escape from this event. It must eventually happen. And until it does, all plans for the future of the planet could not be assured. There was a definite need to put this worldly imbalance behind them.

It was decided to prematurely bring about the timing of the flood. A planned inundation had many benefits. The inside race would have time to prepare. They could save their created "Man" along with most of the evolved species. And they would use the event to rid the world of the less desired races of humanity. This would resolve the situation and end the risk forever. But they would need to use their accumulated technological know-how to control the flow of the waters.

The great plan was put into place. Preparations began for the coming event. The race of Noah was called together. They were told the end of all life was to come upon the Earth. They must prepare for a great devastation, for they were the ones specially chosen to be saved. All the rest will perish under the waters of a great flood, a flood that will come to inundate the earth, a flood sent by their powerful God to cleanse the Earth of all its evil.

Genesis 6 : 13, 14 *"And God said to Noah, the end of all flesh has come before Me, for the earth is filled with violence through them. And behold, I will destroy them along with the earth. Make an ark of Cyprus timbers for yourself. You shall make rooms in the ark; and you shall cover it with asphalt inside and out."*

Genesis 6 : 17 to 20 *"And behold, I even I, am bringing a flood of waters on the earth in order to destroy all flesh in which is the breath of life from under the heavens. Everything which is on the earth shall die. And I will establish My covenant with you. And you shall come into the ark, you and your sons and your wife, and your sons' wives with you. And you shall bring into the ark two of every kind, of every living thing of all flesh, to keep alive with you; they shall be male and female; from the fowl after its kind, and from the cattle after its kind, from every creeping thing of the ground after its kind - two from each shall come in to you to keep alive."*

The crucial plan to bring about the flood was set. Careful consideration had been given to all possibilities. The waters must be released in a certain manner. Damage would be greater if they were to escape from the one single point. There would need to be more than one path for the flood, several evenly spaced over the Earth's surface. This way the rate of flow will be divided and flooding more even. The wall between the two worlds would be breached. Channels will be cut through from the ocean floor. Each to be broken through at precisely the same moment when all preparations are complete. The great weight of deeper ocean and atmosphere within will then force the inside ocean out through the channels in the planetary wall of the Earth in turn flooding the outside world. (Fig. 14.1)

Nearly all the land of the outer surface will be inundated. But then, once the inside ocean has been fully expelled, the way will be clear for the excess inside atmosphere to escape and equalise with the atmosphere outside. (Fig. 14.2)

With the vaults inside the Earth exhausted, and pressures inside and out balanced, the expelled waters will return, flowing back through the planetary wall of the Earth. Only

The Source of the Flood

Fig. 14.1
The instigation of the Great Flood - The outcoming.

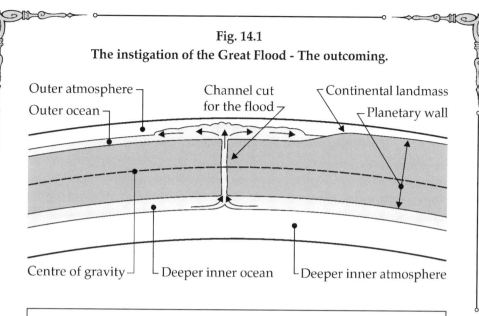

Outer atmosphere
Outer ocean
Channel cut for the flood
Continental landmass
Planetary wall

Centre of gravity
Deeper inner ocean
Deeper inner atmosphere

Greater pressure inside the Earth forces the inside ocean out through the channels and the outside surface floods.

Fig. 14.2
The instigation of the Great Flood - Atmospheric equalisation.

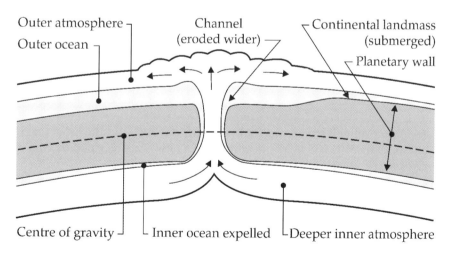

Outer atmosphere
Outer ocean
Channel (eroded wider)
Continental landmass (submerged)
Planetary wall

Centre of gravity
Inner ocean expelled
Deeper inner atmosphere

Once the inside ocean has been expelled, the way will be clear for the excess atmosphere to escape and equalise with the outside.

The Source of the Flood

then will the flood begin to recede. Once again the inside ocean will return. But the levels of atmosphere and ocean will have changed. The inside ocean and atmosphere would be shallower than before. The outside ocean and atmosphere would now be deeper. As a result, all the previous coastlines will have changed. The coastal lowlands of the outside will remain submerged forever. (Fig. 14.3)

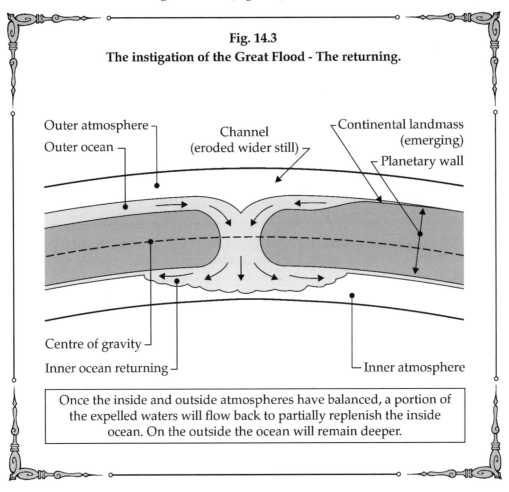

Fig. 14.3
The instigation of the Great Flood - The returning.

Outer atmosphere
Outer ocean
Channel (eroded wider still)
Continental landmass (emerging)
Planetary wall
Centre of gravity
Inner ocean returning
Inner atmosphere

Once the inside and outside atmospheres have balanced, a portion of the expelled waters will flow back to partially replenish the inside ocean. On the outside the ocean will remain deeper.

The races of the Earth will have to adjust to a changed world. But the new world would be safe and in balance. It will be the beginning of a new era, one ruled by God and the saved race of Noah.

Genesis 6 : 22 *"And Noah did so, according to all that God commanded him, so he did."*

The race of Noah, seeing the wisdom of their God, understood the importance of obeying his command. And so, with the help of the inside people, they began preparations for the coming event.

The enormity of the task was obvious. As much of life as possible must be saved. The outer surface was teeming with almost endless numbers of species. Their combined habitats covered millions of square kilometres. Each and every variety was especially adapted for its own particular place in the environment, adapted for conditions that varied from night and day to differing climates across the face of the Earth. Then there were the

The Source of the Flood

dangers to all species inhabiting the sea. They too had to be considered. Life would need to be protected inside the Earth as well, oceanic species there would be threatened or lost as the inside seas drained away. It would not be possible to save all the world's species. Inevitably, some would be lost. But none the less, as many as possible must be preserved.

To increase their effectiveness a variety of methods would be adopted. Mankind would be ordered by his creators to help with the task. Many outside species had been collected by previous generations inside. They had been kept and studied and still survived within the Earth. Their progeny could be used to restock the outside world after the flood. But now it was time to collect as many of the others as possible. In certain areas, species could be appropriately relocated to higher ground. There they would find refuge from the rising waters. Other species were to be collected by the multitudes of the Noah races and protected for the duration of the flood.

Obviously, it would have been impossible for a single man and his family with one ark to save all the species that existed on the Earth. The saving of life was a joint effort between God and "Man" lasting several centuries. The construction of an ark is symbolic of what took place. Noah was a race consisting of many peoples now located in several places over the Earth. Noah building the ark represents the race in total, preparing for the flood. The construction of arks was just one of the methods used. Groups of the Noah race near high country were directed to safety away from the lower ground near the coast.

In addition to those species collected according to God's command, each of the members of the Noah race was instructed to take supplies of food, water, and seed to regenerate life after the flood. The mission of saving so many lives was almost incomprehensible. It was an undertaking unparalleled by any other event in history. It took many generations to complete. But then, just under four and a half thousand years ago, all was finally ready. Preparations for the flood that would ravage the outer world were finished.

The world was on the brink of change. A new era was on the horizon. The world of old was about to become a world new. The new world would be considerably different to that before the flood. The outer pre-flood world had less atmosphere. Less atmosphere meant less protection from the extremes of the Sun. Accordingly weather patterns were considerably different to those experienced today. There was less erosion on the Earth, with fewer carved canyons and river gorges. The original pristine surface was scarred with craters marking the impact points of past meteorites. This was a time when continental shelves the world over were exposed above the sea. And many sections of the Mid-Atlantic Ridge were still dry land. Many great cities had been built beside or near the shore, including one famous city called "Atlantis". There were many more varied plant and animal species in existence, including the mighty Mammoth that roamed the grasslands of the Earth. It hadn't been possible to preserve them all.

The final moment had come to pass upon the Earth. Of all within the spectrum of life, none were aware of imminent destruction. Not even those inhabiting the great cities knew. No-one dreamt of the catastrophe awaiting beyond the horizon. Unknowingly they were all doomed. Most of life was about to be swept away by the waters of the inner sea. This was the time that would cleanse the world of all its evil, and balance the air and sea for all time. It had taken 600 years from the birth of Noah to the end of preparations for the flood. But then, with the threat of disaster forever behind them, an endless fruitful future would be assured for all, a future shared by those of the inside race together with

The Source of the Flood

their created "Man".

Genesis 7 : 6 to 11 *"Noah was six hundred years old, and the flood of waters was on the earth. And Noah went in, and his sons, and his wife, and his sons' wives with him into the ark, because of the waters of the flood. And they went in to Noah into the ark, male and female of clean animals, and of animals that are not clean, and of fowl, and of every thing that creeps on the earth, two by two, as God had commanded Noah. And in time, after the seven days, the waters of the flood came into being on the earth. In the six hundredth year of Noah's life, in the second month, in the seventeenth day of the month, in this day all the fountains of the great deep were risen, and the windows of the heavens were opened up."*

In this section of text, Genesis tells of the waters being released from within the Earth. "all the fountains of the great deep were risen", describes the waters rising from below, likened to that of a fountain. The "windows" of the heavens signifies the linking of two heavens by openings or windows. This is exactly what they were. The channels cut for the flood were these openings between the inner heaven and the outer heaven. Here, Genesis uses the plural form when referring to the fountains and windows because, several paths had been cut to ensure an even dispersion of the flood.

And so, for the first time in the history of the Earth, the waters of the two separate worlds came together and became one.

And the Earth shook...

The air was still. An unsuspecting world returned to silence. But soon distant rumblings could be heard. Vibrations sent ripples across the water. Suddenly a swelling brown ulcer awoke the sea. Like a beast from the deep it burst through the ocean surface, a liquid mountain alive with noise. The land and all its inhabitants were doomed.

The titanic force of nature had been released and no power on Earth could stop it...

Genesis 7 : 12 *"And the rain was on the earth forty days and forty nights."*

Genesis 7 : 17 to 24 *"And the flood was on the earth forty days. And the waters increased, and bore up the ark, and it was lifted up above the earth. And the waters prevailed, and were greatly increased on the earth. And the ark floated on the face of the waters. And the waters were strong, exceedingly violent on the earth, and all the high mountains under the heavens were covered. The waters grew strong, fifteen cubits upward, and the mountains were covered. And all flesh that moved on the earth died; the fowl, the cattle, and beast, and every swarming thing that swarms on the earth, and all mankind; all died in whose nostrils was the breath of life, of all that was in the dry land. And every living thing which was on the face of the earth was wiped away, from man to cattle, and to the creeping things, and the fowl of the heavens. And they were wiped off from the earth, and only Noah was left, and those who were with him in the ark. And the waters were strong on the earth a hundred and fifty days."*

...Fuelled from vaults below, the great oceans grew. Moisture saturated clouds rained upon the Earth. The sea flooded the land as if the very ground itself was sinking. For the animals there was no escape. They feared instinctively, but found nowhere to run. Huge waves thick with

The Source of the Flood

sediment and marine life crossed the continents. Forests were bulldozed and valleys were carved. The prevailing water swept everything in its path on a destructive journey into the continents. Mountains of trees and animals were piled high and layers of sediments buried all. Huge boulders were washed great distances from their place of origin. Growing black clouds swirled together blotting out the sun. As the flood encroached on the poles frozen white sheets were lifted. Enormous icebergs joined the mixture and travelled with the tide.

The Earth was drowning. Our once blue planet was turning brown as the thin veneer of life was wiped clean. The water continued to rise, suffocating the world and causing massive pressure on the submerged land. Layers of debris were compressed and flattened under the tremendous weight, preserving the remains of life trapped within. Tall mountains were covered and still the water rose.

The almighty power of nature was catastrophic...

Genesis 8 :1 to 3 *" And God remembered Noah and every living thing, and all the cattle, which were with him in the ark. And God made a wind to pass over the earth, and the waters subsided. And the fountains of the deep and the windows of the heavens were stopped, and the rain from the heavens was restrained. And the waters retreated from the Earth, going and retreating. And the waters diminished at the end of a hundred and fifty days."*

Nearly all the inner ocean had been expelled to the outside world, forced through Earth's planetary wall by pressure from within. And now the way was finally clear for the higher pressure inner atmosphere to escape and equalise with the atmosphere outside. The expulsion of the excess atmosphere was the wind passing over the Earth referred to by Genesis. The waters were now finally able to flow back, diminishing the level of the flood. The expulsion of the inner ocean had taken 150 days.

...A wind filled the air and the waters came to a crest. The vaults from the deep had been exhausted. But this was just the eye of the storm. The tide had turned and the ocean brew embarked on its return journey. As the waters flowed within, the mountain peaks once again touched the sky. The Earth began to emerge. As the sea fell, the swirling tide crossed the continents tattooing their entire length. Deep water flowing off the land carved grand canyons and giant river beds...

Genesis 8 : 4, 5 *"And in the seventh month, on the seventeenth day of the month, the ark rested on the mountains of Ararat. And the waters were going and falling until the tenth month. In the tenth month, on the first of the month, the tops of the mountains were seen."*

At last the land was beginning to reappear, ten months after the rains started.

Genesis 8 : 13 to 18 *"And in the six hundredth and first year, at the beginning of the first of the month, the waters were dried up from off the earth. And Noah removed the covering of the ark and looked. And behold! The face of the earth was dried. And in the second month, on the twenty-seventh day of the month, the earth was dry. And God spoke to Noah, saying, Go out of the ark, you and your wife, and your sons and your sons' wives with you. Bring out from you every living thing that is with you, of all flesh, of fowl, of cattle, and of every creeping thing that creeps on the*

The Source of the Flood

earth; and let them swarm on the earth, and bear, and multiply on the earth. And Noah went out, and his sons, and his wife, and his sons' wives with him."

One year had passed since the races of Noah sought refuge from the flood. But now the great inundation was over. And so the inside race advised Noah to return to the land, for the time had come for life to start anew. The new era had begun.

Genesis 8 : 20 to 22 *"Then Noah built an alter to Jehovah, and took of every clean animal, and of every clean bird, and offered burnt offerings on the alter. And Jehovah smelled the delightful odour, and Jehovah said in His heart, I will never again curse the ground for the sake of man, because the imagination of the heart of man is evil from his youth. Yes, I will not again smite every living thing as I have done; while the earth remains, seedtime and harvest, cold and heat, summer and winter, and day and night shall not cease."*

The flood had greatly changed the Earth. Yet, its rotation and axis had remained intact. Night still followed day and seasons followed seasons as they did before the inundation. And while the Earth remains in this present format it is not possible for the inner seas to again flood the outside world. The Earth's oceans and atmospheres were now in balance. This is confirmed when Jehovah states he will not again smite every living thing as I have done. The words, "while the earth remains, seedtime and harvest, cold and heat, summer and winter, and day and night shall not cease", indicate humanity's place is now to remain as a permanent species on the outside surface of Earth.

Genesis 9 : 1 *"And God blessed Noah and his sons. And He said to them, Be fruitful and multiply, and fill the earth."*

Genesis 9 : 8 to 13 *"And God spoke to Noah, and to his sons with him, saying, Behold I, even I, am establishing My covenant with you, and your seed after you, and with every living creature which is with you, among fowl, among cattle, and among every animal of the earth with you, from all that go out from the ark, to every animal of the earth. And I have made stand My covenant with you, and all flesh shall not be cut off again by the waters of a flood; nor shall there ever again be a flood to destroy the earth. And God said, This is the sign of the covenant which I am about to make between Me and you, and every living soul which is with you, for everlasting generations; I have set My bow in the cloud, and it shall be a sign of a covenant between Me and the earth."*

A rainbow appeared in the changed atmosphere over them, a sign the earth was now in balance.

> **...Eventually the ocean surface receded to a final level. A new coastline formed. But the brown foamy sea was almost indistinguishable from the land. The Earth had been poisoned. The sun shone through and warmed the world. A rainbow filled half the sky. Its kaleidoscope of colours contrasting against the black atmosphere and the turbid earth below.**
>
> **Nature was ready to begin again...**

The surface of the new Earth had been extensively reshaped by the abrasive action of the inner sea. The flood had stripped the land bare of its soils, vegetation and life. Remnants of ancient meteor impact craters had all but disappeared. All had been swept away into huge deposits of silt, sand and conglomerate stone. Life the world over had been buried

The Source of the Flood

to become coal deposits and fossil beds familiar across the Earth. Deposits, accepted so casually today, reflect the violent nature of the recent past. Thick oceanic sediment choked low lying ground everywhere. Huge blocks of stone, torn away from mountain ranges, were scattered in fragments across the land and ocean floor. Areas of once fertile ground had become endless wastelands of sand. And new islands of silt and sand had appeared, left by swirling oceanic currents. There were massive grand canyons and new river courses, scoured by the power of sediment laden waters cascading off continents. Ancient river deltas had disappeared forever along with whole glaciers swallowed up by the rising waters.

The inner ocean would never be fully replenished. The sea level there was now considerably lower than before. Much of the waters had remained outside, as an equalising balance between the two worlds. Consequently the oceans of the outer Earth were now deeper. All the coastal cities had been destroyed. Their ruins submerged forever beneath the surface of the sea, seas now deeper not through the melting of an ice age, but from a balancing of pressures between the inside and outside worlds.

The Mid-Atlantic Ridge, along with its great cities, had all but disappeared, swallowed up by the rage of an unforgiving sea. The lands of the legendary Atlantis would never be seen again. Today, only its memory remains as lost images from somewhere in our mysterious past. And Iceland is all that stands above the level of the sea, our last visible point of this major geological feature, the Mid-Atlantic Ridge Spreading Site.

Today, continental shelves the world over, are submerged. The surface of the sea conceals life as it was in the pre-flood world. Ruins, ancient forests, riverbeds and other remnants remain to tell of times when the sun warmed the dry land. Now, all that remains is silence. They serve as reminders of this recent inundation event, a world changed forever less than four and a half thousand years ago.

Chapter 15

Secrets of the Sea

Fear of the unknown escalates thoughts of the cause.

Secrets of the Sea

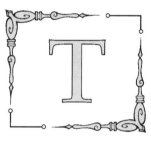he outer Earth had been shaped and eroded by the great flood. Lands were stripped bare and mountains were carved into canyons. Flowing waters laden with stone and sand had extinguished much of life. The land was scored from horizon to horizon. But there were other scars as well, those that extended beyond the erosion and destruction visible on the surface. The ocean floor had borne its own share of devastation brought on by the flood.

In a mere 150 days, virtually all of the inner world's oceans had passed through the channels cut in the ocean floor. This was followed by the cyclonic power of escaping excess atmosphere from within. After expulsion of the atmosphere, the waters were then able to flow back. More than half of the volume of the original inside oceans returned to replenish the expelled inner seas. But now, the waters travelling in the opposite direction were heavily laden with abrasive sediment and stone stripped from the outer world. The forces generated were tremendous, and so resulting erosion within the channels was extensive.

The ocean crust at the site of each channel varied in thickness. Where the crust was thinner, erosion had a greater effect on enlarging the hole. As a consequence each individual channel eroded differently. Some became gaping openings between the two worlds.

After the inundation, the world's seas were fouled with impurities. As the waters calmed and stabilised, sediments settled to the bottom under the natural action of gravity. However, in the vicinity of the channels, there was no longer any sea floor. Direct openings existed through the Earth's crust from one side to the other. These openings, passed through the planetary wall, leaving the centre of gravity exposed.

Sinking sediments settled into the openings from both sides. Because downward attraction ceases to exist at the centre of gravity, settling matter reaching this point could fall no further. Debris and other loose sediment built up on the centre of gravity filling the

Secrets of the Sea

openings to level with the normal surrounding sea floor on both sides. Once full, the openings were totally obscured. A false sea floor had been naturally formed. Today, these areas look no different to any other sediment covered bottom. But unknowingly, all that remains beneath is loose sediment held in place by the force of gravity. There is no longer any solid crust. Sea floor suspended in this way can be unstable. Being non-solid, it acts differently to the normal sea floor surrounding it. (Fig. 15.1)

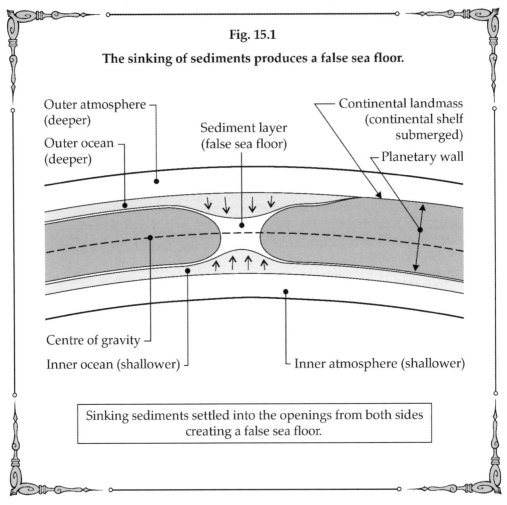

Fig. 15.1

The sinking of sediments produces a false sea floor.

Outer atmosphere (deeper)

Outer ocean (deeper)

Sediment layer (false sea floor)

Continental landmass (continental shelf submerged)

Planetary wall

Centre of gravity

Inner ocean (shallower)

Inner atmosphere (shallower)

Sinking sediments settled into the openings from both sides creating a false sea floor.

The atmosphere is constantly on the move. Because of this, air pressure varies from region to region. Pressures vary in accordance with thermal currents generated by heat from the Sun. High and low pressure systems exist right throughout both atmospheres inside the Earth and out. As pressure systems change, the surrounding environment is effected. A high pressure system is a region where the atmosphere is more dense. The process of gravity acting on increased volumes of atmosphere converts to extra weight pressing down on the Earth's surface beneath. The opposite is a low pressure system. This is where the air is less dense. Accordingly with less matter to attract downward, pressure on the surface beneath is less. Consequently, highs and lows exert varying levels of pressure on the surface of the sea and in turn the ocean floor beneath. Depending on their strength. loose sediment within the channels responds by rising and falling in accordance with atmospheric pressure differences between the two worlds. The greater the pressure difference the greater the movement. (Fig. 15.2)

Secrets of the Sea

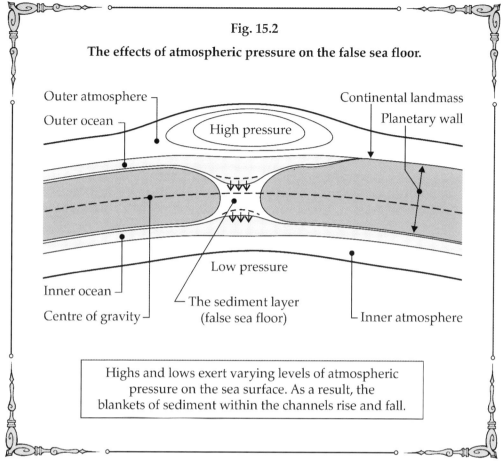

Fig. 15.2

The effects of atmospheric pressure on the false sea floor.

Outer atmosphere

Outer ocean

High pressure

Continental landmass

Planetary wall

Low pressure

Inner ocean

Centre of gravity

The sediment layer
(false sea floor)

Inner atmosphere

Highs and lows exert varying levels of atmospheric
pressure on the sea surface. As a result, the
blankets of sediment within the channels rise and fall.

Most of the time pressure differences over these sites is minimal and the false sea floor remains relatively stable. But, when pressure differences are sufficient and movement does occur, the surrounding ocean is effected. As a result, sudden changes in sea currents can develop. Until now these anomalies have never been fully understood.

Occasionally, if weather conditions inside and out are severely opposed, pressure levels exerted on the sediment layers can become extreme. As pressure systems naturally flow from highs to lows, the false sea floor is pushed away by the weight of high pressure towards the lower pressure side. If these pressure extremes exceed a certain level, movement of the false sea floor is no longer sufficient to compensate. Then, under pressure from above, the ocean will find the weakest point and break through the sediments. With that, vertical currents run through the false sea floor to balance with the lower pressure on the opposite side. Such currents, travelling straight down through the planetary wall, have a dramatic effect on the flow of the ocean over the site.

This vertical flow of ocean through the channels can happen in either direction. Firstly, depending on the severity of conditions, when the sea breaks through as a result of inside pressure, the vertical movement of water is sometimes witnessed as an aqueous white water eruption on the surface of the sea. The size and duration of these eruptions depends on the size and intensity of the pressure imbalance. Surface currents flow outward from the eruption to form level sea. The eruption process is the same action as occurred at the time of the great flood but on a much smaller scale. (Fig. 15.3)

Secrets of the Sea

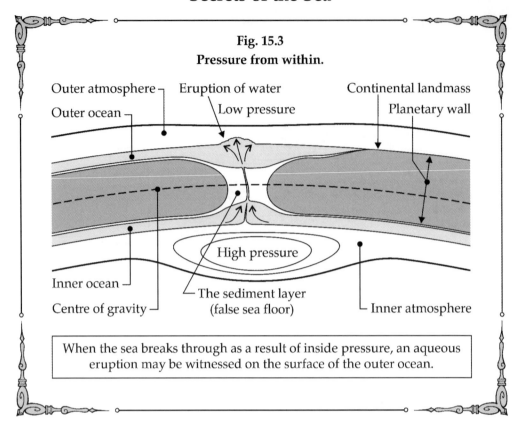

Fig. 15.3
Pressure from within.

Outer atmosphere ─ Eruption of water   Continental landmass

Outer ocean ─   Low pressure   Planetary wall

High pressure

Inner ocean ─

Centre of gravity ─   The sediment layer
(false sea floor)   Inner atmosphere

When the sea breaks through as a result of inside pressure, an aqueous
eruption may be witnessed on the surface of the outer ocean.

Secondly, if the situation is reversed with high pressure on the outside, again depending on the severity of conditions, whirlpools can develop on the surface as the water is drawn down. Whirlpools can vary from relatively minor disturbances to large vortexes. When conditions are at their extreme, the air above may be drawn down to join the vortex system. When this happens, its size can increase immensely as it spirals outwards to envelop the surrounding atmosphere. Strong currents within both the ocean and atmosphere circle around the vortex's centre. Rapid movement of air and sea near the mouth of the vortex atomises the surface water into localised mists or fogs. This can be likened to the working action of an aerosol can. Air masses outward from the centre, circle the disturbance at high speed. The air rotating in this way can extend for many kilometres from the phenomenon. As a result, large volumes of atmosphere near and towards the outer edges can travel considerable distances in a relatively short period of time.

Rapid atmospheric turbulence within a thunderstorm is responsible for the generation of electrical anomalies within that region. For those nearby, lightening is frequently experienced together with varying degrees of electrical interference. Vortexes are atmospheric disturbances too, and so produce similar electrical anomalies in much the same way. However, because the speed of atmospheric movement associated with major vortexes is considerably greater than that of a thunderstorm, electrical disturbances are accordingly much more extreme. In this situation, lightening of all types, including the rare variety known as "ball lightening", is often produced.

Like that of a dynamo, the spinning action of the vortex generates an electrical field. Accordingly the Earth's natural magnetic field is effected in the immediate area of the

Secrets of the Sea

disturbance. This results in varying degrees of magnetic anomalies. With the loss of magnetic direction, compasses wander aimlessly.

The drawing down action of the vortex curves the surface of the ocean, distorting it into a large depression. This changes the appearance of the horizon in the immediate area. It may look unusually close.

The vortex process of drawing water down through the floor of the ocean is the same action as occurred when waters abated through the planetary wall to replenish the inner world seas during the great flood, except of course on a much smaller scale. (Fig. 15.4)

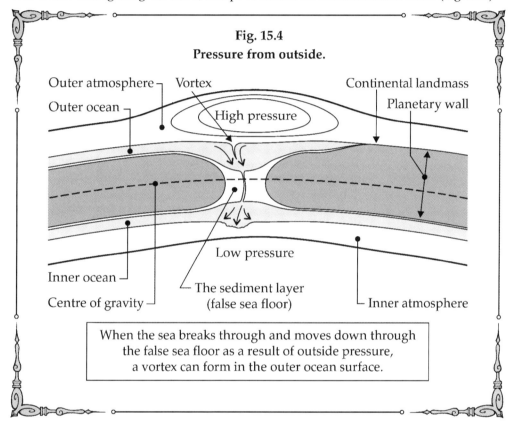

Fig. 15.4
Pressure from outside.

Outer atmosphere — Vortex

Outer ocean

High pressure

Continental landmass

Planetary wall

Low pressure

Inner ocean

Centre of gravity

The sediment layer
(false sea floor)

Inner atmosphere

When the sea breaks through and moves down through
the false sea floor as a result of outside pressure,
a vortex can form in the outer ocean surface.

The phenomenon of oceanic eruptions and vortexes are interconnected. They are both part of the same disturbance produced by pressure displacement. One action does not occur without the other. The effects of such pressure movements are not always strong enough to reach all the way to the ocean surface. However, when an outer surface eruption does occur, it is a fair indication of a substantial vortex taking place on the opposite side within the Earth. And vice versa, if an intense vortex develops in the outside ocean the corresponding forces are likely to reach all the way up and erupt on the inside surface.

Such disturbances travelling through the wall of the Earth, can effect considerable areas of oceanic surface on both sides. This is because of two factors.

Firstly, oceanic currents can penetrate through the false sea floor at any given point within its extremities. In some channels, erosion has been more extensive than others. Here, large areas of the original sea floor have been swept away and replaced by the sediments

Secrets of the Sea

of an unstable false sea floor. In these regions, developing pressure currents occur randomly over a wide area.

And secondly, vortex currents often wonder considerable distances from their point of origin as they wind their way up to the surface kilometres above. Therefore, vortexes appearing on the surface do not necessarily pinpoint the location of the sea floor disturbance beneath. It may be many kilometres away. The combination of these two factors is the cause of how such disturbances influence wide areas of certain sections of the Earth's oceanic expanses. (Fig. 15.5)

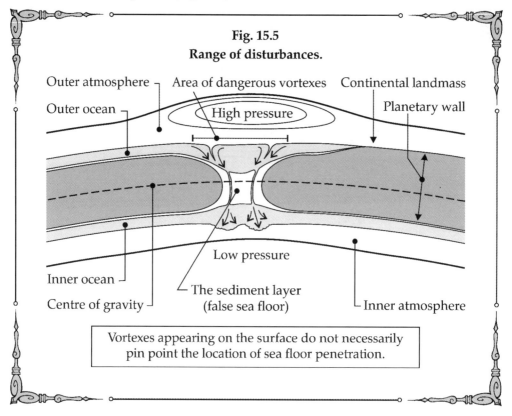

Fig. 15.5
Range of disturbances.

Vortexes appearing on the surface do not necessarily pin point the location of sea floor penetration.

Such phenomenon produces hazardous environments for those navigating the sea surface or flying immediately above. Unknowingly, vortex forces have been responsible for numerous unexplained disappearances at sea. Whilst tragedies do occur throughout the oceans of the world, there are certain areas where multiple unexplained disappearances are grouped. Many of these pinpoint the location of eroded flood channels. They remain as hidden openings beneath the ocean floor, unknown hazards able to consume those unsuspecting above.

In one such location more than 100 planes and ships have been claimed and 1,000 lives have been lost. Investigators, unaware of the perilous nature of the ocean floor beneath, have been puzzled as to what is actually happening here and why. Many have put forward a variety of theories in an attempt to seek satisfactory answers. Ideas range from those of naturally occurring oceanic currents to strange powers from other dimensions beyond understanding. But, because the correct knowledge of the ocean floor's structure has never been known, the mystery has remained unsolved.

Secrets of the Sea

Without a solution, many instinctively fear these huge graveyards of the sea. One section of ocean in question is located off the shores of Bermuda. Its boundaries dominate an extensive triangular portion of the Western Atlantic ocean. It covers an area bounded by Bermuda in the north, Southern Florida in the west and past Puerto Rico to about 40 degrees west longitude in the east. Today, with its history of perilous events, this section of mysterious ocean has become known to all as the infamous "Bermuda Triangle".

This unsafe expanse of ocean is home to a wide range of strange reported occurrences. These occurrences are believed to have been the cause of so many tragic disappearances in the past. Built up records reveal some details of experiences encountered by those facing catastrophe within the triangle. Despite the unusual nature of the events encountered, all can be easily explained as part of the natural phenomenon taking place there.

Early investigators were puzzled as to why so many disappearances occurred during the day in fine weather conditions. They considered it more likely for disappearances to take place in a stormy environment, not in safe calm weather. Unfortunately, calm fine weather is an indication of a developed high pressure system in the atmosphere of that region. High pressure cells weigh down on the sea surface. This in turn exerts downward stress on the sediments of the false sea floor below. A high pressure system, with other conditions present, is the recipe for disaster.

The weather over the western Atlantic is fine and sunny. All is well aboard the 130 metre freighter as it cuts its way through the glassy surface of a reflective sea. Including its cargo, the ship displaces a weight to in excess of 15,000 tons. The crew of 39 are anticipating a normal and uneventful voyage. The unusually calm conditions are making the job of being on board more pleasant than normal. Each member of the crew is busy going about his own duties, enjoying the summery atmosphere provided by the building high pressure system around them. But, for the unsuspecting occupants of the ship, the building pressure, has serious implications that directly effect their safety. Inside the Earth an intense low has positioned itself directly beneath them. The perils of the hidden false sea floor are yet to be discovered. And so, no-one on board has the slightest inclination of the dangers presented by the opposing pressure over the inner sea. Like a great power from the deep, the potential for disaster is looming.

Their final radio message confirms all is well.

But by now the false ocean floor has distorted and is giving way under the forces pressing down on the sea surface above. A small cloud, warning of catastrophic currents has developed in the near distance off the starboard side of the ship. Completely unnoticed by the preoccupied crew, the unusually shaped cloud is growing at ever increasing speed. Deep sea currents have broken through the sediments obscuring a flood channel. Vertical currents are racing through the wall of the Earth at ever increasing speed. With each passing second, pathways penetrating the sediment barrier are opening wider and wider. Millions of tons of oceanic water is travelling straight down at frightening speed. Water pulled under at the surface reveals a developed vortex. But, from the ship, all that is visible is a harmless looking symmetrical cloud. Those who have noticed it, make light comment on how strange the formation looks as it moves towards them. However

Secrets of the Sea

unbeknownst to the crew, the situation has turned critical. Even though it is still not too late to avoid tragedy, no-one on board is at all aware of anything amiss. The crew are totally ignorant of the terrifying secrets concealed below them.

It is noticed the ship is a little off course. Those in control don't understand why. It is given little importance as a minor correction is made. Still mindless of any problem, their progress continues. But now the cloud has intensified. Its symmetry is reaching higher and higher, changing the look of the atmosphere above it. Its appearance has suddenly turned from one of amusement to eerie and threatening.

Again the ship has veered off course. But this time more than before. There seems to be no reason as to why this is happening. All vital checks reveal nothing. To the crew at the helm, it appears almost as if the ship is being pulled off course by the brewing storm. But how could this be possible? No-one understands what is happening or the seriousness of their situation.

Having weathered many ferocious storms in the past, the hardened crew feel little threat by this curious unusual cloud formation and so sail on regardless. Those watching notice the horizon beneath the storm doesn't look quite right. It appears to be closer than normal, much closer than the horizon on the opposite side of the ship. This is beyond explanation. They have never seen anything like this before.

All of a sudden the crew have become noticeably nervous. Perhaps it would be best if the incident were reported back to port. But all attempts to make radio contact are in vain. For some reason the airways are filled with static. With tension building it is decided to again check the ships course. But to the alarm of the captain this task is also not possible. Instead of indicating north, the freighter's compass is spinning aimlessly. It is as if the ship is besieged. A bewildered crew stop and stand in amazement. Then in an instant all electricals shut down. The sound of the engines die as their power is cut off. The ship stands in silent peril. And now, for the first time, the sounds of the storm can be heard over the hushed ship and crew. Controlled minds overcome panic as urgent attempts are made to restart the generators and engines. But it is hopeless. It is now too late.

The ship has gone beyond the point of no return. There is no way back. Nothing on Earth can change their fate now. All aboard are hopelessly doomed.

The wind picks up. And rapidly builds in strength towards the storm. Suddenly it is upon them. The horizon has moved in with the storm. The ocean surface is seen to be distorted, bent downward forming a large depression. This is the cause of the appearance of the false horizon. The clouds of the storm are seen to be concentrating and descending right into the ocean, pouring into the centre of the depression like a large funnel. The whole formation is several kilometres wide from one side to the other. In its centre the division between the sea and air is blurred by ocean spray atomising into mist. Nothing can be seen beyond. Through the howling wind a thundering roar can be heard. The air is charged with electricity. Ball lightening is seen descending from above entering into the sea. As they look back nothing can be seen. The storm has completely enveloped them. Agitated water, penetrating the atmosphere turns the sky green. As the ship pitches and rolls orientation is lost. It is impossible to tell from which direction they had come. A state of confusion brings chaos. No-one can hear over the roar of white water ahead.

All on board see their fate as their ship is drawn over the lip of the oceanic depression.

Secrets of the Sea

The distorted ocean surface bends ever steeper as it curves inwards reaching down into the centre of a huge fearful vortex. The sea and air ahead combine as one into a chaotic turbulent mass. The very surface of the sea is disappearing, spiralling into the centre of the rotating force. Following the same course, the ship distorts and breaks under the strain. With no time to reflect, all on board are consumed in seconds. Every part is drawn down into the depths of the crushing abyss beneath.

The power of the vortex has briefly linked the two worlds as one. As atmosphere meets atmosphere a balancing of pressures settles the disturbance for now. Returning sediments once again separate the individual worlds. Peace and tranquillity returns the sea surface to glassy smooth.

Nothing is left. There is no evidence to attest to the tragic event. Devastation is complete. Every part has been consumed, locked for all time deep in the filtering sediments of the false sea floor, kilometres below the surface. Nothing will ever be found of the 15,000 ton freighter, its cargo, or its crew. And now, with no answers to give, only a puzzling mystery remains. Yet another unexplainable disappearance has occurred within the boundaries of the infamous Bermuda Triangle.

Unexplained disappearances within the Bermuda Triangle are not restricted to shipping. As stated earlier, many planes have been lost as well. Most aircraft disappearances have occurred within normal contact of land with no hint of trouble. In the few occasions when distress messages were actually received, happenings reported seemed strange and bizarre. Details within the messages described malfunctioning compasses and loss of electrical equipment. Often their experiences were associated with the mists and strange lights. Others, appeared to be lost, not knowing where they were. In some cases pilots told of a loss of orientation with confusion as to which way is up or down. They claimed the sea didn't look right and of not being able to see the horizon. Some, just before losing contact, stated they seemed to be entering white water. Those receiving the messages were totally mystified by what they heard. Yet the descriptions sent, reflect normally occurring events associated with an encounter with the vortex phenomenon.

An incident in Aug. 1963, demonstrates the power and range of currents that can be generated in a vortex system. Two KC-135 jet Stratotankers disappeared. When some wreckage was found it was assumed the two planes must have collided in midair. However a few days later more wreckage was found some 250 kilometres distant. This was thought to be from the other plane. But, investigators couldn't begin to explain as to why the wreckage from a midair collision was so far apart. If they didn't collide, then what caused the two planes to crash simultaneously? However, air currents in a vortex phenomenon, are sometimes extreme. This particular incident helps give some sort of idea as to how large an area can be effected by these disturbances.

The spinning force within a vortex disturbance creates streams of fast moving atmospheric currents throughout the system. Currents, in the mid to outer layers, have been responsible for previously unexplained reports of early and late arrivals of some plane flights.

In 1970 a group of C-130s flew from North Carolina to the Azores. All planes except one landed on schedule. The other arrived three and a half hours early. During the flight one crew member noticed the ground speed indicator registering a speed of some 1,300 kilometres per hour faster than the air speed indicator, suggesting they were flying with an extreme tail wind.

Another remarkable case of an early arrival caused by a vortex encounter was reported in December 1970. In this incident the pilot with his father embarked on a flight from Andros Island to Palm Beach Florida. Shortly after take off, whilst still over the waters of the Bermuda Triangle, they came upon an elliptical cloud approximately 25 kilometres across. Unable to fly around the formation, they reluctantly entered it only to emerge soon afterwards. The sudden clear air beyond was unexpected. Looking back they saw the cloud had formed into a huge semicircle to a height of over 18,000 metres and was surrounding them rapidly. The bottom of the cloud seemed to be penetrating right down into the ocean below them.

Before they could fly out of the area the cloud completely encircled them with the exception of one small hole. They made the decision to head for this rapidly disappearing space to escape the region. By the time they reached the hole, it had reduced to a tunnel through the cloud running for approximately one and a half kilometres. Blue sky could be seen on the other side. As they flew through the narrowing tunnel, the clouds making up the walls were seen to be rotating in a clockwise direction. Then as the walls closed in and touched the wing tips of the plane, both on board experienced weightlessness for several seconds. This unusual effect was brought on by the rotation action within the vortex tunnel spinning the plane.

After escaping the spiralling tunnel they found themselves surrounded by a strange greenish haze. All the instruments on board the plane were malfunctioning. As the clouds slowly cleared away they were surprised to see Miami was already below them. They landed at Palm Beach 45 minutes after take off, 30 minutes earlier than normal. Despite having a maximum speed of 313 kilometres per hour, the plane had completed the 402 kilometre distance in just 45 minutes. This was equivalent to a ground speed of 536 kilometres per hour. On further inspection, the plane had only consumed 70% of the required fuel. It was concluded, to account for the anomalies, the plane must have encountered a substantial tail wind within the cloud with an estimated wind speed velocity of around 1,600 kilometres per hour.

Planes unknowingly flying against the airflow direction of a vortex disturbance are at greater risk. This situation has been responsible for many flights ending up off course or arriving at their destination much later than expected. In these cases, forced to fly for longer periods to pass through the opposing air currents, fuel consumption has been considerably higher than normal. Others, becoming hopelessly lost, never arrived at all.

Outer surface currents, generated by ocean drawn towards whirlpool formations, effects shipping in a similar way. The many reports include various ships suddenly and mysteriously veering off course, following new circular paths in the middle of the ocean. This unusual occurrence is not easily understood by those who are unaware of the vortex phenomenon. However, rather than changing course, the ships were simply being carried along by the curving oceanic currents drawn around a vortex system.

Some of the more descriptive reports, detailing happenings within the vortex phenomenon, have come from incidents involving vessels under tow. One typical report told how, on a clear fine day, a towed barge was suddenly shrouded in a strange mist and pulled back away from the towing vessel by some seemingly powerful force of unknown origin. The same force was seen to control the surrounding ocean, drawing it in from all directions. The water in the area of the barge was noticeably more choppy and confused. Strange lights descending into the sea, spinning compasses and electrical malfunctions were all experienced in the incident. The captain told of how he was forced to use full throttle to free his load from the phenomenon. But again, these are all normal occurrences associated with vortex development. Other reports tell of captains, fearing for their safety, cutting towlines to free themselves from impending disaster. In one incident in 1966, a 20 metre tug disappeared altogether leaving its 65 metre barge, towline and cargo intact. No trace of the tug or crew was ever found.

Another eerie and bizarre twist to the Bermuda Triangle involves the frequent discovery of abandoned ships. Known as derelicts, these perfectly seaworthy craft, mostly intact, are devoid of all crew and passengers. Most have been discovered with sails set, cargo intact and ample stores on board. Common amongst the finds is a certain amount of minor storm damage with partial flooding below decks. Whilst compasses, navigation charts and often lifeboats have been taken, other valuables, supplies and sometimes even pets have all been left behind. This evidence seems to indicate those on board left in great haste for some definite reason. But with no sign of bloodshed, looting or any other obvious problems, the reason why has remained one of the most baffling mysteries of the famous triangle. The puzzling question for those investigating has always been, why? For what reason would a crew and passengers desert a perfectly seaworthy craft in the middle of the ocean with nowhere to go? With no-one ever found to tell of what happened, it is as if these crews and passengers somehow vanished into thin air.

But an all important clue lies with other reported happenings. Some crews have recalled strange incidents where extreme pressures had been exerted on the hull of their ship. This coincided with other anomalies encountered at the same time within the Bermuda Triangle. It was likened to as if some force was holding the ship and trying to wrench it apart. Again this can be explained as a typical consequence of the vortex phenomenon. The stresses experienced are those caused by an imbalance between normal pressure within the ship and low pressure outside produced by a smaller vortex pulling down on the hull from below.

It is this action that has been responsible for the repeated occurrences of derelict ships in the triangle. Developing vortexes can be of any size from minor disturbances beneath the surface to others, kilometres across, capable of consuming whole ships and even aircraft above. The derelict ship enigma results from a chain of misunderstood circumstances.

It all starts with the formation of a smaller vortex near a passing ship. Sea drawn into the disturbance carry the ship with it. Once over the mouth of the vortex the ship is subjected to suction from beneath. This drags down on the hull of the ship pulling it lower into the water. All of a sudden the sea unexpectedly floods across the decks, through all open hatches and pours below. It is as if they are sinking. Those on board, totally unaware of what is really happening, believe disaster has struck. They are going down fast. With no time for questions everyone rushes to escape. They grab whatever they can, compasses, maps, etc., and flee the ship as quickly as possible. But the ship is not sinking. It only appears to be. Partially submerged, the force from below is not strong enough to completely consume the craft. The ship's buoyancy coupled with its size out competes the vortex's power. But for those in the smaller lifeboats, their fate is sealed. Once in the

Secrets of the Sea

water there is no escape. There is no way back. The power of the vortex instantly pulls them under, beneath the churning sea.

As the pressure imbalance neutralises, the vortex weakens and subsides. The partially flooded craft, once released, and still buoyant, rises back onto the surface. Having sustained minor damage, it is left to drift minus those on board. Later, when found, yet another mystery derelict ship is added to the growing list of unexplained happenings within the Bermuda Triangle.

There are times when the vortex phenomenon is reversed. Aqueous eruptions on the ocean surface are symptomatic of pressure moving outward from within. Vertical sea currents have penetrated through the false sea floor and forced upward by a high pressure system over the inner sea. Though spectacular and still quite dangerous, the eruption side of the phenomenon is less hazardous than the vortex counterpart. Eruptions are more frequent in poor weather conditions and during the night. The reason being, these are normal times of low pressure.

Several sightings of aqueous eruptions have been reported in certain areas of the Bermuda Triangle.

In March 1963 a captain and two crew members on a Pan Am flight from New York to Puerto Rico witnessed a giant symmetrical bubbling shape on the surface of the ocean. The captain likened it to an airport size cauliflower formation that lasted for three minutes before subsiding to a dark patch of blue water.

Just over a week later a similar incident was again witnessed. This time on a Boeing 707 flying in the opposite direction. The location given was over the Puerto Rico Trench. This is one of the worlds deepest oceanic canyons, a tectonic formation where the ocean floor drops to in excess of eight kilometres beneath the surface. The ocean was seen to rise into a giant mound, again likened to that of the form of a cauliflower. Its size was estimated as measuring from one to one and a half kilometres in diameter and to a height of perhaps half its width. Subsequent checks with relevant authorities for any recorded seismic activity in the area revealed nothing.

Other reports have told of strange experiences whilst on board craft at night. Details include not being able to make forward progress sometimes for several hours. Many times vessels have found themselves pushed back several kilometres by unexplained strong opposing currents. The most noticeable feature of these experiences is the presence of an unusual dark shape ahead of them. Just above the horizon, like a patch in the sky, it was seen to obscure the stars. In most cases, all the usual anomalies associated with the Bermuda Phenomenon were experienced such as malfunctioning compasses, electrical equipment and ball lightening entering the ocean. In all cases everything returned to normal once the dark shape disappeared.

Without knowledge of the vortex phenomenon, those aboard were totally confused by their experiences. None were aware they were sailing against the outflow currents of an oceanic eruption. The disturbance ahead, had risen up creating the dark patch in the night sky. Both forward progress and vision were inhibited by the event. The stars lay hidden behind a mountain of erupting water, forced up by immense pressures escaping through the ocean floor from the world beneath their feet.

Secrets of the Sea

The Bermuda Triangle is not the only area where these unusual happenings have taken place. There are other locations as well. One noted region is in the Western Pacific off the east coast of Japan. Today it is known as the "Devil's Sea". Studies of the ocean floor in both the Bermuda Triangle and the Devil's Sea have revealed some of the world's deepest oceanic trenches. In places the floor is 11 kilometres below the sea surface. Here, echo soundings are used to calculate ocean depths. However, in certain areas, repeated measurements contradicted those taken before. The depth of the ocean floor seems to be in a state of continual fluctuation for some unknown reason. Investigators likened the rising and falling of the bottom, as if floating. Unknowingly, they were examining the false sea floor sediments within flood channels. As expected, no satisfactory explanation has come forward to solve the floating sea floor problem. One prominent incident of ocean floor movement took place in May 1973. Investigators were surprised to find the floor of the Bonin Trench, located off the coast of Japan, had suddenly risen 1,800 metres. Their only theory as to why the ocean floor ascended nearly two kilometres was, it could have been caused by some sort of unknown tectonic movement.

Several channels had to be cut for the flood. Each one eroded differently, acquiring its own individual characteristics. Whilst the positioning of channels beneath the Bermuda Triangle and Devil's Sea are more apparent, others still exist at various locations beneath the floors of the world's oceans. The positioning of each channel depended on the suitability of the site. All sites picked had to be evenly spaced around the globe and located in regions with ocean on both sides. As already stated, the crust making up the ocean floor is thinner. And of course, the deeper the ocean the thinner the crust. Ideal sites can be weighed up by overlaying the contours of the Geoid onto a world map. Lower elevations indicate which areas of the inside surface are below sea level. In this way we can perceive an approximate map of the inner world. When viewing this Geoid map, the Bermuda Triangle appears over one of the lower elevations. This was naturally a suitable site for one of the channels. But, because at this point the crust is considerably thinner, the channel sustained extensive erosion. With a greatly enlarged false sea floor, the area is more hazardous during times of atmospheric imbalances.

Another channel exists near the North Pole. Whilst it poses little threat to shipping and airline routes, unusual phenomenon has been reported in the area. Warm sea currents containing remnants of tropical and aquatic type plant life have been known to appear without apparent reason. Such remnants and warm currents present a dilemma in this frozen environment of the outer world.

Fortunately, knowledge of the Earth's structure provides the simple answer. The phenomenon occurs because the environment within is different. When sediment layers in the channel are breached, warm currents impregnated with inner world matter occasionally flow through the planetary wall to the outer world. This is a natural occurrence because of the existence of the North Polar hole.

Other channels are less active. Some situated in more remote oceanic locations have little effect on passing marine travellers. Others are no longer active. Having sustained much less erosion, they have now resealed.

Today there are less mishaps. Technology has advanced. Planes and ships, with the latest equipment on board, are larger and more sophisticated. And fewer lives are lost to the secrets of the sea.

Secrets of the Sea

Chapter 16

Gravity's Grand Reign

The truth is universal.

Gravity's Grand Reign

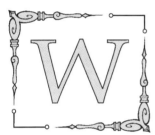 e have failed in our attempt to solve many of the Earth's great mysteries. This is due to a lack of understanding. Each mystery is not a singular problem but instead one piece of the bigger jigsaw puzzle of Earth, and the Earth one piece of the infinite picture of the universe. Nothing is isolated. Everything is a part of everything else. Each has its own place. If one thing changes, all other things adjust along with it.

All too often humanity focuses on the immediate problem becoming blind to everything else. Multiple mysteries do not exist at all. There is only one. It lies in the understanding of the universal network. For us, mysteries remain unsolved because this network is not yet fully understood. With just one piece of the puzzle in hand it is not possible to see the whole picture. However, only when the completed picture is before us do all things become apparent. Essential answers have eluded us because this important fact has not been properly considered or fully understood.

The purpose of this book has been to provide the answers. However, just answers on their own would fail to complete the picture, and so the reasons and workings behind them have also been given. This allows the full map of understanding to be achieved.

Understanding gravity is the answer. It brings the chaos of the universe into common order. This is the primary rule that controls everything. All things that exist from atoms to planets, from stars to galaxies are made from the same common ingredients moulded naturally by gravity. The only difference between all things is their size, their position in the universe and which ingredients they are made of. The same laws govern them all.

The primary force of gravity interacting with the mass of the cosmos is the key. Understanding this is understanding the complete network. The way the ingredients of the cosmos are built upon the foundations of gravity, is the blueprint of universal existence. Earth's incredible structure is a reflection of this blueprint.

Gravity's Grand Reign

Because everything everywhere is created under the same rule, the mysteries we encounter here on Earth we also encounter on other planets and beyond.

Ruled by the same law, the sequence making up the Solar System follows similar lines to that of the Earth. Attraction from the Sun's mass is the controlling factor for all the Solar System's matter. But, because the strength of attraction reduces with distance outward, the closer a planet is to the Sun, the more dense its matter is likely to be. Accordingly, the structure of planets vary depending on their location in the order of the Solar System. This rule applies to all solar systems throughout the universe.

Each individual structure has its own inherent questions waiting to be answered. In order to unravel just a few enigmas, it is necessary to take a journey from the Sun, out past the planets, through the Solar System, and observe the workings of gravity along the way.

Gravity's journey through the Solar System

Our voyage starts in the centre with the Sun. This is our star, the energy source that lights, heats and holds the Solar system together. It contains the most matter, is highest in density and retains the heaviest elements. The total mass of the Sun is consumed by heat radiating outward from its central solar reaction. Without heat, the Sun would be no more than a huge hollow terrestrial (rocky) planet.

Out from the Sun we encounter the orbiting planets. Each of the nine recognised planets of the Solar System are identified as either rocky or gaseous. Planets that are composed mainly of rock are known as terrestrial planets. These are higher in density. Gaseous planets are those composed mainly of gas and so are lower in density. However, most of the planets are a combination of both. High density terrestrial planets are located closer to the Sun. Gaseous planets are found further out.

As we travel out from the Sun, the first planet we encounter is Mercury. With a diameter of 4,878 kilometres, it orbits the Sun at an average distance of 58 million kilometres. Due to its close proximity to the Sun, its surface temperatures are extreme. Mercury is the first in a line of the terrestrial planets. Being the closest to the Solar System's centre, its mass density is high. The planet is devoid of atmosphere and has a surface completely pitted with crater marks.

Crater mysteries from the past

Most of us are familiar with this type of terrain. Looking at the Moon we see a surface bearing scars from countless numbers of impacts. These tell of a past time when incoming meteorite and asteroid material relentlessly bombarded the Moon's exposed outer crust.

Meteorite and asteroid material is the matter left over in space after the Sun and its planets came together forming the Solar System. Over eons of time, this material, piece by piece, has been gravitating in towards each of the planets. With each piece of debris that falls to ground, there is one less left behind in space. So today, meteorite and asteroid collisions are greatly diminished. The period in the Solar System's past, when impacts occurred more frequently, is known as the "great bombardment".

Variations in structure from crater to crater is one of those confusing issues awaiting a

Gravity's Grand Reign

satisfactory explanation. Craters exist not only on Mercury, but in fact on all terrestrial planets and moons. They occur in all sizes. Some are no bigger than a human hand. Others are more than a thousand kilometres across. The features of each individual crater vary depending mainly upon its size. By examining these variances, we get a clearer understanding of the planet's structure beneath.

Small craters below 25 kilometres in diameter have a typical deep bowl structure. Those between 25 kilometres and 130 kilometres usually have a central peak and by comparison a much shallower bowl shaped floor. Once the diameter of a crater exceeds 130 kilometres its structure completely changes in design. No longer is the floor bowl shaped. Instead it is convex, following the natural curvature of the planet, and terraced by concentric rings. (Fig. 16.1)

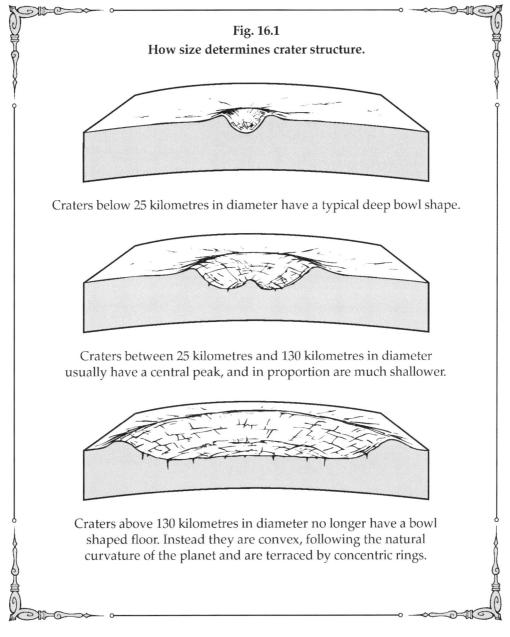

Fig. 16.1
How size determines crater structure.

Craters below 25 kilometres in diameter have a typical deep bowl shape.

Craters between 25 kilometres and 130 kilometres in diameter usually have a central peak, and in proportion are much shallower.

Craters above 130 kilometres in diameter no longer have a bowl shaped floor. Instead they are convex, following the natural curvature of the planet and are terraced by concentric rings.

Gravity's Grand Reign

The question to be answered here is; why don't larger impacts leave the same bowl shaped depressions as do smaller ones? What factors are in play to cause changes in crater structure? This anomaly has never been properly addressed. Without the correct understanding of natural hollow planet structure, vital answers are not achievable. But now the solution is once again simple. Crater features on the surface reflect planetary structure beneath, structure that is hollow.

So, how does hollow planetary structure effect crater format? In order to find out, it is necessary to examine what actually happens at the point of celestial impact.

With smaller impacts, the full force throws material out from the site forming a deep hole and surrounding crater wall. And so the classic bowl shape is left behind.

With impacts a little larger, a different set of circumstances come into play. The force is sufficient to slightly deflect the planetary wall. Or in other words the planetary wall distorts inward away from the force of the collision. Matter is thrown outward producing a normal crater wall much the same as with smaller impacts. But the difference here is; to achieve its perfect balance, the forces of gravity rebound the planetary wall back to its normal spherical shape. This rebounding action ejects matter upward in the centre of the crater forming the familiar peak. The function is similar to that of a rebounding droplet thrown up after a marble is dropped into water. The crater depression is not proportionately as deep as smaller craters because the planetary wall has absorbed a share of the force, reducing the impact's ability to displace matter.

This is the same action as hammering a nail into an unsupported plank of wood. The springing of the plank, like the planetary wall, reduces the effect of the hammering force. This is because some of the force is used up in flexing the plank. And so it requires a greater impact force to hammer in the nail. When the plank is properly supported, that portion of the force, previously used in springing the plank, is now directed to drive the nail in much deeper.

The larger the impact, the more the planetary wall is flexed. In major collisions, a massive amount of impact energy is spent by deflecting the planets surface inward out of shape. On occasions in the past, whole areas sometimes a thousand kilometres in diameter, have given way and distorted under the weight of a huge celestial collision. On impact, the planetary wall is pushed inward out of shape. As a result, the matter of the planet is distorted out of its natural spherical balance. After the incident, gravity from the planet's mass takes over, returning the wall back out to its spherical form around its centre of gravity. This action changes the shape of the new crater floor. It is not depressed or even flat. Instead, as it rebounds, the crater floor becomes convex as it follows the natural curvature of the planet. This only happens because the planet is hollow and returns back into spherical shape after the depression of a major impact.

Such is the case on Mercury. One major crater known as "Caloris Basin" is more than one thousand kilometres across. This represents a huge celestial collision. The floor of the crater is not depressed or flat. It is convex, following the natural curvature of the planet. The planet's original surface within the crater floor is extensively cracked, similar in appearance to that of a flattened egg shell. This was caused as the planet surface depressed inward under the weight of the impact. If Mercury had been a solid planet, as is currently believed, this crater would have been completely different in structure. The floor of the crater would not follow the curvature of the planet as it does. Instead the full force of the

Gravity's Grand Reign

impact would have excavated a huge hole in the planet's surface. The Caloris Basin Crater and almost endless numbers of other craters on Mercury and other planets are so structured because they were formed by the rebounding surface of planets and moons that are structured hollow. (Fig. 16.2)

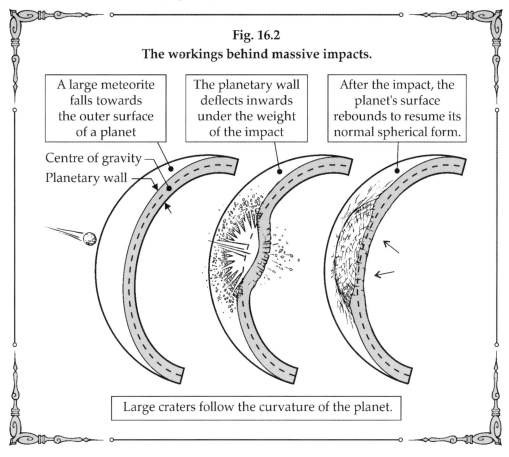

Fig. 16.2
The workings behind massive impacts.

| A large meteorite falls towards the outer surface of a planet | The planetary wall deflects inwards under the weight of the impact | After the impact, the planet's surface rebounds to resume its normal spherical form. |

Centre of gravity

Planetary wall

Large craters follow the curvature of the planet.

Directly opposite the Caloris Basin, on the other side of Mercury, there exists an area of chaotic terrain. This was formed by shock waves travelling out in all directions from the impact site, following around the planetary wall and converging together on the opposite side. Again, if Mercury had been solid, this formation would not have occurred.

Beyond Mercury

Continuing our voyage beyond Mercury we next encounter Venus. With a diameter of 12,104 kilometres, Venus is only slightly smaller than the Earth. It orbits the Sun at an average distance of 108 million kilometres. Venus again is a terrestrial planet. It has an atmosphere comprised of mainly carbon dioxide. This produces a greenhouse effect helping to maintain a ground temperature as high as 480 degrees Celsius. Despite thick atmosphere obscuring vision of the surface beneath, radar echoes have been reasonably successful in mapping most of the features of Venus's terrain. This planet too faced the great bombardment. However, it is considered the high density atmosphere would have prevented a large proportion of incoming matter from reaching the surface. As happens on the Earth, most would have disintegrated and burned in the upper levels of the atmosphere.

Gravity's Grand Reign

Next in line is the Earth. This dense terrestrial planet 150 million kilometres out from the Sun, is mankind's sole abode. At this location heat radiation from the Sun is ideal. The Earth's atmospheric pressure is such that water is able to exist in liquid form. Because all the right elements are present and conditions are suitable, life as we know it is able to exist. The Earth bears few of the familiar crater scars found on other terrestrial planets. Remains from past impacts have been mostly washed away by ensuing catastrophic flooding from its oceans.

Beyond Earth is Mars. After Venus and of course the Moon, Mars is our closest neighbour. A rocky planet like Earth, its orbit varies from 206 to 249 million kilometres. At 6,794 kilometres, it is half the diameter of Earth and twice the diameter of the Moon. It too has polar ice caps. Tilted on an axis of 24 degrees, Mars experiences four seasons as does the Earth. The Martian year is nearly double ours being equivalent to 23 Earth months. Each Martian day is a mere 41 minutes longer than Earth's. But despite the similarities the Martian environment is quite different to that experienced here on Earth. The atmosphere there is less than one hundredth of the density of Earth's. As a result, surface temperatures vary greatly. On the equator, summer temperatures may reach 26 degrees C. But during the night it drops to below -100 degrees C. Mars is the lowest density of all the terrestrial planets, being only slightly higher than the Moon. Whilst a magnetic field has been detected, it is much weaker than the Earth's.

Secrets from within Mars

Mars has its own set of unsolved mysteries. In 1971 the Mariner 9 space craft, and again in 1975 the Viking Orbiter, transmitted back detailed pictures of the Martian surface. Apart from the normal cratered and volcanic terrain expected, the images revealed something else quite different. The Martian surface was not eroded solely by atmospheric winds and celestial impacts, but also by flowing water.

Mars too has suffered a great flood.

This presented those investigating with an unsolvable problem. It was considered not possible for flowing water to exist on the Martian surface. The reason being, the pressure of the atmosphere is too low to support water in its liquid form. If exposed to the conditions on the surface of Mars, liquid water would simply boil away to vapour or, if cold enough, turn to ice. Liquid oceanic expanses are able to exist on Earth because of the presence of its higher pressure atmosphere.

To further complicate the mystery, the volume of water involved is by no means minimal. Such is the amount of erosion across the Martian surface, it is now apparent Mars experienced a similar inundation event as did the Earth, although to a lesser extent. But the unanswered question for science is, how could this be? How could so much water exist on the surface of a planet with so little atmosphere? But the indisputable evidence is there for all to see, revealed in these pictures from Mars.

By examining the returned images we can learn many things. The source and flow direction of the flood is clearly seen. Areas of broken blocks in the crust mark the point where the full width of the great flood emerged from beneath the planet's surface. From here it carved a path for hundreds of kilometres across the dusty Martian terrain. The "Ma'adim Vallis" is just one of the carved channels. It runs for a distance of 600 kilometres. Other channels are fretted with tributaries. Elsewhere, there are areas crossed by drainage

Gravity's Grand Reign

networks, left as water flowed down from higher ground. In places, flow patterns have been created by water diverting around higher ground and crater formations. Occasionally, the flow of the flood was interrupted by elevated lava flows. It is clearly seen how water backed up behind ridges and then broke through forming erosion gaps.

These amazing pictures have left scientists guessing. There is no disputing that the markings have been caused by an aqueous event. But no-one has been able to explain exactly why the water existed and where it came from. However, some suggestions have been made. One works on the possibility of the atmosphere being different in the past. A more substantial atmosphere may have been sufficient to sustain water in its liquid state. A second idea suggests the flood originated from the melting of ground ice locked within the planet's crust. The theory works on the concept of volcanic heat melting the ice and forcing water up to the surface. From there the waters flooded across the Martian terrain, leaving the erosion behind. The water left on the surface then boiled away in the low pressure to become part of the atmosphere.

Whilst science admits these ideas are only hypothetical and cannot be proved, there are still several problems with them. Initially, in answer to the first theory of the loss of atmosphere, how or even why a planet would lose most of its atmosphere is yet to be explained. There is no evidence to support this line of thought. Then, as for the second theory, how sufficient quantities of ice, to produce such an extensive erosion event, could exist in the crust is a problem in itself. This is more apparent if we examine the process of surface formation. When the crust first forms, it solidifies from a molten mass. Consequently, there is no possible way ice could form or exist in this super heated environment. Then, as the molten material cools, a solid compressed rocky mass results, just as happened here on Earth. There is no way the required volume of ice could penetrate it. And of course, it is not possible for water to flow into any unexplained gaps beneath the surface to later turn to ice, because the air pressure is too low for liquid water to exist. Even if, by some unexplained way, small quantities of ice could exist below the surface, volcanic heat would simply vaporise the ice as it melted because again, liquid water cannot exist. The vapours would then ventilate through the surface as gasses.

Other theories such as the water arriving from an ice meteorite are likewise not credible. The force of a celestial impact produces so much heat that the shattered meteorite fragments instantly turn to vapour and become part of the atmosphere. No liquid water would be left after such an event.

Melting of ice is not the solution. The reason for the great flood catastrophe on Mars is simple and straight forward. Once again the law of natural hollow planet formation provides us with the essential answer. We now know, as with all similar celestial bodies, Mars too is hollow. As with the Earth, out-gassing from the molten mass of the planet produced two Martian atmospheres, the outer atmosphere we know of today and one on the inside. Again, due to the properties of a hollow sphere, with its reducing area above the inner surface, gasses inside built up deeper. This converted to extra atmospheric pressure at ground level. Out-gassing outside spread out thinner over the ever increasing area above. The shallower atmosphere there converted to less atmospheric pressure. And so, as happened on the Earth and other similar planets, a pressure imbalance naturally developed between the inner and outer atmospheres.

This pressure difference is the critical factor in understanding the origins of the great flood on Mars. Whilst the outer atmosphere was too low for liquid water to exist, inside

Gravity's Grand Reign

the planet the environment was different. Here the additional depth of atmosphere provided sufficient pressure to support water in its liquid form. Water vapour was able to condense. It collected together to form lakes and eventually small oceans. Outside water vapour remained in the atmosphere or became ice at the Martian poles. Over time, like the Earth, Mars expanded. This progressively thinned the planetary wall. The extra pressure of atmosphere, now combined with increasing oceans, weighed heavily on the inner surface. Eventually, with ongoing expansion further thinning the wall, and the weakening effects caused by endless meteorite impacts, the planetary wall fractured.

After millions of years, pressure inside now found the weakest point. Huge volumes of inside ocean surged through the planetary wall and past the centre of gravity. The ancient Martian surface erupted as outflow from the inner depths burst forth. For the first time in the history of the planet, water, flowing as a liquid saturated the dry earth. The ensuing flood carved its way across the Martian terrain. Cascading watercourses cut channels for hundreds of kilometres. Diverted water eroded flow patterns around mountains and through craters. For a time there were fast flowing rivers and great lakes. Erosion was extensive. The Martian surface had been changed forever by the tide of water expelled from within.

In order for the inside ocean to be expelled, inner pressure must have built sufficiently to overcome frictional resistance encountered through the planetary wall. Accordingly, as inner pressure was released, the rate of flow through the subterranean channel slowed. Once the inside pressure reduced to a level equal to the resistance encountered through the wall, the aqueous eruption stopped. The expelled waters then remained isolated on the outer surface. There, in the low pressure, they boiled away to become part of the Martian atmosphere. Today, all that remains is hundreds of kilometres of erosion, left by an ocean that no longer exists. A seemingly unsolvable mystery remains for those unaware of natural hollow planetary structure.

Travelling out from Mars, we leave the terrestrial planets behind and arrive at the first of a line of gas planets, Jupiter. This is the largest planet in the Solar system, and the closest gas planet to the Sun. It has a diameter in excess of 140,000 kilometres. As the fifth planet, it orbits the Sun at a distance of more than 740 million kilometres. Jupiter, unlike Earth, is not terrestrial in structure. This is a planet of swirling gas clouds.

Obscured processes within gas planets

Jupiter, just visible to the naked eye from Earth, is noted for the many varying sized spots swirling throughout its atmosphere. Among these, one is most prominent. It is a giant red blemish situated in the southern hemisphere. Oval in shape, it measures approximately 26,000 kilometres in length and nearly 14,000 kilometres in width. Its size is such that the whole Earth would fit within its boundaries. Today this feature is known as the "Great Red Spot". Although many other spots exist throughout Jupiter's gaseous atmosphere, the Great Red Spot is by far the largest. Observations have revealed gasses within the spot rotate in an anticlockwise direction. And the whole formation is not fixed but instead wonders a few degrees in latitude.

Jupiter is not alone with its strange spots. They are found on all the gas planets of the Solar System. A satisfactory explanation as to the existence of so many spots has never been given.

Gravity's Grand Reign

To date, Jupiter's Great Red Spot has generated the most interest. Scientists have been puzzled by this strange red shape ever since its discovery more than 300 years ago. Of the many theories that have been put forward, none so far have offered any sort of satisfactory explanation as to what it actually is. Some have suggested it is simply a storm. But if this were true, where is the central eye as is normally found in this sort of atmospheric disturbance? There isn't one. The atmospheric structure of the red spot is not correctly configured to satisfy this theory. Secondly, how can one storm last for hundreds of years? And, why have no others of a similar size developed? The Giant Red Spot is unique. Nothing else of such magnitude exists on the face of the planet. It is alone.

Others have suggested the red spot is merely a disturbance in the atmosphere caused as gasses swirl around and over mountainous terrain beneath. But, if this were true, the spot would not vary its position in latitude. And besides, no evidence has ever been found to suggest the existence of any solid crust beneath Jupiter's clouds.

None of these concepts go anywhere near to solving this great enigma in Jupiter's atmosphere. This is because, without an understanding of natural hollow planetary structure, the cause of the red spot and indeed all the spots is unsolvable. However, with the correct key in hand, another part of the incredible universal picture takes shape. The solution is simple and straight forward.

Firstly, Jupiter is formed like all other planets. It is hollow. As a gaseous planet, the planetary wall is made up of various layers of gasses. There is no solid crust. Because nothing is firmly connected to anything else, movement within Jupiter's mass is not even. The planet does not have a particular speed of rotation because different latitudes rotate at different speeds. But, whilst Jupiter does not have a solid crust of its own, its planetary wall does contain considerable quantities of solid matter such as dust and rock fragments. All these materials, being heavier than Jupiter's gasses, have sunk down to the centre of gravity. There they remain obscured from view. Lighter and lighter gasses are layered over the heavier matter upward from the centre of gravity. The very lightest gasses of all make up the cloud tops in the uppermost reaches of Jupiter's atmosphere. It is these gasses that are visible from space.

None of the planets were exempted from the almost endless impacts of the great bombardment. Each took its share. This is evident by the sheer numbers of craters visible on the rocky (terrestrial) planets and moons. But, when it comes to the gas planets, impact evidence there is a little more subtle.

Incoming matter did not encounter a solid barrier. Instead, the gaseous wall of planets such as Jupiter, offered resistance of a different type. Smaller meteorites burned up in the outer layers in much the same way as shooting stars do here on Earth. In the event of larger meteorite impacts, any pieces that did survive the frictional forces encountered in the atmosphere, ultimately sank down to the centre of gravity. There they remained to be eroded to dust by the abrasive winds of Jupiter's violent atmosphere, joining the increasing volumes of loose sands and other rock fragments left from previous impacting matter.

The largest surviving pieces on Jupiter's centre of gravity interrupt the normal flow patterns within the atmosphere. Eddies develop as gasses flow around them. Heavy sands at the centre of gravity are disturbed and flow with the gasses around and over following the outlines of the new shape.

Gravity's Grand Reign

Such atmospheric disturbances are observed from above in space as swirling spots across the face of Jupiter. Spots that have been misinterpreted ever since their discovery, show the positions of celestial pieces trapped on the centre of gravity, matter being worn down by Jupiter's constant abrasive winds. The larger the spot the larger the body. Varying colours indicate the depth of disturbance through the many layers of the planet's atmosphere. Colour changes are more noticeable when heavier materials such as red dust from deeper within flow over and around the mass. (Fig. 16.3)

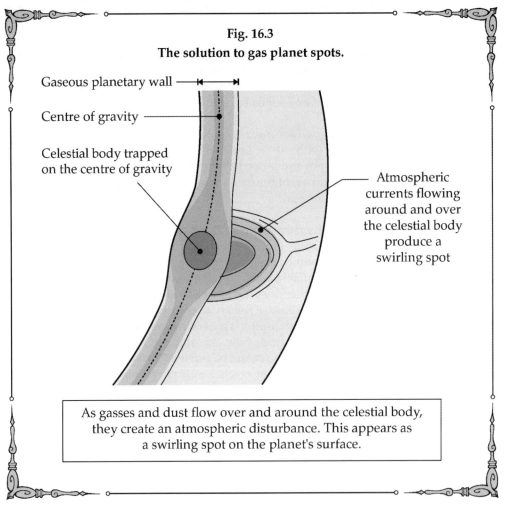

Fig. 16.3

The solution to gas planet spots.

Gaseous planetary wall

Centre of gravity

Celestial body trapped on the centre of gravity

Atmospheric currents flowing around and over the celestial body produce a swirling spot

As gasses and dust flow over and around the celestial body, they create an atmospheric disturbance. This appears as a swirling spot on the planet's surface.

The mystery behind Jupiter's Great Red Spot

Jupiter's Great Red Spot is one of these disturbances. It is not a storm or the site of a volcanic eruption as various theories propose. Like all other spots, this giant blemish indicates the position of a solid mass on the planet's centre of gravity. One that is much larger. But it doesn't end here. The Great Red Spot is different. It is not the remains of an impacted celestial body as with the others. This giant terrestrial mass originates from another source.

The story of the Great Red Spot begins with the very birth of Jupiter itself.

Like all other celestial bodies, Jupiter too was structured from the multitude of matter

Gravity's Grand Reign

drifting in space. It is clear by analysing the planet's present structure that at this distance from the Sun the vast majority of building material available was not rock but instead, gas. Despite the terrestrial matter being by far the smaller portion, its density is considerably greater than that of gas. This means it possesses a stronger force of attraction. And so, as gravity's force consolidated matter together into the first stages of Jupiter, a high proportion of the first materials to arrive were these heavier terrestrial elements.

This is a natural process similar to the settling of muddy water in a pond. Sediments that are more dense and therefore heavier, sink to the bottom first followed by other silts that are progressively lighter and finer.

As the mixture of rock and gas began to consolidate, the first part of the planet Jupiter came into being. At this stage, the mass of the young planet was small and contained a high concentration of terrestrial matter. And so, under the force of gravity, the heavier terrestrial elements sank down through the gasses and converged in the centre of the mass. Soon a solid central unit had formed. Jupiter's format at this time was not unlike the early developmental stages of the Earth. It was structured as a solid centrally compressed mass enveloped by an atmosphere. Like Earth, the atmosphere was by far the smaller portion of the mass of the planet.

With its dense rock composition, the central unit attracted the surrounding gasses down onto its surface. This produced highest atmospheric pressure at ground level decreasing with elevation. In other words, the atmosphere was internally compressed. This is similar to the present configuration of the atmosphere on Earth. Here too, air pressure is greatest at ground level. (Fig. 16.4)

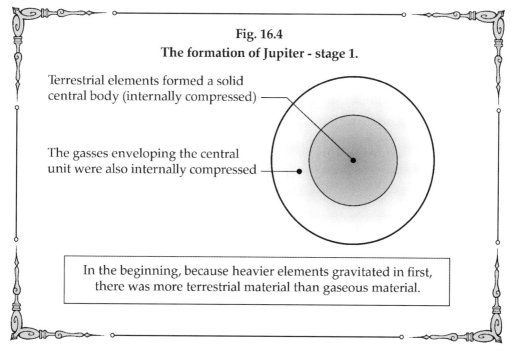

Fig. 16.4
The formation of Jupiter - stage 1.

Terrestrial elements formed a solid central body (internally compressed)

The gasses enveloping the central unit were also internally compressed

In the beginning, because heavier elements gravitated in first, there was more terrestrial material than gaseous material.

With incoming matter continuing to arrive, both the atmosphere and central mass increased. Eventually, as the size of the central mass outgrew the depth of its surface effect, it evolved externally compressed.

Gravity's Grand Reign

By now a large percentage of the terrestrial matter available had already gravitated in to join Jupiter's early stages of planetary growth. Because of this, further incoming matter was now increasingly more gaseous. So as the planet grew, the enveloping atmosphere built exceedingly faster than the central unit. The terrestrial mass was becoming a lesser and lesser portion of the total volume of the planet. Jupiter quickly progressed from a terrestrial planet with an atmosphere to a gaseous planet with a small rocky centre. (Fig. 16.5)

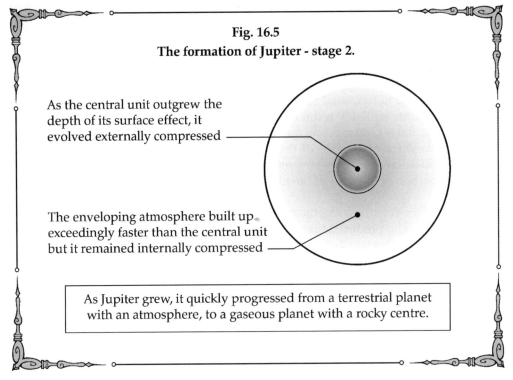

Fig. 16.5
The formation of Jupiter - stage 2.

As the central unit outgrew the depth of its surface effect, it evolved externally compressed

The enveloping atmosphere built up exceedingly faster than the central unit but it remained internally compressed

As Jupiter grew, it quickly progressed from a terrestrial planet with an atmosphere, to a gaseous planet with a rocky centre.

Responding to outward attraction from its own externally compressed mass, matter in the middle of the central unit moved out. With that, the central unit became hollow.

As incoming matter continued to join the planet, the atmosphere extended ever outward. Now, the distance between the central unit and the outer reaches of the atmosphere was far greater than ever before. For the first time, the depth of gasses surrounding Jupiter exceeded the depth of the surface effect within the atmosphere. This meant, no longer could weight from gasses arriving at the outer limits of the atmosphere compress the gases all the way down to the central unit. And so, as Jupiter continued to grow, its atmospheric mass also became externally compressed. (Fig. 16.6)

Eventually the next stage of planetary development took place and the hollow central unit began to expand.

As more and more matter arrived, Jupiter's depth of gasses extended ever outward into surrounding space. Accordingly, external compression in the atmosphere increased. Up until this point, inward gravity from the central unit had been responsible for holding the inner mass of Jupiter together. But now, outward attraction from this increased externally compressed atmosphere was becoming much stronger than before. This was neutralising the level of inward attraction from the central unit. (Fig. 16.7)

Gravity's Grand Reign

Fig. 16.6
The formation of Jupiter - stage 3.

The central unit became hollow

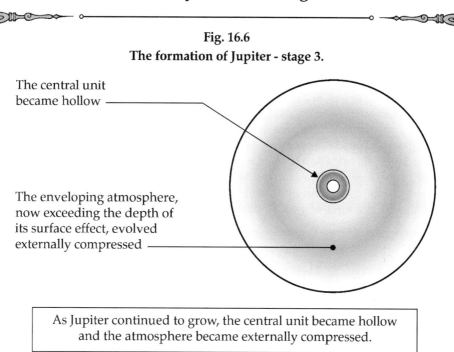

The enveloping atmosphere, now exceeding the depth of its surface effect, evolved externally compressed

As Jupiter continued to grow, the central unit became hollow and the atmosphere became externally compressed.

Fig. 16.7
The formation of Jupiter - stage 4.

The central hollow unit expands as its planetary wall thins

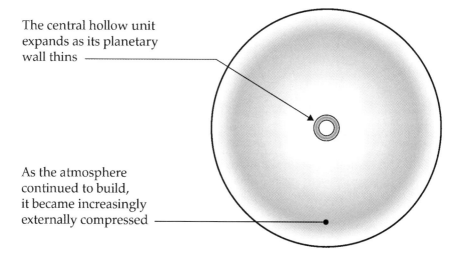

As the atmosphere continued to build, it became increasingly externally compressed

Inward attraction from the central unit, responsible for holding the inner mass of Jupiter together, was being increasingly neutralised by opposing attraction from the mass of the atmosphere.

Gravity's Grand Reign

Eventually, as the process of planetary development continued, a point was reached when the force of outward attraction from built up gases strengthened beyond the level of inward attraction from the central unit. Gravity from the mass of the atmosphere was now greater than gravity from the terrestrial unit in the centre. No longer was the central unit in control of Jupiter's structure. Under the new direction of resultant attraction, the central mass was finally pulled outward towards the greater gaseous matter surrounding it. With the unit surrendering its central position, the force holding the middle of the planet together was immediately removed. Accordingly, responding to the strong outward force, the gases of Jupiter moved rapidly out leaving behind a void in the centre of the planet. Suddenly its mass had formed into a huge planetary wall. The displaced central unit settled away from the centre to the new centre of gravity within the wall. From here, expansion was rapid and immense, and only ceased when the mass of Jupiter reached equilibrium with the force of gravity. (Fig. 16.8)

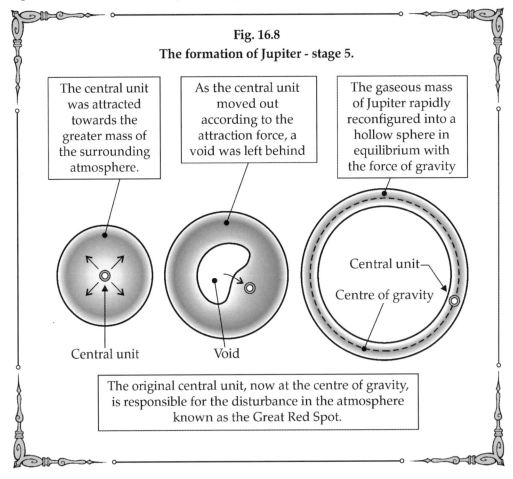

Fig. 16.8
The formation of Jupiter - stage 5.

| The central unit was attracted towards the greater mass of the surrounding atmosphere. | As the central unit moved out according to the attraction force, a void was left behind | The gaseous mass of Jupiter rapidly reconfigured into a hollow sphere in equilibrium with the force of gravity |

Central unit

Void

Central unit

Centre of gravity

The original central unit, now at the centre of gravity, is responsible for the disturbance in the atmosphere known as the Great Red Spot.

The central terrestrial mass, now at the centre of gravity, remains to this day to disrupt the natural flow patterns within the atmosphere. Like all other terrestrial debris, as currents displace gasses and dust from deep within the atmosphere, they flow over and around the terrestrial mass. This is seen from space as a giant swirling red spot. It is not a storm or the site of volcanic activity. It is the remnants of the beginnings of Jupiter itself.

Eventually this great swirling blemish will disappear forever. The abrasive winds of Jupiter are slowly wearing it away. But, the very fact that this piece of celestial history still remains

Gravity's Grand Reign

is testimony to the youthful age of our Solar System.

Beyond Jupiter

The next planet beyond Jupiter is Saturn. This is the sixth planet of the Solar System and the second in line of the gas planets. It has a diameter of 120,000 kilometres and orbits the Sun at a distance of 1,427 million kilometres.

The most distinguishing feature of Saturn is its complex system of surrounding rings. This incredible sight is the result of sunlight reflecting off particles of matter orbiting the planet in a narrow plane around its equator. This feature however, is not unique to Saturn. Similar but lesser rings have formed around two other gas planets, Jupiter and Uranus.

Like Jupiter, Saturn too has swirling spots in its atmosphere. Again they are caused as terrestrial matter, trapped on the centre of gravity, disrupts the normal flow of atmospheric currents. The largest spot is found in the northern hemisphere. Named "Big Bertha" it measures 10,000 kilometres by 6,000 kilometres. There are many other smaller spots such as "Anne's Spot" in the southern hemisphere. This one is approximately 3,000 kilometres in diameter. It is red in colour and is similar in appearance to Jupiter's Great Red Spot.

As we journey on, out through the Solar System information about the remaining planets becomes less. Uranus and Neptune are respectively the seventh and eight planets. Both are gaseous in structure. Uranus is just over 51,000 kilometres in diameter and orbits at a distance of 2,870 million kilometres. Neptune is just over 50,500 kilometres in diameter and orbits at a distance of just under 4,500 million kilometres. There is little detailed information on these two outer planets. However, Neptune has one definite prominent feature. Named the "Great Dark Spot", this huge blemish is comparable to Jupiter's Great Red Spot. This swirling feature indicates the location of the remains of Neptune's original central unit created in the beginnings of its evolution.

The last recognised planet is Pluto. Apart from its diameter being less than 2,500 kilometres, nothing much is really known about this small planet. Pluto's true composition remains a mystery. It has an elliptical orbit that varies from between 4,425 million kilometres to 7,375 million kilometres. Despite its position as the ninth planet, for a short section of its orbit it moves closer to the Sun than Neptune, and so for this period it actually becomes the eight planet.

Further discoveries beyond Pluto await our curiosity.

Life within our Solar System

As with all the constituents of the cosmos, the Solar System falls into gravity's universal format. Every celestial body is complete with its own unique environment. They reflect a range of natural physical elements within the universe. This brings us again to the most important and exciting aspect of all. Life and its possible existence elsewhere throughout the cosmos has always been of great interest to humanity.

Does life exist elsewhere other than on Earth? Mankind often asks this obvious and intriguing question. Surely, in the infinite vastness of space there must be countless planets with similar environments to Earth's. Science is forever scrutinising the far reaches of space in a never ending search for life's subtle signs. At times, humanity has directed its

Gravity's Grand Reign

attention towards Mars.

Mars is one planet that is surprisingly similar to Earth. The possibility of life having evolved there has been weighed up over centuries ever since its discovery. It is an issue that no-one has been able to positively answer. Unfortunately with the recent discovery of the low pressure Martian atmosphere, the likelihood of life having once existed is now considered less likely. But those investigating were only analysing the environment on the hostile exterior of the planet. They knew nothing of its interior.

So, what kind of environment can we expect to find within Mars? Could life have evolved there? Conditions within would have been very different to those on the exterior surface.

The fact that the inside environment supported the waters of the Martian flood, provides us with information that is both interesting and significant. Water flowing as a liquid from within the planet is the important clue. Apart from pressure, there is one other essential ingredient which must be present for water to exist in its liquid state. That ingredient is heat.

Not only did passing space probes record the marvel of the Great Martian Flood, but they also detected a weak magnetic field surrounding the planet. Although not as strong as the Earth's, like the Earth, it originates from the centre of the planet. Its presence indicates the existence and location of a similar but lesser solar reaction occurring within.

Mars too has a central sun.

Prior to the flood, the internal environment of Mars appears to have been surprisingly favourable. An inner ocean was maintained by a suitably pressurised atmosphere. In this amazing enclosed world, the warmth of the sun prevented the oceanic waters from freezing. The environment was constant and even, under the gentle rule of low gravity. Most of the conditions found inside Mars are expected to have been remarkably similar to those of the habitat inside the Earth. If the miracle of life did actually take place, the constant elements would have been ideal for its development. And it would have been likely that little existed to stand in the way to slow its progress.

So just how close was the inside environment of Mars to that of Earth? Was there enough evaporation to support precipitation? Would there have been dousing rains to dampen dry continents creating rivers and lakes? Did life evolve within the waters or on the landmasses elevated above the level of the sea? If so, how far did the evolutionary process patiently develop its creations before being devastated by the great flood? Surely, the destiny of millions of life forms would have been sealed, swept away by the waters to perish in the hostile outer world, their remains left to be one day found somewhere in the sands of the flood ravaged outer surface of the planet?

For those of life left inside, the onset of the flood would have changed things forever. With the inner atmosphere released and equalised with the low pressure outside, pressure essential for supporting water as a liquid was gone. As remaining oceans evaporated away, nature's creations would have sadly faded into extinction. Millions upon millions of Martian years of evolution surely lost for all time.

But, is this what really happened?

Gravity's Grand Reign

Did the inner atmosphere escape or not? Is it possible, the breach through the planetary wall resealed before all the ocean was expelled?

One important factor is still to be considered. A large portion of the expelling force, produced by atmospheric pressure, would have been consumed in overcoming adding up friction encountered along the path through the planetary wall. The situation can be likened to water passing through a garden hose. The longer the hose the less water pressure at the other end. This is because of friction which adds up along the length of the hose. The flooding Martian ocean could only reach the outer surface providing the force expelling it is greater than the level friction encountered. As the water escaped the force of inner pressure naturally reduced. And so the outflow of ocean accordingly slowed. Reduction continued until a level was reached when the expelling force became equal to the value of friction. From here on, nothing more could be expelled. The crucial question here is; was this point reached before or after all the oceanic waters had escaped?

If the flow ceased before the full contents of the ocean had been expelled, the original atmosphere would not have escaped. If this is the case, and the inner atmosphere is still intact, surface pressure would be much the same as it was at the time of the flood. This means, pockets of ocean will have survived. And if life did evolve, it may still exist today.

The question of life on Mars may seem significant to most. But really, this is only the tip of an endless entity of unknowns confronting mankind today. Each planet and moon conceals its own set of individual characteristics awaiting an answer, just as does the Earth. We witness seemingly miraculous events everywhere. They begin within our bodies, leading out to the far reaches of the galaxies and beyond the boundaries of space. But ultimately, there is only one answer. It is the one solution that leads to all others. A wondrous new era of awareness is upon us. It is born from the final understanding of the universal network. An understanding that clarifies the picture infinitely outward, growing from the knowledge of gravity. With this tool at the fingertips of our minds, the way is open to answer all other things.

The direction forward, towards new understanding, is now available to all mankind.

Chapter 17

Future Unity

One world, one people, one truth...
one day.

Future Unity

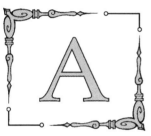nd then we are told of the future, a time of equilibrium within the Earth...

We see progressing expansion slow the scales of balancing matter. Counteracting forces of friction are wasting the waning powers of planetary wall thinning. Expansion is beginning to slow. Over time we see the force weaken until finally overruled by the demands of resistance within the matter of the wall. From that time, gravity is powerless to thin Earth's planetary wall any more.

We see how continental movement has come to a halt. The land no longer trembles. The ground is forever still. No longer will fault lines rule to divide land from land. The power that forged them is spent. Gravity and matter are in balance. And now, as the crust lies still, the Earth's diameter is forever sealed.

But there remains a power beneath, that of heated molten matter. It provides a division between the two worlds, a division between the two peoples. But it too will cool in time. As the heat escapes from its place within, the two crusts will fuse. And so we see a future unity of the two worlds joined as one.

All volcanic life has ceased. Erosion wears down mountains never to be rebuilt. No longer will the stones crack from forces within. The land is volcanically at rest. The Earth is silent.

The stillness of the ground is disturbed by the movement of light. Shadows are cast from the endless voyage above. This we see as the Sun continues its task upon the land. And a world of sea and air following in its rhythmic path. Rotating cycles never end. The land is washed and life is replenished.

But there is another event before all this comes to pass. We are told of another future. It is one that is different. It is the future belonging to all of humanity.

Future Unity

There is a time following a great learning, a common understanding. Mankind will have come face to face with truth. Greed will diminish. And the environment will be repaired. It will provide for the generations that follow, ensuring the ongoing survival of the human race, one that will last to the end of the life of the Earth. All the peoples will share the same knowledge. For there is no other way. The world must be saved at all costs. A new set of values will come into play. And a resurgence of interest will follow. There will be a collective effort, an effort shared by all for the benefit of all. After generations of conflict, mankind will come together. Times of despair will have turned to times of fulfilment. The land of old will be rediscovered anew. Wisdom will show, no-one wins from conflict. Only then will the time come when peace and harmony reign across the face of the Earth.

Ultimately mankind will feel a great need. We will seek out our creators from within. And we will walk as one with those thought of as our gods. We will abide as a combined race in the one world, sharing the one understanding, ruling the land together.

We will rule under the elevated banner of one unified trinity, a trinity formed by the union of mankind and our creators, a trinity fused by three entities; our creators as our fathers, we the created as the sons, joined together as one united spirit by the Earth we both share.

> **And then suddenly we are back....**
>
> **We feel the weight of gravity instantly upon our being. It is as if we will never readjust. Our consciousness awakens as the clock of life is restarted. And the Sun resumes its path across the sky.**
>
> **The outside world is the same place we left. But somehow, something is different. A change has come about. We have brought back a new understanding, a vision that alters things forever. We now know why we are here. And we now know from where we came. Our purpose on the Earth is clear. But in our knowledge we are alone. Stopping for a moment to reflect back we see the wonderful truth. It is a truth that all the people around us do not know.**

We stand in a world where we do not fully belong. But there is nowhere else to go. This strange yet familiar land is our only home. This is the land we must accept as our own. Only in the passage of time, will the fabric of mankind be helped by natural evolution and transform to become in tune with the outer world environment. Until then, future generations must face and cope with the difficulties we encounter each day, hardships that have been inherited from others not adapted to the different conditions that surround us.

The peoples of the Earth must know the truth. The origins of humanity is their rightful heritage. For the benefit of everyone, ignorance must come to an end. We feel an urgency to tell all. But will the world believe our incredible story? It may take time to change. We must provide humanity with the essential map, a direction into the future. The difficulty of the task is before us. There may be many who don't wish to agree. But eventually truth will prevail. There is so much to tell and so much to be learnt. Words must be compiled for the understanding of all mankind. Words will complete the unknown picture. And then all will see. But the words must explain the reasons why, for without the reasoning behind it, the answer on its own is less than complete. A book must be written

Future Unity

to tell of our heritage. And provide the knowledge of "The Land Of No Horizon".

We are distracted by the difficult environment around us, and reflect back to the ease of life within. But then, as the Sun sinks slowly beyond the horizon, the colours of sunset remind us; this primitive world has beauty too. This is a world with peoples worthy of protection for all time.

As the coolness of night replaces the warmth of day, we see one era of humanity come to an end to be replaced by a new era of future unity.

www.thelandofnohorizon.com

Bibliography

Avers C. J., *Process and Pattern in Evolution* (1989)

Baltscheffsky H. And others, ed., *Molecular Evolution of Life* (1987)

Bendall D. S., *Evolution from Molecules to Men* (1983)

Berlitz C., *The Bermuda Triangle* (Doubleday & Company Inc., 1996)

Berry R. J., *Evolution, Ecology, and Environmental Stress* (1989)

Birx J. H., *Theories of evolution* (1984)

Burnat P., *20,000 Years Under the Sea* (Readers Digest, November 1992)

Calow P., *Evolutionary Principles* (1983)

Carey S. W., *The Expanding Earth* (Elsevier Scientific Publishing Company, 1976)

Cattermole P., Hunt G., Moore P. & Nicolson I., *The Atlas of the Solar System* (Mitchell Beazley Publishers, 1990)

Clark A. M., *Understanding Science Through Evolution* (1987)

Edward O. And Dodson P., *Evolution: Process and Product* (3d ed. 1985)

Fasold D., *The Ark of Noah* (Wynwood Press, 1988)

Grant V., *The Evolutionary Process* (1985)

Green J. P. Sr., *The Interlinear Bible* (Hendrickson)

Laing D., *The Earth System* (Wm. C. Brown Publishers)

Lamprecht J., *Hollow Planets* (World Wide Publishing)

Leakey R., *Origins Reconsidered* (1992)

Lewin R., *Human Evolution* (2d ed. 1989)

Montgomery J. W., *The Quest For Noah's Ark* (Bethany House Publishers)

Noorbergen R., *The Ark File* (New English Library Times Mirror)

Ollier C., *Tectonics and Landform* (Longman Inc., 1981)

Poirier F. E., *Understanding Human Evolution* (1987)

Porter S. C. & Skinner B. J., *Physical Geology* (John Wiley & Sons)

Richards G., *Human Evolution* (1987)

Velikovsky I., *Earth in Upheaval* (Victor Gollanz Ltd. in association with Sidgwick and Jackson Ltd., 1956)

Wilson J. T., *Continents Adrift* (W. H. Freeman, 1972)

Index of Diagrams

Index of Diagrams

Index of Terms

Index of Terms

Index of Terms

Index of Terms

Index of Terms

Index of Terms

W